Jewish Education and Society in the High Middle Ages

Jewish Education and Society in the High Middle Ages

Ephraim Kanarfogel

Wayne State University Press   Detroit

Manufactured in the United States of America.

96 95 94 93 92 5 4 3 2 1

Library of Congress Cataloging-in-Publication Data

Kanarfogel, Ephraim.
Jewish education and society in the High Middle Ages / Ephraim Kanarfogel.
p. cm.
Includes bibliographical references and index.
ISBN 0-8143-2164-X (alk. paper)
1. Jewish religious education—Germany—History. 2. Jewish religious education—France, Northern—History. 3. Jewish learning and scholarship—Germany. 4. Jewish learning and scholarship—France, Northern. 5. Jews—Germany—History—1096–1800. 6. Jews—Germany—Intellectual life. 7. Jews—France, Northern—Intellectual life. 8. Tosafists. 9. Hasidism, Medieval. 10. Germany–Ethnic relations. 11. France, Northern—Ethnic relations. I. Title.
BM85.G4K36 1992
370′.89′92404—dc20 90-26160

Book design by Mary Primeau

For Devorah

Published with the assistance of
The Louis and Minna Epstein Publication Fund
of the American Academy for Jewish Research
and the
Lucius N. Littauer Foundation

Contents

Preface

The Jews of medieval northern France, Germany, and England, known collectively as Ashkenazic Jewry, have commanded the attention of scholars since the beginnings of modern Jewish historiography. Over the past century historians have produced significant studies about Jewish society in medieval Ashkenaz that have focused on a wide range of topics: the nature of communal self-government; the economic and political profiles; the ability of Ashkenazic Jews to interact with rulers, clergy, and laypersons; responses to restriction and persecution; and intellectual and spiritual creativity.

Ashkenazic Jewry has emerged from these investigations as a well-organized, creative, steadfast community, able to overcome most obstacles that were placed before it. The twelfth and thirteenth centuries were its heyday. This period of remarkable achievement began with the recovery from the First Crusade of 1096 and lasted until the expulsions of English Jewry in 1290 and northern French Jewry in 1306 and the sustained persecution of German Jewry from the end of the thirteenth century through the Black Death. It was, on the whole, a period of prosperity and enhanced spirituality despite the increase of different forms of pressure. Brushing off a variety of physical, political, and religious attacks, Franco-German Jewry produced an impressive corpus of Talmudic and halakhic compositions symbolized by the genre known as *tosafot,* which revolutionized the study of rabbinic literature.

The literary creativity of the Tosafists has been cataloged and analyzed, and the scope and policies of communal government in Ashkenaz have been fixed and compared. Yet no sustained attempt has been made to integrate these crucial dimensions of Ashkenazic society. This study of Jewish education in the high Middle Ages will address some of these relationships by examining the degree of communal involvement in the educational process as well as the economic, societal, and halakhic factors that affected this process from the elementary level to the production of the Tosafist corpus. Comparisons will be made throughout to pre-Crusade Ashkenaz, the period following the Black Death, Spanish and Provençal Jewish society, and general medieval society. By drawing parallels and highlighting differences, what emerges from twelfth- and thirteenth-century Ashkenazic sources can be sharpened and clarified.

M. Güdemann, one of the earliest scholars of medieval Jewish education, noted in 1880 that the Tosafists studied and wrote a great deal but, paradoxically, wrote very little about how they studied or how the educational process in their day was structured. Indeed, despite the substantial amount of evidence now available and the substantive methodological developments that make this study possible, gaps do still exist. For example, the precise transition from one phase of the educational process to another is difficult to reconstruct. Equally difficult to pinpoint are the connections between the Tosafist academies and less prestigious study halls. Some of the discussion of higher education—most notably that concerning curriculum—will be restricted to the Tosafist academies, since the documentation within the literature can only be applied with certainty to the schools that produced it.

I will not describe in any detail what might be termed "informal education," that is, the ongoing educational involvement of an adult who was not part of an academy setting. In addition, the education of women will not be discussed. The education of women clearly lagged far behind the education of men. On the basis of a handful of citations, some scholars have argued that just as Jewish males in Ashkenaz were better educated than the general populace, so too Ashkenazic women were more enlightened than their Christian counterparts. One might reasonably suggest that the education that women received took place solely in the home in an informal, irregular manner and is thus not reflected to any significant degree in extant Ashkenazic literature. The entire topic requires separate treatment.

A complete portrait of the educational theories and practices that were prevalent in the Jewish communities of medieval Europe still cannot be painted. Nevertheless, this study aims to demonstrate that a close reading of the rich rabbinic literature of the Tosafist period can yield coherent and comprehensive answers to many of the critical questions facing the student of medieval Jewish education and society.

Acknowledgments

Over the years, I have carefully read and scrutinized numerous acknowledgments in an effort to formulate something clever and original when my turn came. At this moment of truth it seems to me that genuine gratitude reads best. I am deeply grateful to the many teachers, colleagues, friends, and students who have been subjected to my questions and even to my answers. Above all, I wish to thank Prof. David Berger, under whose guidance an earlier version of this book was completed; Rabbi Hirsch Fishman, who has had a profound influence on all my endeavors; and Dr. Karen Bacon, whose vision and integrity have made my role at Stern College for Women a most rewarding one. My friend and colleague Prof. Moshe Sokolow, and my students Rivka Landau, Chaviva Levin, and Batya Zuckerman provided invaluable assistance in checking the galleys. Professors Arthur Hyman, Jacob Katz, and Isadore Twersky have given wise and effective guidance.

Various stages of my research were supported by grants from the Memorial Foundation for Jewish Culture, the National Foundation for Jewish Culture, and Yeshiva University. I also wish to acknowledge publication grants from the Louis and Minna Epstein Fund of the American Academy for Jewish Research, and from the Lucius N. Littauer Foundation.

My parents have always been a source of inspiration and encouragement. My wife Devorah and our children Tova, Dovid, Moshe, and Atara know that they are more important to me than my work; but they also appreciate just how important my work is to me. Dedication of this book to Devorah is but a token of the love that I feel for her.

1

The Structure of Elementary Education in Ashkenaz

ASHKENAZIC JEWRY IN the twelfth and thirteenth centuries produced a corpus of Talmudic commentaries, codes, and works of biblical exegesis that revolutionized the study of biblical and Talmudic literature and deeply impressed all succeeding generations of Jewish scholars. While there were leading personalities who stood head and shoulders above the rest—scholars such as R. Tam, Ri, and Rabiah—Ashkenazic society as a whole was literate (if not learned) and intellectually motivated. A brief look at the level of literacy in medieval society will place these achievements into proper perspective.

The regnant perception of the late-Victorian period that illiteracy was widespread throughout medieval Europe held sway until the 1930s. In that decade several studies modified this view by demonstrating that the ability to read and understand the vernacular was not unusual among members of the nobility.[1] Recent research has shown that while laypersons knew more Latin than had been previously thought, the general public was not able to express itself in writing or take advantage of the written word even for the practical purposes of daily living. Among the nobility a rather limited degree of literacy prevailed. Some read or wrote the requisite amounts of Latin or French to keep or at least decipher public records.[2] By the end of the twelfth century a competing body of literature in French and English had emerged, and the degree of latinity, even among the royal families, was greatly diminished. Giles of Rome (c. 1260) exhorted the sons of noblemen to use their knowledge of Latin to study the seven liberal arts, metaphysics, ethics, and politics and even law, medicine, and theology. But he conceded that they would not have time to do so if they attended to the business of the world. They should therefore concentrate on learning the faith and morality of Christianity and at least learn Latin. If they could not manage even that, they should be taught manners, in French.[3] In addition, clerical education throughout this period was uneven. Many clerics remained illiterate.[4]

Christian scholars were aware of the heightened commitment of Jewish parents to the education of their children and of the spiritual motivation behind that commitment. A student of Peter Abelard writes,

> If the Christians educate their sons, they do so not for God, but for gain, in order that the one brother, if he be a clerk, may help his father and his mother and his other brothers. They say that a clerk will have no heir and whatever he has will be ours and the other brothers. . . . But the Jews, out of zeal for God and love of the law, put as many sons as they have to letters, that each may understand God's law.
>
> A Jew, however poor, even if he had ten sons would put them all to letters, not for gain as Christians do, but for the understanding of God's law, and not only his sons but his daughters.[5]

Historians have viewed the Tosafists and their achievements as sure signs of the high intellectual level of Ashkenazic society and of the high quality of education in Ashkenaz. Thus, R. Chazan writes that in the absence of explicit sources indicating the quality of schooling, "the literacy demanded by the business pursuits of the Jews and the already high level of cultural achievement indicate a successful educational system." In enumerating the services provided by the Jewish communities of northern France, such as court systems and philanthropic agencies, Chazan writes, "The Jews of northern France possessed a well-developed school system for both elementary and advanced education." His documentation for the elementary school system is the quotation from the student of

Abelard, which Chazan characterizes as a "curious encomium to the Jewish school." The *yeshivot* of Paris, Sens, and Troyes are mentioned by Chazan as part of the school system for advanced education.[6] Indeed, the academies of northern France and Germany were noted throughout the medieval Jewish world as exceptional centers of study and erudition. Their hegemony over Talmudic studies was unchallenged.[7] Chazan implies, in his assertion that the Jews of northern France had a well-developed elementary school system, that if Ashkenazic Jewry could produce such outstanding scholars and institutions of higher learning, there must have been lower echelons of the educational system to feed the schools of higher learning. This sort of deduction has been employed in regard to medieval Christian educational institutions. L. Thorndyke, among others, assumes that the existence and development of medieval universities proves the existence of a network of elementary and secondary schools beneath the universities.[8]

That there was an organized system of elementary education in the Tosafist period had been suggested by M. Güdemann in 1880. Describing elementary education in northern France, Güdemann writes that in each Jewish community there were schools supported either by the community at large or by a separate fund specifically for this purpose. There were also private schools, staffed by special teachers.[9] Güdemann repeats his description when he discusses elementary education in Germany. Teachers taught either in private rooms at a fixed fee per year or in communal schools supported by each community. Indeed, German Jewry subscribed to the motto *It is better to give charity so that youngsters may study than to give charity to the synagogue.*[10]

The academies of the Tosafists were populated, to be sure, by students who had some prior training. But the presence of these students in Tosafist academies (which were smaller than the universities since they clearly drew from a smaller pool of students) does not prove that such training was received in an organized communal school system open to any child who wished to enter it. Indeed, the existence of Tosafist academies does not even prove that formal elementary education was widespread in Ashkenaz.

The relatively few great scholars who created the *tosafot* were concentrated in a handful of towns and cities in northern France and Germany.[11] Assuming that they were actually products of a highly developed system of elementary education, the system itself may have been a limited one. Moreover, the type of elementary education available to Tosafists probably placed them at the fringe of any system. The young Jacob Tam, living in the house of his father R. Meir and exposed at a young age to the teachings of his brothers R. Samuel and R. Isaac, would have been able to master the study of Talmud even if there was no educational system at all. To phrase it differently, if young Jacob had a tutor or if he participated in some elementary school system, would it have mattered if the system suddenly collapsed? His family would have seen to his training regardless of any other educational opportunities that were available. All of Rashi's Tosafist descendants studied within the family in their early years. Rashbam studied with Rashi himself while growing up in his house. Ri studied with R. Isaac b. Meir in his younger years and then with R. Tam. Ri's son Elḥanan studied and ultimately taught with Ri, and Ri's grandson Samuel also studied with him.[12] Thus, the achievements of a Rabbenu Tam do not necessarily prove that the elementary system in Ashkenaz at the preacademy level functioned well or even existed.

There were other Tosafists who grew up in homes or in families where they would have been educated irrespective of or despite the education available to others. Rabiah sat at the feet of his great-grandfather R. Elyaqim when he was less than ten years old.[13] Similarly, R. Meir of Rothenburg, whose father was not nearly as distinguished as Rabiah's, was perhaps ten when he studied with R. Isaac Or Zarua' for the first time.[14] There are strong indications that R. Judah Sir Leon, R. Elijah of London, and others also began to study with recognized Tosafists at an early age.[15] When students entered an academy at such an early age, the existence of a formal system of elementary education cannot be assumed. If the child was privately taught the rudiments of biblical and Talmudic studies and found to be bright, the father's initiative would be more than enough to place the child in an academy and set him on the path of scholarship. There is evidence for the presence of very young students alongside senior students in the academies of Ashkenaz.[16]

Thus far, we have argued that the presence of Tosafists in France and Germany does not force us to presume that there was a well-developed school system for elementary education operating in Ashkenaz in the twelfth and thirteenth centuries. We must now proceed further to examine all references to elementary education in this period to see if Güdemann's picture of the educational system is an accurate one. On the basis of the available sources, can we accept the position that there was a communally funded and administered system of elementary education in Ashkenaz, as Güdemann maintains? After all, we are aware of *battei midrash* scattered throughout northern France and Germany which were not Tosafist academies.[17] Perhaps this cadre of lesser scholars was trained in organized communal elementary schools.

A look at the education of young children in Ashkenaz will reveal that the *melammed,* or tutor, was the central figure in the educational process. The hiring of the *melammed* was done by the child's father, at which time the terms of employment were specified.[18] In many cases the tutor was hired for just one student, but sometimes he taught several. In the latter situation each father would reach an agreement with the *melammed* for his child, or a parent or group of parents might collectively promise the *melammed* a certain sum.[19] From the extant literature, it appears that there was no elementary school per se in northern France and Germany; that is, there were no school buildings or groups of teachers maintained by the members of the community for the children of the community. Elementary education was the result of agreements between parents and teachers. If the parent did not wish to hire a teacher or if there were no teachers available, there was no village or town school to which the child could turn. It was in this context that R. Meir of Rothenburg ruled that a father should be forced to hire a *melammed* for his son or teach the boy himself.[20] The need for such a ruling indicates that some fathers were not concerned about these matters and that as a result, there were children who were not being taught.

Two halakhic formulations of R. Tam should also be understood in light of these circumstances. An ordinance promulgated by R. Tam[21] demanded that a father who had taken leave of his family must continue to pay not only their living expenses but also adequate funds for Torah education in accordance with the Talmudic requirement.[22] In a case where A hired a young tutor (*baḥur*) to teach the son of B, R. Tam ruled that B was obligated to pay the tutor as long as he didn't object to the arrangement made by A.[23] While this ruling was primarily an application of the halakhic principle that silence is tantamount to acquiescence, its implication is that B is merely doing what is incumbent on him in any event.

The structure that placed the *melammed* in the center and left the hiring up to the parents obviously placed children whose fathers were too poor to hire tutors (and orphans as well) at a disadvantage. Several passages in *Sefer Ḥasidim* show this disadvantage very clearly. For example,

> One person should not do a kindness for another where a transgression will result. For example, if A and B both have sons and B says to A: "You are wealthy and I am poor and have nothing with which to hire a tutor for my sons. But you do not have so much that you can hire a [separate] tutor for my sons. Instead, do me a favor and let my sons study with your sons and the teacher that you hired for them." If B's sons are ill-qualified and lazy and will disturb and deter the sons of A, A should not allow the sons of B to study with his sons.[24]

The Jews of western Europe were not alone in having to deal with the problem of disadvantaged children who remained uneducated. In 1179 the Third Lateran Council decreed that all cathedral churches had to provide a teacher who would teach poor children and orphans at no cost.[25] This statute was confirmed and then extended by Pope Innocent III at the Fourth Lateran Council in 1215. Not only cathedral churches but all churches of sufficient resources were to provide for a master who would give free instruction to poor students in reading and writing Latin and in elementary logic. Innocent also required each metropolitan church to provide a master to teach theology.[26] The opening of municipal and guild schools in Germany in the late thirteenth century was also undertaken as a response to these problems.[27]

Apparently, there were instances where wealthy Jewish fathers paid, as an act of charity, for separate *melammedim* for poor children. The giving of charity for this purpose is evident in another section of *Sefer Ḥasidim.* A young man tried to dissuade some other youngsters from dice playing and tried to get them to study the Bible by playing a word game based on biblical verses (perhaps for money). The father of the young man rebuked his son because he had induced the youngsters to study Torah while making it frivolous in their eyes. The father dictated the following:

> This shall be your expiation. Do not meet with them any more. For each letter that came out of their mouths, you must either fast or donate money to poor people who have nothing with which to hire tutors for their sons. Your donation will cause [these sons] to learn an amount commensurate to the amount of wrongdoing that you caused [the youngsters]. You must teach those who do not yet know how to learn, e.g., young children, in order to achieve atonement.[28]

The poor children who were to receive this money would not have been able to study otherwise. On the other hand, the wealthy father or dedicated father willing to expend additional sums could ensure that his son would continue to study even when there were not enough tutors available to fill the demand.[29] In the words of R. Tam, "There are several heads of households who would rather expend large sums than have their children remain idle."[30]

All of the forty responsa emanating from Ashkenaz that deal with the hiring and terminating of *melammedim* are based on situations where the child's parent is the hirer.[31] While many of the questions asked were unusual and did not reflect the norm, the background against which they are asked—that the father hires and pays the *melammed*—never changes; this context seems to have been uniform. The same observation may be made regarding rulings that deal with *melammedim* in Ashkenazic codes and legal commentaries: never is the community referred to as the hirer or supervisor of *melammedim,* as the Talmud describes[32] and as several medieval Sephardic authorities and Geniza documents indicate.[33] For example, R. Meir ha-Levi (Ramah) penned the following comment on a Talmudic passage delineating the city's responsibilities in hiring elementary teachers: "We derive from here that the community must appoint teachers in every city. . . .

Their salaries must be paid by the community. This is best because it allows the children of the poor to learn in the same manner as the children of the wealthy."[34] In his *Kad ha-Kemaḥ,* R. Baḥya b. Asher wrote, "It is incumbent upon the *gabba'im* to ensure that the young children attend school. . . . The communal leaders in each city must strive to achieve this. . . . If they are lax concerning this matter, they will be punished."[35]

If we look at R. Meir of Rothenburg's list of services that a community was required to provide and for which funding could be extracted from even the newest members, specific references to educational services are glaringly absent:

> The *Tosefta* records: Residents of a city can force each other to build a synagogue and to purchase Torah scrolls and scrolls of the Prophets and Scriptures. R. Meir ruled that this is also the case when it comes to providing for guests and distributing charity to them. And similarly if there is no quorum in the city and the residents wish to hire one . . . they can force each other to contribute to the communal fund. . . . It is evident that a newcomer can be forced to contribute even if he has never participated with them and, in the same vein, he may be compelled to participate with them in [paying] taxes.[36]

There was one piece of communal legislation enacted in Ashkenaz that dealt with support for education. It is an ordinance promulgated by Rhineland scholars in Mayence in 1220 and repeated in Speyers with slight variation in 1223:

> In a place where people are not paying the tutors of children enough because there is not enough in the charity fund [*heqdesh*] since they do not have so much, they can take from the other funds [*she'ar heqdeshot*] which those who passed away had set aside for their souls and give to the tutors, if the deceased did not specify, on his deathbed, the purpose for which his money should be used. The remainder should be utilized according to the desire of the community.[37]

This ordinance does not demonstrate that there were *melammedim* under the employ of the Rhineland communities, nor does it mandate the giving of funds by members of the community to support the educational services of that community. It deals with the problem of *meshaneh mi-ẓedaqah li-ẓedaqah*—Can funds not specifically pledged for the instruction of children be used for that purpose? The existence of the ordinance confirms the fact that funds for education were not always abundant in Ashkenaz and that education depended on charity.[38] These findings will be further corroborated when we study the role, if any, that communities took in supporting their local study halls.

The term *beit sefer* that appears in rabbinic literature of this period in connection with the education of young children does not refer to a community school. Rather, it refers most often to either the home of the *melammed* or rooms rented by the *melammed* to which students came.[39] This term also refers to the home of the student, where some *melammedim* lived. They taught the children of the household and occasionally other children as well.[40] In addition, the term might refer to the local synagogue where the *melammed* taught children from the surrounding community. But even in this type of arrangement the community was not the administering agent, and the fathers made the appropriate arrangements with the *melammed.*[41]

There are several references to *scholae inferiore* (= *petites écoles*) in Provençal cities. Historians of Jewish education in Provence, on the basis of other sources as well, have posited the existence of lower, or elementary, schools. There is one reference to such an institution in Orléans.[42] An unresolved question is whether the term *schola* refers to a school or to a synagogue.[43] Do these texts refer to a lower school or to the smaller synagogue of a particular city? In the Orléans passage the context appears to favor the synagogue interpretation.

There were people in certain cities who were recorded in memorial records as carrying the title *melammed.*[44] These *melammedim* lived or worked in the city; they were not hired by the city. Fathers would occasionally bring particular *melammedim* from other locations to teach their children exclusively.[45] In his Talmudic commentary, Rashi describes a *sofer mata* who served as a supervising *melammed,* but that interpretation could easily have been dictated by the Talmudic passage in question. Indeed, *tosafot* notes that

Rashi interpreted the same title differently in another Talmudic passage.[46]

The small size of the Jewish communities in medieval Germany and northern France may be the single most important factor in explaining the hiring of *melammedim* not by the town or the city, as was the practice in Talmudic times, but by individual residents.[47] When the Talmud discusses the hiring of elementary-level teachers (*Bava Batra* 21a), the determinant for how many teachers a city must hire was the number of students in that city. Up to twenty-five students required the hiring of one teacher. A survey of Ashkenazic halakhic code-commentaries such as *Sefer Raban, Sefer Or Zarua*ʿ (or more precisely *Simmanei Or Zarua*ʿ), and *Sefer Mordekhai* shows a complete lack of interest in this part of the *sugya*. The only Talmudic guidelines cited are that residents of a city cannot restrict the presence of teachers of children even if their teaching is noisy and that a teacher of young children who errs may be dismissed immediately.[48] Rambam, on the other hand, does note class size and the number of teachers required based on the Talmudic formulation.[49] A responsum of R. Meir ha-Levi Abulafia's, as well as a passage in his Talmudic commentary *Yad Ramah,* also give the impression that the numbers in the *sugya* were considered to be relevant as well.[50] The halakhic position of the Ashkenazic *posqim* tallies with what we know about class size in Ashkenaz. In most cases the *melammed* worked with only one child (usually in the child's home) or with a small group of perhaps two or three students. A single Ashkenazic source refers to a *melammed* who might have taught ten children at one time.[51]

It would appear then that the claims of both Güdemann and Chazan that a well-developed system of elementary education existed in medieval Ashkenaz are not sustained by a thorough study of the sources.[52] While there was, as we shall see, ample educational opportunity for a boy growing up in Ashkenaz, his taking advantage of these opportunities depended on where he lived, what his parents could afford, and the interest they displayed in his education.

The preceding discussion has shown the dominant role played by the *melammed* in the educational process of children in Ashkenaz. As we would expect, the quality of *melammedim* varied greatly.

For every experienced, competent tutor there might be one who was a gambler,[53] one who was unqualified to teach either because he was ignorant[54] or because he was lazy,[55] and one who wasn't much older than his pupil.[56] In light of the *melammed*'s crucial role in the education of children and precisely because there was no system of elementary education in Ashkenaz, it would seem that the qualified *melammed* should have been a valuable commodity in Ashkenazic society.

There is conflicting evidence about the social status of the *melammed* in this society. On the one hand, while the tutor spent a good deal of his time teaching some form of Torah, the nature of his teaching disassociated him from scholars who taught Talmud to older students and were respected for their teaching. Aside from obvious considerations, several specific factors were responsible for this diminished esteem. We shall see that while teaching Torah for gain was unacceptable in Jewish law, there was no prohibition against receiving a fee for teaching young children.[57] The *melammed* could receive direct compensation for his teaching, but his prestige was thereby lessened. He was not included in the class of teachers who must theoretically teach without compensation in emulation of God. Talmudic law rendered this teacher no more important in his profession than any other layman.

Moreover, we shall see that an academy head—or even a lesser scholar who lectured to senior students—often had the opportunity to earn a living in some other profession and did not have to rely on any of the Talmud-approved methods of being compensated for teaching Torah. His students did not require constant supervision, as did students of the *melammed.* The *melammed* did not have time to pursue other professions and was halakhically constrained from diminishing his teaching capacity by moonlighting.[58] R. Isaac of Corbeil maintained that the scriptural allowance for compensation should be extended to any teacher who had to expend effort to make sure that his students grasped the material.[59] This would ostensibly include even teachers of Talmud who were teaching older students. But the right of these teachers to be compensated was not the same as that of the *melammed* on the elementary level. The more advanced Talmud teachers were comparable to the teachers of the temple rites to priests who, because of the nature and importance of what they taught, were compensated even though they were thus being rewarded for performing a *mizvah.*[60] The *melammed* who taught young children was entitled to compensation not because of his subject matter but because he was watching the child and protecting him from harm (*sekhar shimmur*). The *melammed* was thus in a class lower than any other teacher of Torah.

Other aspects of economic reality might further limit the esteem accorded the *melammed.* While being poor, in and of itself, might not lower the social status of the *melammed,* the possibility of having to endure a life of poverty might deter qualified people from becoming *melammedim. Melammedim* did earn low salaries. The salary structure that emerges from the sources is that if a *melammed* could teach eight or ten students for an entire year, he could earn a livable wage.[61] As we have noted, most *melammedim* taught fewer students than that.[62] A tax exemption for *melammedim,* based on their low incomes, is recorded in a responsum of R. Meir of Rothenburg. The *melammed,* like the servant (*mesharet*) and the scribe, is not to have his income taxed unless he makes more than two *zequqim* a year.[63] This exemption was not granted to the *melammed* as a scholarly privilege.[64] It was an indication that the *melammed,* like the servant or the scribe, provided a needed service, for which he usually earned a small amount of money. The relative poverty of the *melammed* as compared to other workers is also clearly seen in another responsum of R. Meir:

> Q. A mother demanded support for her three sons. One son had no money except for his salary as a teacher [*ha-'eḥad ein lo kelum akh mah she-mistakker be-limmud*]. The second son has fourteen marks [*zequqim*]. The third son is rich but does not live in the same town. Who must support the mother?
> A. . . . Children of means must be forced to support their mother as an act of charity. Therefore, any son who would himself be thrown upon charity were he forced to support his mother, cannot be forced to do so. But those sons who have means should support their mother in proportion to their wealth.[65]

Some *melammedim* were provided with room and board in addition to the compensation that they received.[66] Others, however, worked for room and board alone. The existence of this kind of arrangement was attributed to the difficult economic conditions of the period, which forced even some prominent tutors (*melammedim ḥashuvim*) to work under disadvantageous terms.[67] An arrangement of this type might have been suitable for a young man who was supporting himself while continuing his own studies but would hardly have yielded sufficient income for someone who had to support a family. There were calls made to pay *melammedim* promptly, but these calls were not always heeded.[68] At least one industrious *melammed* used the home in which he lived and taught as the base for a pawnbroking business.[69] Undoubtedly, there were other *melammedim* who were able to earn additional income, perhaps as scribes.[70] Overall, however, the *melammed* lacked not only professional prestige but also the security of a comfortable livelihood.

An additional factor that contributed to the relatively low social status of the *melammed* was the availability of tutors for hire. Ri describes, in the course of a responsum on the financial liabilities of a tutor who has resigned, the circumstances that often led to a surplus of tutors: "If at the time that this tutor was hired there were more tutors available than there are now, because there were more passersby who needed employment [*ki yoter meẓuyim maḥmat she-rabbu ha-ẓerikhim ha-ʿoverim ve-shavim*] and were willing to hire themselves out, such that the student would only be idle for a short while. . . ." The glut of *melammedim* meant that if one *melammed* quit, another could be obtained very quickly with little loss to the student.[71] Based on a Talmudic ruling concerning the elementary-level teacher (*maqrei dardeqei*) Raban ruled that a *melammed* could not be denied settlement in the location of his choice.[72] In the mid–thirteenth century R. Isaac of Evreux found it necessary to take steps to prevent one tutor from stealing away the position of another.[73] According to R. Isaac of Corbeil, this ruling is to be attributed to R. Tam.[74] The availability of increasing numbers of *melammedim* was due to the fact that especially at the elementary level, many knew enough to teach reading and Bible and perhaps the rudiments of Talmudic study. Although not as many had the ability to be good teachers, it appears that the *melammed* was considered, by Ri at least, to be a nonskilled worker. The position could be left to *'overim ve-shavim,* the travelers or wanderers from town to town.

It should be noted that several halakhic formulations that appear to downgrade the social status of the *melammed* severely must be discounted. A *mishnah* in tractate *Ketubot* discusses the laws of a recalcitrant wife and husband. The Talmud defines recalcitrance on the part of the husband as his abstention from marital relations and economic abandonment of his wife.[75] R. Elijah of Paris deduces from this passage that a husband must hire himself out for any type of labor in order to support his wife. Otherwise, R. Elijah maintains, the Talmudic definition of recalcitrance makes no sense. Indeed, the language of the *ketubah* itself (*ana afalaḥ*) obligates the husband to this extent. In describing the type of work the husband must accept in order to support his wife, R. Elijah includes the following: "A person must hire himself out as a tutor [*melammed tinoqot*] or to do any other labor [*melakhah*] in order to feed his wife."[76] This formulation ostensibly indicates that a *melammed tinoqot* is a quite lowly and undesirable position. Moreover, it implies that becoming a *melammed tinoqot* requires no real skills or qualifications and that these positions are readily available. All these factors would render this position exceedingly low on the social ladder.

In fact, R. Elijah's position does not single out the *melammed.* The lowliness of the *melammed* is subsumed under a much broader category of workers who are hired hands. Thus, in a fuller version of R. Elijah's position, the *melammed* is not specifically mentioned: "From here R. Elijah derived that a person must hire himself out [*meḥuyyav le-haskir et 'aẓmo*] to do work in order to feed and support his wife."[77] The absence of any reference to the *melammed* in this comprehensive statement of R. Elijah's position and the nature of his argument with R. Tam (who held that the husband can only be compelled to do work that can be done around his homestead such as plowing and planting) show that the *melammed* per se was not a crucial figure in this controversy. The tutor is part of a group of professions that is being evaluated. Any work that is characterized as *sekhirut* is considered by R. Elijah to be more lowly than self-employment. This view may be understood both psychologically and socially. Being a hired hand often meant that the *melammed* or any other *sakhir* had to live and function in the house of the employer as a quasi servant. This type of employment would certainly impinge on the *melammed*'s role as head of his own household. Indeed, a *melammed* who is hired by the father but teaches in his own home might have a more desirable and respected position.[78] While the position of R. Elijah places the *melammed* on the lower end of the spectrum of desirable occupations, as we have noted, it cannot be presented as a source categorically maintaining that tutoring of young children is the lowest and most undesirable position available to an unemployed husband.

Restraint must also be employed when analyzing other halakhic sources that categorize the *melammed.* In the rabbinic literature of Ashkenaz the *melammed* is not only compared to a *sakhir* or a *po'el* but sometimes to a servant (*mesharet*), a nursemaid (*meineqet*) and even to a Jewish slave (*'eved 'ivri*).[79] These comparisons are made based on the nature of the *melammed*'s obligations to his employer, and the latter comparisons are not necessarily reflections of an exceptionally low social status accorded to the *melammed.*

At the same time, we find several Tosafist positions that attribute some measure of pedagogic skill or teaching ability to the average *melammed.* Tosafists ruled that a *melammed* who was unable to perform his duties not because of malfeasance on his part but due to actions of his employer was to be paid not as a *po'el batel* (a furloughed worker who receives half pay for the time that he is idled) but rather like the Talmudic porters of Meḥoza, who were paid in full. The porters of Meḥoza preferred to work because idleness hampered their ability to resume working at full strength. The *melammed* was placed in this category for two reasons: first, the *melammed* might forget, as a result of his being idled, the material that he was prepared to teach as well as the most effective way to teach it; second, he might be adverse to a layoff since teaching involved him in a noble pursuit (*melekhet shamayim*).[80]

In another context, *tosafot* describes the *melammed* as a *ba'al ummanut* (skilled artisan), comparable to a tailor or to a piercer of pearls. A *melammed* who is disabled and cannot continue to teach is not to be paid when unable to work as if he were a watchman in a field. The Talmudic law setting compensation for a disabled worker at this rate applies only to unskilled laborers.[81] Like the tailor and the pearl piercer, the *melammed* is a skilled worker who must be compensated for his disability on a higher scale.

Finally, there are scattered references in memorial records from Ashkenaz to individuals who bore the title *melammed.*[82] This title, like the title *sofer* found in these records, does not signify that the bearers occupied official posts. Its use does show that the societal status of the tutor may have been above the status of ordinary workers in the Jewish settlements of Christian Europe.

We find, then, a degree of conflicting evidence when evaluating the social status of the *melammed.* On the one hand, the *melammed* was thought to possess certain skills. In a society where Torah study was the noblest pursuit, a skillful *melammed* who could properly prepare his students for advanced study was performing a valuable service. There is some recognition of the *melammed*'s skills and the difference that a qualified *melammed* could make. At the same time, it seems that the position itself was not accorded great societal respect. This attitude was caused by—or perhaps led to—the notion that teaching young children was the province of the *ʿoverim ve-shavim* (wayfarers) who needed a job and might as well hire themselves out as tutors. It is significant that the statements of both R. Elijah and Ri link the potential *melammed* to one who is seeking to hire himself out in any capacity. Ashkenazic society as a whole assumed that provided the student became able to study on an advanced level, the exact quality of his early training was unimportant. Systematic, communal supervision of *melammedim* and attempts to alleviate the tutor's economic plight were unknown.[83]

While it is possible to document the economic and social aspects of the *melammed*'s position, ascertaining precisely what he taught is somewhat more difficult. R. Eleazar Roqeaḥ, in the introductory programmatic section of his *Sefer Roqeaḥ,* offers the following sequence of beginning studies, which seems to correspond to the reality of his day: "At first [the child] should learn to recognize the letters and then to put them together. These are called words. And then he should study the verse and then the *parashah* and then the *Mishnah* and then the Talmud."[84] It is possible that the very beginning of the process was undertaken by the father himself. Several Ashkenazic commentators, basing themselves on a *mishnah* in *Avot* and a passage in *Midrash Tanḥuma,* charge the father with the responsibility for initiating the child into the recognition of the Hebrew alphabet, the reading of verses, and even the beginning of more formal biblical studies.[85] Of course, the father could hire a *melammed* for this purpose. *Sefer Ḥasidim* refers to a *melammed ʿivri,* whose job was to teach the student to recognize and read Hebrew words.[86] The well-known Ashkenazic educational initiation ceremony (see Appendix B) presumes that the child can recognize Hebrew letters and perhaps read words but calls on the *melammed* to reinforce both these skills by having the new student read after him and recite a series of verses.[87]

We will discuss later whether Mishnah was in fact taught as a separate discipline in Ashkenaz and whether biblical studies were found in the curriculum at a higher educational level.[88] M. Breuer has suggested that just as biblical studies were downplayed for mature students in the Tosafist period, Bible was also not systematically taught to elementary level students.[89] Only from pre-Crusade Ashkenaz are there sources describing tutors teaching Bible to their students.[90]

As the formulation of Roqeaḥ clearly indicates, Scripture was in fact taught to elementary-level students in the later period as well. The biblical text served as an introduction to the reading and understanding of Hebrew.[91] R. Isaac Or Zaruaʿ refers to *melammedei tinoqot* who taught the weekly portion, ostensibly with either Targum Onqelos or Rashi's commentary.[92] The sections in *Sefer Ḥasidim* that discuss biblical studies for children attempted to guide that study, not create it.[93] In discussing the halakhic status of the tutor who resigns, Ri described a *melammed* who was hired to teach an entire "*sefer*" or half the "*sefer,*" without any time limit. The "*sefer*" referred to was a book of the Bible.[94] R. Gershom discusses, in a responsum, the case of a *melammed* who was contracted to teach his young pupil "all of Scripture" and subsequently claimed that he had done so.[95]

It appears that the *melammed* in Ashkenaz was involved primarily with younger students. The tutor is very often referred to as a *melammed tinoqot.* Moreover, the Ashkenazic responsa dealing with the employment of the *melammed* consistently address issues that reflect a fairly young student pool, such as the responsibility of the tutor in cases of prolonged student illness.[96] As we have seen, the average *melammed* taught material that did not require great breadth or depth of knowledge. We can therefore assume that *melammedim* usually taught biblical reading, translation, and basic interpretation or else perhaps the rudiments of Talmudic study.

In general medieval society a nobleman retained a tutor for his child until the basic educational process was complete. A student striving to become a scholar had to seek a school and its master or a university.[97] In Jewish society, once the rudiments of Talmudic study were assimilated, the student either sought out a local teacher, who delivered lectures to a group of students, or traveled to an academy. In the responsum referred to above, R. Gershom described an arrangement whereby A was hired by B to take charge of the latter's son and to "enter him into the gates of the scholars in the morning and at night." Presumably, the father hired this "tutor" to help his son make the transition from private study to studying in an academy or study hall. While the teacher in these institutions had certain responsibilities toward the student, he was not as responsible to the father as the *melammed* was.[98]

2

Attitudes toward Childhood and the Educational Process

IN 1960 PHILLIPE ARIÈS published a controversial book entitled *L'enfant et la vie familiale sous l'ancien régime.*[1] The book was translated into English in 1962 and entitled *Centuries of Childhood: A Social History of Family Life.*[2] Ariès maintains that in western Europe until the sixteenth century, no one paid much attention to children during the *enfances* stage of childhood (birth to age seven). This does not mean that all children in the Middle Ages were necessarily despised or neglected. Rather, the awareness of what distinguished a child from an adult was lacking; and as a result, there was no appreciation of childhood for its own sake.[3] Citing evidence from iconography depicting the "ages of children," the history of both games and children's dress, and a vast array of medieval texts, Ariès argues that in medieval society, there was a complete lack of attribution of any special character to childhood.[4] Parents did not accept children on their own terms, enjoy them, or coddle them.[5] There was also no attempt made by parents to inculcate self-control or supervise the young child's moral development.[6] The newborn baby who had not yet acquired certain physical and intellectual skills was treated with indifference.[7] The death of a small child was not a cause for great sorrow.[8] Indeed, Lynn White, who accepts Ariès's thesis, sees the relative indifference of adults toward children as directly related to the high infant and child mortality rate. It did not pay to invest great emotional capital in a child whose chance of survival was less than 50 percent.[9]

Ariès further claimed that once the child reached the post-*enfances* stage and did not need to be cared for as much as before, he immediately became part of the adult world. Thus, medieval education was not geared to children but to "little adults." There was no structured primary education at all. When children did begin their schooling, there was no attempt made to separate students of different ages and abilities.[10] The educational process was such that in most cases the child was removed from his family and was taken by the teacher or tutor to live in a different household or location. This further loosened the bonds between parents and children and encouraged these students, because of a lack of discipline, to become rowdy.[11] The loosely knit family prevailed throughout the Middle Ages, and it was not until the modern period that the concept of a nuclear family centered around children and their parents became firmly established.[12]

Ariès's book evoked varied responses but most certainly revitalized interest in children and childhood. Some scholars, while generally accepting his thesis, attempted to blunt the force of some of his conclusions by finding sources that ran counter to the thesis. Thus, U. T. Holmes, in a 1968 review of Ariès's work, gathered some anecdotal texts showing an appreciation of childhood on the part of the texts' central figures.[13] For example, in *The Life of William Marshall* little William's cute childish talk and mannerisms while at play gave pleasure to King Stephen and indeed saved William's life while he was being held hostage.[14] Chrétien de Troyes writes of a father who embraces his young daughter and protects her from being teased by her older sister.[15] Holmes claims that children had their own toys and amused themselves with a variety of games. The fact that adults would also play some of these games (which led Ariès to conclude that children did not have their own "childish" games) is considered by Holmes to be inconsequential. Evidence from art, which shows that children were not well depicted or were drawn as little adults, may result from the poor drawing techniques employed before 1400. As for education, Holmes shows that in the upper strata of society a child was often given a *maistre* or *garde,* who, while not much older, supervised the child's studies and served *in loco parentis*. Holmes concludes, however, that in the majority of cases children between the ages of seven and fourteen were sent away from the home to be educated or receive training without any form of parental control.

In the 1970s, new interest in the history of childhood fostered directly and indirectly by Ariès's work brought forth additional material. Most of the research centered around the first part of Ariès's thesis, that childhood as a distinct entity and parental appreciation of childhood were not to be found in medieval society. David Hunt, writing in 1970, questioned the plausibility of some of Ariès's conclusions in light of the basic tenets of human psychology. If the indifference of the parents to their younger offspring was as deep and pervasive as Ariès suggests, the very lives of these children would have been threatened.[16] In the midseventies several papers presented additional sources and materials showing, among other things, that medieval art did portray children's faces and bodies as distinct from those of adults.[17] The most significant and heavily documented article produced at this time was an article by Mary McLaughlin entitled "Survivors and Surrogates: Children and Parents from the Ninth to the Thirteenth Centuries" and published in a volume entitled *The History of Childhood*.[18] Using a wide range of sources, McLaughlin showed that from the twelfth century on, tenderness toward children, interest in the stages of development, and responsiveness to the beauty of children can be documented in poems, tales, philosophical and scientific works, and hagiography.[19] Greater interest in developing the morality of children can also be found especially in the thirteenth century encyclopedia of Bartholomew of England and the work of his contemporary Vincent of Beauvais on the education of noble children.[20] It is striking, however, McLaughlin notes, that few of these sources represent the views of actual parents. They may reflect an ideal rather than a practice, although the ideal itself is significant. Indeed, in entitling her paper "Survivors and Surrogates," McLaughlin claims to sum up the actual, unenviable position of children in medieval society. There is ample evidence of children who were neglected, beaten, and even murdered. The enactment of corrective legislation, ecclesiastic and secular, indicates that such occurrences were not rare.[21]

If Ariès's questions are asked about Jewish society in medieval western Europe, the same answers will not always apply.[22] Consider a passage found in the commentary to *Pirqei Avot,* hitherto attributed to R. Yedaʿyah ha-Penini of Béziers.[23] M. Saperstein has shown that this commentary is in reality not the work of R. Yedaʿyah but of a certain R. Isaac b. Yedaʿyah, who flourished in Provence in the thirteenth century.[24] The passage is found in R. Isaac's comments to a *mishnah* in the third chapter of *Avot:* "Sleep of the morning and wine in the afternoon and the conversation of children remove one from the world."[25] In explaining why children's conversation causes this result, R. Isaac writes that the nature of man is to love the small child more than the older one. The child teaches or causes the father to speak of idle matters (*ledabber siḥah beteilah*), perhaps to talk baby talk; and whatever the child says is pleasing to the father.[26] R. Isaac further asserts that it is the nature of man that the father expends more effort with the younger child than with the older one who knows the difference between right and wrong and who is weaned and can take care of himself.[27] The small child who cannot tell the difference between right and wrong will die an abrupt death if his father does not help him. The purpose of this *mishnah* in R. Isaac's view is to teach that devoting excessive unstructured attention to the child will harm both father and son. When the father is supposed to be developing his own intellect, the child burdens him with his idle talk and his playing. The time that the father should spend teaching the son will likewise be occupied with childish inanities.

The child being discussed in this comment is one who has not yet been weaned. It is precisely this child who, according to Ariès, did not count. Ariès finds no evidence for parents' enjoying the childish behavior of their offspring. R. Isaac assumes that quite to the contrary, there is a natural yearning on the part of a parent to play with the child as a child, to talk baby talk with him and almost to resist the notion that he will grow up. While R. Isaac's comment is the teaching of a moralist and is based on a rabbinic text, it would make no sense to preach these principles if the parents he was addressing did not do as he claims.[28]

Similar attitudes toward childhood were also evident in Ashkenazic society. *Sefer Ḥasidim* is a particularly rich source for the attitudes of parents in Ashkenaz toward childhood. While many sections of this work are devoted to a theoretical exposition of proper beliefs and practices in the Pietist community and while the actions attributed to a particular rabbi or scholar in *Sefer Ḥasidim* cannot very often be taken as historical fact, attitudes or practices that *Sefer Ḥasidim* seeks to correct or embellish or that form the silent backdrop of the author's discussions can be considered to approximate the actual attitudes of the period. Thus, a recent article uses *Sefer Ḥasidim* as an important source for shedding light on medical practices in medieval Germany.[29] Bearing this methodological caveat in mind, we can find several sections in *Sefer Ḥasidim* indicating that parents truly enjoyed playing with, or being with, their small children; that they normally took time to do so; and that they were concerned with, and attuned to, the emotional well-being of their small children.[30] For example,

> Towards evening, a man should not take a child onto his lap, lest the child dirty his clothes. If you were to suggest that he can wash his clothes, [still] they will not be as clean as before. Also, while the father looks for water, the time for praying the *Minḥah* service may pass . . . and he will arrive late, after the congregation has begun to pray. In addition, it is possible that when the father tries to put the son down, the child will cry. The father will be most concerned with the child and not with giving honor to his Creator [*yaḥus 'al ha-yeled ve-lo yaḥus 'al kevod qono*].[31]

Talking or playing with a small child was a source of pleasure for the parent. The author of *Sefer Ḥasidim* welcomed these activities at the appropriate time as helpful diversions while cautioning that they should not cause the father to be remiss in his religious duties such as prayer and study. Hence, "A person who is troubled and [whose] mind cannot comprehend because of the pain, should remove the pain by taking a walk, and then return to the study of Torah. Also, a person of troubled mind on the Sabbath should speak with a youth in order to remove the melancholy from his heart. But he should not stroll idly with the child or kiss him in the synagogue."[32]

It is interesting that just prior to the first passage quoted, too, the author of *Sefer Ḥasidim* seeks to restrict the father's kissing of the child in the synagogue in order that the father show his love and devotion only for his Creator. In other sections *Sefer Ḥasidim* wishes to minimize this practice because it would show insensitivity to those who did not have, or who had lost, children.[33] The synagogue was a place where children were normally treated in a way that would encourage their attendance. While a child was in attendance, the father would pay great attention to him and display his love for him.[34]

A passage found in several volumes of the so-called *sifrut devei Rashi* asserts that a Rhineland scholar (perhaps R. Eliezer ha-Gadol, the great teacher of Mainz in the first half of the eleventh century) would pray with a small child (*tinoq*) in his lap (or perhaps on his shoulders). He would remove the child only when it came time to recite the Shema.[35] Moreover, a passage in *Sefer Or Zarua*ʿ encourages parents to bring little children, both male and female, to the synagogue. Thus, R. Isaac Or Zaruaʿ heartily endorses the prevalent custom of allowing the children to kiss the Torah while it is being rolled up. This will heighten the sensitivity of the children to the performance of religious precepts, and their attendance generally will inculcate the fear of heaven. Such practices could only flourish in a society where the special character of children was understood and appreciated.[36]

When R. Eleazar Roqeaḥ mourned the loss of his twelve-year-old daughter at the hands of Christians in 1197, he eulogized her as a girl of great piety and wisdom who had learned the liturgy in its entirety. She served her Creator through her prayer and her honesty and served her father and household by preparing the beds and untying her father's boots at night and by sewing and weaving. When R. Eleazar described his six-year-old daughter, who was also killed, he noted that she read the first portion of Shema each day and could also sew and weave. But in addition, R. Eleazar mourns her loss because she "played with me and sang [*me-shashaʿat oti u-mezammeret*]."[37] On the one hand, R. Eleazar was pleased that she had begun to master sewing and the recitation of prayers, which were appropriate for a young adult. On the other hand, he appreciated the childish innocence and frivolity that she shared with him.

The sources that we have reviewed show that in Jewish society of northern France and Germany parents did enjoy their children and that some were clearly cognizant of the distinct nature of childhood. These examples also attest to the fact that Jewish parents in Christian Europe did pay attention to their children during the *enfances* period. They were certainly not indifferent toward their children. Ariès argued that the indifference that he uncovered in society at large could be explained in part as a function of the parents' belief that the small child, who had not yet developed certain intellectual skills, simply did not merit the investment of time at this point in their lives.[38] Thus, no attempt was made to inculcate self-control or supervise the moral development of the young child. By contrast, Jewish scholars of this period wished to caution parents that it was never too early to begin to develop the child's intellect and moral sensitivities and sensibilities. The Tosafist R. Pereẓ writes,

> The child emerges from his mother's womb, from darkness to light, and [God] prepared his sustenance, purity from impurity, the milk of the breasts from the menstrual blood, until the child is weaned. From then on, [God] put the favor of the child in the eyes of his mother and father and they will procure his food and his clothing. They will teach him Torah and guide him in the ways of Heaven and the precepts and good deeds. They strive and work for his benefit, in order that he be able to study Torah in purity and with ease. They are partners with God, and He gave the child the intellect to grasp the teachings.[39]

Other thirteenth- and fourteenth-century scholars, such as Shem Tov Ibn Falaqera,[40] R. Menaḥem ha-Meiri,[41] and R. Menaḥem b. Aaron Ibn Zeraḥ,[42] refer to the development of good character traits and acceptable social behavior in children before they are five.[43] We have already noted that Christians recognized that their Jewish counterparts taught modesty and purity of speech, in addition to religious precepts, to their very young children.[44]

We have seen that elementary-level classes were held either in the student's or tutor's home or in rented rooms in the same town.[45] As such, the beginning of the educational process in Jewish society was very closely connected to the child's home. This process was much less disruptive to family life than the prevalent practice in Christian society.[46]

With regard to one aspect of its attitudes toward childhood, however, Ashkenazic Jewish society seemed to have been no different from its Christian counterpart. Jews tended to educate their elementary-level students as little adults. The schoolboy's primer was the biblical text, which was followed by the Talmudic corpus. He was introduced to education in order that he might become a scholar, and he was to emulate the scholar from the start.[47] There is no evidence for any effort undertaken in normative educational practice to separate children of different abilities or to teach children of varying abilities differently. Moreover, because there was no actual system of elementary education in Ashkenaz, as we have demonstrated, little attention was paid to the qualifications of teachers or to monitoring the progress of the students.[48]

Sefer Ḥasidim alone was sensitive to these issues and made concrete suggestions to aid both the stronger and the weaker student. It urged that attempts be made to monitor the elementary-level student to see if he was making progress. This policy was suggested to help both the weaker and the stronger student by letting the stronger advance and the weaker improve.[49] The only other medieval text to exhibit similar concerns was the enigmatic *Sefer Ḥuqqei ha-Torah.*[50] The author of *Sefer Ḥasidim* also displayed a noteworthy appreciation of a child's abilities to question and to learn.[51]

To be sure, the sensitivity of *Sefer Ḥasidim* in these matters emerged from more than just the general concern that children should not be educated as "little adults." As we shall see, the monitoring of teachers' qualifications and fitness for instruction and students' abilities to grasp what they are being taught is to be continued, according to *Sefer Ḥasidim,* as the student moves from elementary studies to the study of the Talmud. The struggling Talmud student should be directed to remain with simple biblical studies or to study Midrash or codes.[52] The teacher who is a knowledgeable Talmudic scholar but does not set a standard for the transmission of moral values should not be retained.[53] I. Ta-Shema has described the educational policies of *Sefer Ḥasidim* as being formulated, in large measure, to ensure that the average student in Ashkenaz would also be able to learn:

> "In the main [the German Pietists] were concerned about the average, in-between students who, in the final analysis, were the majority of the student population. They were likely, from the very beginning, to drop out of the [Tosafist or dialectic-oriented] academy, whose members consisted of an elite group of intellectuals. For them, in the main, *Sefer Ḥasidim* proposes an alternate curriculum of study which would prepare them to be good Jews, who were truly God-fearing, as well as knowledgeable in Jewish law and anxious to do the will of God."[54]

The author of *Sefer Ḥasidim* sought to de-emphasize, from the start of the educational process, the link between Torah study and the achievement of lofty intellectual goals. He also wished to mute feelings of superiority in the bright student and feelings of inferiority in the weaker one. Students of different abilities should be separated and all students should be taught first and foremost to see the moral and ethical values of the text. The young student, beginning the study of the same biblical and Talmudic texts that he would continue to study throughout life, should not necessarily approach these texts as a budding dialectician or Tosafist but as a good Jew.

3
The Economics of Higher Education

MODERN SCHOLARSHIP HAS been able to describe and analyze with great clarity the literary creativity of the Tosafists and the impact of this material on the development of *halakhah* in medieval Ashkenaz. Very little progress has been made, however, in determining how the Tosafist academies and other *battei midrash* functioned within Ashkenazic society. Significant issues that have hardly been addressed include the degree of communal involvement in the support of scholarship and maintenance of *battei midrash* and *yeshivot;* the community's formal role, if any, in the opening of academies and the appointment of scholars to head those academies; and the impact of academies and study halls on the governance and religious life of their host communities.[1] Our first task is to characterize the economics of education in Ashkenazic society. Were teachers, scholars, and students the recipients of salaries, subsidies, or charitable contributions? If so, who were their benefactors? In short, what was the nature of professional scholarship in Ashkenaz?

Ashkenazic Jewry had to deal with the obvious tension between the need to provide teachers and scholars with a livelihood and the halakhic problems inherent in receiving payment for teaching Talmud. Compensation for the teaching of Torah was not acceptable in rabbinic thought except in instances where it was perceived that Scripture permitted compensation. Teaching of the Oral Law for gain was categorically proscribed by formulations in both the Babylonian and Palestinian Talmuds.[2] The passage in the Palestinian Talmud noted that in reality there were teachers of Oral Law who were compensated. This arrangement was permitted when the compensation was viewed as the teacher's opportunity costs (*sekhar battalah*). If the teacher could have worked in another job or profession, he was paid for teaching Torah up to the amount that he could have earned in the other position.[3]

Tosafists concluded from their analysis of parallel sources in the Babylonian Talmud that it was permissible to receive compensation for teaching Talmud if the teacher had no other means of support. Even if the teacher had the ability to do other work, he was entitled because of the importance of his chosen vocation to *sekhar battalah* provided that he did not receive compensation from any other position.[4]

R. Isaac of Corbeil maintained that any teacher whose students did not comprehend immediately but required the teacher to expend effort (*toraḥ*) to ensure that they grasped the material being taught might also receive payment. On the other hand, teachers of students who grasped the lessons as they were being taught could not be compensated. R. Isaac does not identify the students in the last group further. His formulation perhaps implies that Talmudic scholars who lectured to students in an academy or *beit midrash* were not permitted, in general, to receive payment for their teaching.[5]

Other Tosafists rejected the utilization of any form of *sekhar battalah* and contended that in practice an instructor of Talmud ought to teach without compensation and earn his livelihood in a profession other than teaching. The author of a twelfth-century Ashkenazic commentary to *Avot,* perhaps Rashbam, interprets the phrase *and despise rabbinic position* in *Avot* 1:6 to mean that one must "lower himself in order to secure employment" and not receive payment for rabbinic functions, including teaching.[6] Elsewhere in his commentary, the author states that Torah must be taught to others neither for self-aggrandizement nor for compensation. The author explicitly rejects the practice of paying a teacher *sekhar battalah,* although he notes that there are those who accept payment through reliance on this concept. Only teachers of young children may be compensated.[7] R. Eliezer of Metz writes that Rabiah "ran away from honor in order not to appear haughty and in order not to receive compensation because of his knowledge of Torah."[8] Several rabbinic texts reveal the nonteaching occupations of important Tosafists, including Rashbam. Many Tosafists who taught students did not earn their livelihoods from teaching.[9] Indeed, it was common practice in Ashkenazic society that scholars worked at some kind of profession in order to earn their livelihoods and devote any remaining time to their studies.[10] An ideal profession was thus one that consumed as little time as possible.[11] An academy head—or even a lesser scholar—who lectured to older students often had the opportunity to earn a living in some other profession and did not have to rely on any of the prevailing arguments allowing compensation for teaching Torah. His students did not require constant supervision, as did the young students of a *melammed*.

Interestingly, the twelfth century saw a change in the attitude of Christian scholars toward the receiving of payment for teaching God's Word. The masters in the new urban schools that were opened in numerous cathedrals in the twelfth century received payment for their teaching. These teachers were paid for their instruction in the form of salaries from public authorities, ecclesiastical prebends, or (most often) monies paid by the students themselves. This was, of course, not the practice in the monasteries. Opposition to the practice of paying the masters was neutralized by the claim that the teacher's payment was the result of the labor and time expended in the service of his students rather than payment for his knowledge. However, while a number of famous twelfth-century scholars were wealthy men, some Christian thinkers still clung to the notion that to live a scholarly life meant to live a life of poverty.[12]

Undoubtedly, there were teachers of Talmud in Ashkenaz who did rely on the justifications we have described and received payment for their teaching. To be sure, the teacher who accepted compensation could have done so in order to spend additional time studying Talmud; so these arrangements might be perceived as a form of professionalized scholarship. Nevertheless, the payment of *sekhar battalah* was made only to someone who taught and thus provided a service to others, not to one who was engaged solely in study.[13] There is no evidence for any salaries or stipends paid to scholars in the period prior to 1348 so that they could engage solely in Talmudic study.[14] No effort was made to establish a cadre of scholars in Ashkenaz that would be supported by individuals or communities to make Torah study their profession.[15] Even if the formulations that sought to curb the payment of *sekhar battalah* were not always heeded, they reflect a strong desire within Ashkenazic society to withhold compensation from those who were engaged in Torah study. Some forms of support could not be withheld for practical reasons. But the ideal that a scholar should not earn a livelihood from his studies retained its prominence. As we shall see, its influence was felt with regard to other aspects of a scholar's livelihood—such as tax exemptions, where the scholar's privileges were curtailed.

Although no salaries were offered to scholars by virtue of their studies, it was deemed appropriate to aid scholars so that they could earn a living as effortlessly as possible. R. Gershom was asked a question concerning a scholar who taught Talmud to a group of older students. He had no salaried or official position and did not receive compensation for his lessons. He earned his livelihood from business dealings with Gentiles who were his clients exclusively. R. Gershom ruled that the monopolistic business relationship that the scholar had developed must be protected by the community even though this community was not accustomed to allowing its members to retain monopolies:[16] "The community is mandated by Talmudic law to protect and aid this scholar, whose work is the work of heaven [*melekhet shamayim*] and who teaches Torah without compensation, in order that he not be distracted from his studies."[17]

There is almost no discussion in Ashkenazic rabbinic literature about providing tax exemptions for scholars. *Sefer Ḥasidim,* one of the few sources in medieval Ashkenaz to refer to this issue, maintains that tax exemptions for scholars, which were mandated by Talmudic law, were reserved for scholars who earned no livelihood and spent all of their time engaged in study (*toratan ummanutan*).[18] Since the practice in Ashkenaz was that all scholars who needed to earn a livelihood and were capable of doing so had to work at an occupation of some type, none of these scholars qualified for a tax exemption. Only a scholar who was independently wealthy or was completely impoverished could qualify for a tax exemption. Thus, the absence of discussion concerning the granting of tax exemptions for scholars in Ashkenazic rabbinic literature may be explained by the fact that in practice Ashkenazic communities did not grant tax exemptions to scholars.[19] A. Grossman and D. Berger have argued that the small size of the pre-Crusade Ashkenazic communities, the high percentage of scholars in the communities even as they grew larger numerically, and the leadership roles that many scholars took in these communities rendered the granting of tax exemptions to scholars almost impossible.[20] I. Ta-Shema has shown that a more lenient Ashkenazic position developed after 1348, but even then there was still stiff opposition to exemptions for scholars.[21] R. Ḥayyim Paltiel (a younger contemporary of R. Meir of Rothenburg)[22] writes that the greatest scholars of his day paid taxes.[23]

To better understand the positions of Ashkenazic Jewry regarding professional scholarship and privileges for scholars, a comparison to Jewish society in Spain will be helpful. As an inheritor of the legacy of the Geonim, whose academies developed extensive systems of support and fundraising, Andalusian Jewry was predisposed to providing financial support for its scholars.[24] Jewish communities in Spain continued to do so throughout the Middle Ages, despite Maimonides' well-known position that Torah scholars who decided not to work but to live on the salaries provided by willing benefactors were profaning the name of God. Indeed, Maimonides notes that his position is against the dominant [Sephardic] communal practice of his day.[25] R. Shmuel ha-Nagid (d. 1056) had already endorsed the very practice that Maimonides condemns when he proclaimed that he would support and maintain any scholar who wished to make Torah study his profession (*lihyot torato ummanuto*).[26] R. Avraham ibn Daud refers to important scholars who were supported by patrons and to scholars and judges who received salaries from their communities.[27] R. Yehudah b. Barzilai (c. 1100) provided Talmudic justification for these practices. Moreover, R. Yehudah maintained that communal support for judges and scholars is both prevalent and obligatory.[28]

Spanish halakhists of the thirteenth century were sensitive to the Maimonidean view that a scholar should derive his sustenance from secular pursuits. The scholar who was able to earn a livelihood from other endeavors should not denigrate his Torah scholarship by seeking to make it the major source of his livelihood or by reaching out to others for financial support.[29] But at the same time, the communities were obligated to provide for scholars in order to ensure their uninterrupted study. Members of the community were encouraged to identify and support scholars who needed their help in order to continue to study seriously or to maintain their academies.[30] These scholars could accept the support of communities or patrons if it was offered. The Maimonidean ideal was thus preserved only in part.

The carefully nuanced position of Rabbenu Yonah of Gerona clearly reflects this dichotomy. R. Yonah provided ample justification in a number of formulations for the compensation and support of scholars who were dedicated to their studies. In a comment on Proverbs 14:4, R. Yonah explained that the farmer must tolerate the slovenly habits of the ox and allow the animal to fulfill its needs because the ox is so productive for the farmer. So too, scholars should be tolerant of the masses. Such tolerance will enhance respect for scholars and facilitate the acceptance of religious instruction and admonition, but it also fulfills a somewhat more temporal purpose. The masses should be treated well "in order that the people carry the [scholars'] burden so that they can be free to study day and night." Just as one suffers the slovenliness of the ox because of its productivity, the scholar must tolerate the burdens that are placed upon him by various people because they can be helpful to him in his scholarly endeavors.[31]

In his *Iggeret ha-Teshuvah,* R. Yonah recommended that one who wished to further the study of Torah should "come to the aid of *rabbanim* and *talmidim* who study for the sake of heaven. He should contribute toward the support of scholars so that they will remain in his city and study Torah because of him."[32] In his *Commentary to Proverbs,* R. Yonah wrote that the purpose of the righteous man in striving to acquire wealth was to be able to devote himself to the support of sacred causes and to assist those who fear God and make his name known.[33] The biblical commentary attributed to Rabbenu

Yonah, which is a product of his milieu and teachings if not of his pen, openly advocated the support of yeshiva students and scholars and noted that this has been in vogue "since the days of the Geonim."[34]

R. Yonah does cite Rambam's well-known diatribe against subsidized scholarship in his own commentary to *Avot* 4:7. But as I have demonstrated elsewhere, careful comparison of Rambam's comment to Rabbenu Yonah's reveals that R. Yonah's citation was suggestively selective. R. Yonah's comment was intended mainly to prevent a scholar from abusing his position and privileges.[35]

According to Rabbenu Yonah payment for teaching Torah in the form of *sekhar battalah,* which was explicitly rejected by Maimonides,[36] could be received without hesitation.[37] This was also the view of Ramban[38] and probably of Ramah as well. Indeed, Ramah discusses the payment of teachers in a community in detail and is receptive to the idea of communal support for education.[39]

All of the aforementioned Sephardic halakhists, including Maimonides, approved the granting of tax exemptions to qualified scholars.[40] Ramah and R. Asher b. Yeḥiel (in a responsum addressed to a Spanish Jewish community) even granted tax exemptions to one who had a profession but devoted as much time as he could to his studies.[41] According to Ramah the scholar is exempt "not because of his poverty but because of his Torah." There were some Spanish communities that would not grant an exemption to a scholar who did not devote himself exclusively to study.[42] But the fact remains that some form of tax exemption for scholars was the norm in Sephardic communal and intellectual life.

In the conflict between the benefits of professional scholarship and the demands of spirituality, spirituality triumphed in Ashkenaz. A scholar had to be self-sufficient and derive his sustenance from some outside form of employment, not from the study of Torah. Perhaps the models for this position were Tannaim and Amoraim who earned their livelihoods from secular pursuits, often enduring great hardships in the process.[43] While some Ashkenazic scholars approved of the Talmudic convention of paying *sekhar battalah* to a teacher of Talmud, no salaries or direct communal subsidies were paid to scholars who wished to dedicate themselves to Torah study.[44] In fact, the only religious functionary who was paid by the community was the cantor.[45] Moreover, Ashkenazic scholars were not even granted tax exemptions. Two additional formal privileges aimed at enhancing the status and economic well-being of scholars were available to Spanish but not Ashkenazic scholars in the high Middle Ages: Spanish scholars were entitled to place anyone who embarrassed or shamed them under a ban;[46] in addition, they were entitled to collect fines from those who embarrassed them.[47] Despite its fierce dedication to the separation of scholarship from livelihood, Ashkenazic Jewry recognized that scholars might need some type of assistance in order to remain otherwise financially independent. Individuals were permitted and even encouraged to help scholars earn their own livelihood with greater ease. The scholars surely benefited from this assistance, yet the ideal that one should not profit from the study of Torah was preserved.

So far our discussion has focussed on support for mature scholars. We must also consider the financial aid that students received. An attempt was made to diminish the financial responsibilities of needy students who studied in *battei midrash* or Tosafist *yeshivot.* The goal was partially to defray the cost of the students' education through charitable contributions. This was not to imply that students could or should make a living through their dedication to Torah study. In the case of a charitable contribution to one who was indigent, the money being paid was not viewed as an exchange for the study of Torah (as was the case when a salary was paid). In order to describe this practice, it is necessary to look briefly at the economic needs of one who studied in a *beit midrash* or *yeshivah* in Ashkenaz.

There were numerous *battei midrash* scattered throughout the towns of northern France and Germany. When they were not busy earning their livelihoods, residents would gather in the local study hall to continue their own studies or to attend lectures in Talmud. Youngsters who had completed their elementary studies with tutors and had the inclination and the ability could certainly study in the local study hall as well.[48] But students who wished to study with an accomplished scholar often had to travel away from home to the study hall or academy where that scholar taught. Just as there were wandering students throughout medieval society, there were wandering

Jewish students who would study in one or more *battei midrash* over a period of time.[49] These students would usually reside in the home of their teacher or in surrounding homes. They ate their meals in the teacher's home, either in their own rooms or with the teacher and his family.[50] We cannot describe with certainty the financial arrangements that were in effect, and they may have varied from academy to academy. Many of the teachers did not earn a livelihood from their teaching, as we have noted. But there is evidence that the students contributed some money (if not the full amount of their boarding costs), depending on the personal resources and generosity of the teacher.[51] *Sefer Ḥasidim* refers to a student who was traveling to a distant location to study and had only enough money to stay for a short while.[52] In addition to living expenses, married men who wandered to study with scholars or even in search of employment were required to support their families during their absence. Even in situations where the students and their families lived in the same town as the *beit midrash* or academy, the students often resided during the day or for the entire week in the *beit midrash* (= teacher's home), returning to their homes only late at night or perhaps for the Sabbath.[53]

Students were expected, at least in theory, to pay their own way. Those whose families were able to cover their costs could devote themselves solely to their studies.[54] Others became *melammedim* in order to pay initial costs or to prolong their stay.[55] Nonetheless, contributions were made in some places to help reduce costs for students who were not able to pay. These donations were often invested in order to generate additional revenue. Evidence for this practice is found in a responsum of R. Asher b. Yeḥiel. R. Asher writes that there was an established practice in Germany to invest funds that had been donated to study halls and synagogues in ways that were in violation of standard Jewish usury law. The monies realized from the investment of funds donated to the synagogue went toward the upkeep of the synagogue, the payment of cantors, and the purchase of supplies needed for services. The funds that were donated and then invested on behalf of the study hall were also used to acquire needed supplies. But in addition, according to R. Asher, "this practice contributed to the teaching of Torah because any poor people could use the funds for study, and [the treasurers] also provided for these students who study in the presence of great scholars." R. Asher concludes that in order to further Torah study the forms of investment that he had described, normally prohibited by rabbinic decree, ought to be permitted. In support of his conclusion R. Asher asserts that R. Meir (of Rothenburg) allowed charity funds and study hall and synagogue funds to be lent out at interest in a manner otherwise proscribed according to rabbinic law. R. Asher adds, "Therefore I have permitted it for charity funds [in Spain] because I have seen people here who usurp for themselves in halakhic matters the office of great scholars and prohibit it. . . . They cast aspersions on the students saying that their learning and support is [achieved through] prohibited [means] and I have thus written to silence those who complain about it."[56]

R. Asher claims that these practices had a positive effect on Torah study in Ashkenaz. It is difficult, however, to gauge how widespread this support for poor students who studied in *battei midrash* was.[57] There is only one other source (a responsum of R. Meir of Rothenburg) describing a charitable contribution that was invested on behalf of poor students or scholars in Ashkenaz.[58] Moreover, the earliest source to which R. Asher refers as justification for the supposedly long-term practice for investing funds donated to the study halls is an unidentified decision of R. Meir of Rothenburg, perhaps the responsum just mentioned.

Even if we assume that this type of funding was prevalent at the end of the thirteenth century and before, it was directed toward a limited group and did not compromise the Ashkenazic ideal concerning support for Torah study. The contributions were made and invested on behalf of indigent students who wished to study in the local study hall as well as of the poor students (*talmidim hallalu*) who wished to attend more prestigious study halls. These donations were intended to aid students who could not otherwise afford to set aside time for study or pay the costs of studying with a qualified teacher.

M. Breuer has argued that the academies of Germany and Austria in the fourteenth and fifteenth centuries became quasi-public. Communal support for students was quite common, although some academy heads did receive payment from their students. By the fifteenth century, several German communities had established a "student tax" that members of the communities paid to support the students in their academies. Across-the-board stipends (*haspaqot*), which covered the expenses of all students who studied in a particular academy, were offered by Ashkenazic *yeshivot* at that time.[59] This change in policy is attributed to the exigencies of the period. For the first time the concept of *sekhar battalah* was extended to all who were engaged exclusively in study, "lest the Torah be forgotten." Some ambitious academy heads offered additional sums to induce students to come to study with them.[60] J. Katz has described how the communal and supercommunal organizations of eastern Europe in the sixteenth and seventeenth centuries fully supported the wandering students who came to study in the academies. This public support was so extensive that no *roshei yeshivah* collected fees from their students.[61] Leading scholars in twelfth- and thirteenth-century Ashkenaz apparently did not accept fees for the Talmud that they taught. On the other hand, it is clear that both students and teachers in this period were heavily involved in, and burdened by, the economics of education.[62]

Here too, a comparison with Spain will prove illuminating. While R. Asher b. Yeḥiel informs us that some Spanish Jews questioned the practice of investing funds earmarked for the support of Torah study, he was not the only Spanish scholar to render a lenient decision in this matter. Rashba was asked about the prevailing practice to invest these funds by lending them at fixed interest to Jews, a biblically prohibited practice that R. Asher and R. Meir of Rothenburg rejected categorically. Rashba offered the standard rationale that perhaps this money had no definable owners (like money donated to the temple) but asserted that this explanation was not satisfactory. Rashba concluded that the money should preferably be invested in a manner that entails only a violation of rabbinic usury law. But he offers one additional justification for the current practice: since the members of this community have accepted the responsibility of supporting certain minors and students, as evidenced by their attempts to lend money for this purpose, those who are borrowing the money and paying back additional sums do not consider themselves to be paying interest. Support of these students was incumbent on them in any event.[63]

In additional to providing funds for students through the investment of charitable contributions,[64] Spanish Jewish society also engaged in several much more aggressive enterprises to provide funds for Torah study—and not only for indigent students. We find instances of people who donated vineyards or set up trust funds to allow Torah study to be perpetually supported by the sums that were generated yearly.[65] Efforts were undertaken in several Spanish communities to tax their members in order to support students.[66]

Perhaps most significant, stipends were granted to students who arrived to study in Provençal as well as Spanish academies. Benjamin of Tudela describes this funding in a number of locations in Provence, most notably in the city of Lunel: "The students that come from distant lands to study the Law are taught, boarded, lodged, and clothed by the community, so long as they attend the house of study." Benjamin writes that for the academy of Posquières, Rabad himself paid the expenses of *mi she-ein lo le-hoẓi.* This subsidy was quite extensive, since it was designed to pay for "all [the students'] needs"; but it was given only to students who required it. However, the descriptions of the practices of the other academies, which were maintained by the cities rather than by wealthy individual scholars like Rabad, do not refer to what the students could afford.[67] In the case of Lunel we are apparently dealing with a stipend extended to all students so that their studies at Lunel would cost them nothing.[68]

Spanish society advocated, as we have seen, the paying of salaries and the granting of support to scholars who made Torah study their profession. Among the forms of funding utilized were hefty stipends that academy heads received from their communities so that they could maintain their academies and remove the financial burdens of their students.[69] When Shmuel ha-Nagid indicated that he would support all those who wished to make Torah study their profession, he did not specify the age or stage of development that a student had to achieve in order to be eligible. Just as he provided texts for all students who needed them, he apparently was prepared to sustain both mature scholars and budding ones.[70] To be sure, it is most difficult to identify the precise point at which a *yeshivah* student became a candidate for professional scholarship. At some point a young man studying Talmud in Spain could receive money from the community or from individuals not merely because he was a student of an academy but by virtue of his own status as a dedicated scholar.[71]

In essence, the provisions to aid students in Spain were simply extensions of the various forms of communal support for mature scholars that we have traced. Salaries and stipends for mature scholars were not available in Ashkenaz. Heads of academies had no salaries or communal stipends to pass along to their students.[72] Many scholars did not even accept or condone payment for teaching through the justification of *sekhar battalah*. Tax exemptions were not granted. Thus, aid extended to students of Talmud was as limited as possible in consonance with the notion that professionalized scholarship was unacceptable. Indigent students in Ashkenaz were eligible for assistance, but this assistance was uneven and never guaranteed.[73]

4
The Relationship between the Academy and the Community

THE PRECEDING ANALYSIS has demonstrated that neither the Ashkenazic academies and *battei midrash* nor the students who studied in them were systematically supported or maintained by their communities. Evidence from the economics of education suggests that academies and study halls were not considered public institutions. We must now ascertain whether the communities had any role in the founding, administration, and governance of the academies. N. Golb has recently argued that most of the *yeshivot* of western Europe, including those in northern France, were founded and maintained by the cities and towns in which they were found. On the basis of literary sources and archival evidence, Golb views these academies as essentially communal institutions.[1]

Golb's thesis cannot be sustained in regard to the academies of northern France. None of the sources that he uses to describe schools supported and maintained by their communities or with the aura of communal institutions are from northern France. These sources are invariably Spanish or Provençal. The only source on which Golb relies that has any possible connection to northern France is *Sefer Ḥuqqei ha-Torah.* He believes that the Jewish communal structure discovered by archeologists at Rouen is a prototype of the communally maintained and funded academy which *Sefer Ḥuqqei ha-Torah* (see Appendix A) describes. But Golb's extensive reliance upon *Sefer Ḥuqqei ha-Torah* is problematic. The issues of where the text originated and whether the institutions described in it actually existed or were theoretical structures are not easily resolved. This text certainly cannot be used as an anchor for establishing educational realia in northern France.[2]

Similar methodological flaws invalidate Golb's contentions that all the leading European academies were quite large and that they were housed in communally owned and maintained structures. Golb claims that the model for the communal schools in all of medieval France were the academies of Iraq, Rome, and Mayence.[3] I shall show that in the case of the academies of northern France this assertion is unfounded.[4] In addition, Golb ignores several issues that are crucial for determining whether an institution is public or private. As we shall see, the leading *yeshivot* in Ashkenaz were centered around a particular Tosafist and were not formally connected to the community in which they functioned. Moreover, the Tosafist academies and the scholars who headed them were not automatically given a role in communal government. Academy heads who sat on rabbinic courts or were consulted in matters of *halakhah* were invited to serve because of their reputations as scholars, not because they headed a local academy.[5]

There were no clear guidelines or requirements for the opening of a *yeshivah* in a particular location, and there was no formal appointment procedure that a prospective academy head had to undergo. The brothers R. Moses and R. Samuel of Evreux, echoing a position of Ri, held that due to the vicissitudes of Jewish history, the most effective teachers of Torah were now texts rather than people. Certain signs of respect that according to Talmudic law had to be shown by a student to his major teacher were no longer in effect. It was therefore usual, at least in the brothers' city or region (*be-ʿiram*), that a student would open a new study hall whenever and wherever he wished, with no regard for the Talmudic dictum that a student cannot decide matters of law in a place proximate to his teacher.[6]

While R. Yoel ha-Levi was officially appointed cantor of Cologne, there is no evidence for his appointment as *rav* or *rosh yeshivah*.[7] V. Aptowitzer maintains that Rabiah replaced his father as *rav* in Cologne.[8] Here, too, there was no formal appointment.

He simply opened his academy there. Ribash writes that the granting of *semikhah* in Ashkenaz in the period prior to his own allowed the student to open an academy (*reshut liqboaʿ yeshivah bekhol maqom*) in addition to giving him the right to judge and decide matters of law.[9] But is not clear how far back the period referred to by Ribash extends and how widespread this practice was. Indeed, the historicity of Ribash's formulation has been questioned.[10] Not until the Ashkenazic *semikhah* that surfaced in the late fourteenth century (*semikhat moreinu*) were students required to secure a kind of license,[11] with the approbation of the community, to open their own *yeshivot.*[12]

All of this is in marked contrast to the structure of the Geonic institutions of higher learning. The surrounding Babylonian communities were closely bound to the *yeshivot* and were expected to provide both support and students.[13] More striking is the fact that these conventions and practices stand in contrast even to pre-Crusade Ashkenaz, where the major component used in identifying the leading local academies was not who the *rosh yeshivah* was but rather in which community the *yeshivah* was located. We usually speak of *Yeshivat Sura,* not of the *yeshivah* of R. Saʿadiah Gaon, of *Yeshivat Pumbeditha,* not of the *yeshivah* of R. Hai, and of the *yeshivah* of Mainz as an entity much larger than the *yeshivah* of Rabbenu Gershom.[14] These academies were tied to their communities; and while *roshei yeshivah* invariably passed on, the community and its *yeshivah* remained. For substantial periods of time these schools existed as centers to which new students and *roshei yeshivah* came. In the Tosafist period, however, a town or city had a first-rate academy only as long as a particular Tosafist lived there. As we have noted, students wandered from the school of one great scholar to the school of the next great scholar; and indeed the scholars themselves often changed locations. The academy of R. Tam, which undoubtedly first made an impact on the Jewish community of Ramerupt and later the community of Troyes, was not controlled or regulated by, or identified in name with, either community. We hear nothing about academies in Ramerupt or Troyes once R. Tam has left the scene.[15]

The different means of identifying academies in the pre-Crusade period and in the Tosafist period in Ashkenaz are evident in other contexts as well. There are dozens of references in Ashkenazic rabbinic literature to commentaries or views of pre-Crusade scholars described as the words of *geonei, rabbanei, ḥakhmei,* or *benei* of a particular locale.[16] Rashbam refers to *zeqenei Paris* of the mid–twelfth century but not without specifying them by name as well.[17] We do not, however, find such a title referring to the several important Tosafists who flourished in Paris circa 1200.[18] One set of the so-called *Taqqanot R. Tam* was addressed to *ḥakhmei gevul ha-Reinus, gedolei doreinu yoshvei ereẓ Lothaire, gedolei Auxerre ve-Sens* and *yeshishei Orleans;* but these titles were used as a means of indicating the locations in which the synod's decisions were to be binding.[19] Addressees of halakhic decisions and public policy might be referred to in this way, but commentaries and views emanating from the important academies of Ramerupt or Dampierre are called *Perush R. Tam* or *Tosafot Ri.*[20] Students were often responsible for the writing down of a particular Tosafist's lectures, a sign of the almost collegial relationship between Tosafists and their students. Yet the *tosafot* that they produced were not called the *tosafot* of *beit midrash* X or town X but of rabbi X.[21]

To be sure, the desire for anonymity, which was an important scholarly ideal in pre-Crusade Ashkenaz,[22] may have also been a factor in the naming of commentaries by the locale in which they were written rather than by an individual author or editor. But the centrality of the school and its location extends far past the realm of authorship. J. N. Epstein has demonstrated,[23] and A. Grossman confirmed with some modifications, that it is possible to identify commentaries, methodologies, and practices that were typical of the *yeshivah* of Mayence or Worms in the pre-Crusade period.[24] The characteristics of each school and its customs hold true no matter who the *rosh yeshivah* was. While advanced Tosafist study in Germany seems to remain concentrated in the same locales as in the pre-Crusade period (i.e., in Mainz, Worms, Cologne, and Spires, with only Bonn and perhaps Regensburg emerging as a new centers of scholarship), schools are identified as the academy or *beit midrash* of a particular scholar rather than by the location.[25]

Moreover, the *rosh yeshivah* was in a less central position in the pre-Crusade period. When a question arose in Mayence concerning the appropriate place in the synagogue service of Rosh Hashanah to perform a circumcision, the pious scholars (*qedoshim*) of that city were consulted: R. Gershom, R. Simeon the Great, R. Judah ha-Kohen, R. Judah the Great. Also consulted were *she'ar benei ha-yeshivah ha-qedoshah*. Many members of the academy at Mayence disagreed with the position taken by the majority of those consulted, which included R. Gershom; and R. Gershom was forced to explain the position. While R. Gershom was considered by his peers and by later generations to be a foremost teacher at Mayence and perhaps the greatest scholar of his day, the members of the academy were not referred to as the *yeshivah* or the students of R. Gershom but as students of the "holy *yeshivah*" at Mayence and as scholars in their own right.[26] In eleventh-century Mayence various rabbis within the congregation did as they wished concerning a particular synagogue custom until R. Yiẓḥaq attempted, acting on his own behalf, to establish a fixed custom for students who were unsure which scholars to follow.[27] Both the freedom of discussion and the absence of a central figure to guide the students until R. Yiẓḥaq stepped in are quite apparent. When a similar situation arose in Mayence just after the First Crusade concerning the order of the sounding of the shofar, a free discussion again ensued, with the heads of the academy participating in the discussion as peers of the members of the *yeshivah*, not as the dominant figures.[28]

A noticeably high degree of academic freedom was prevalent in the Tosafist academies.[29] Nevertheless, leading Tosafist teachers were always identified as the central figures in their academies. Students of R. Tam or Ri are referred to in just that manner. They are never known as members of the *yeshivah* or *beit midrash* of Ramerupt or Dampierre. A suggestive situation, which took place at the end of the twelfth century and is comparable to the question of shofar blowing, involved Riẓba and members of his *beit midrash*. The case is referred to as *Ma'aseh be-Riẓba ve-talmidav*. Riẓba required the one who blew the shofar to repeat an entire line of shofar blasts because he had made one note too long. After the services were over, older and younger students (*ha-ḥaverim veha-talmidim*) stood in front of him outside the synagogue. One student, Nathan of Trinquetaille, queried Riẓba as to why he required the whole line of blasts to be repeated. Riẓba could not parry all of Nathan's thrusts and in the end was quiet.[30] What is important here is not that the student bested the teacher. What is significant is that Riẓba took immediate charge of the situation. It was open to discussion only after the fact. Similarly, when R. Shemariah b. Mordekhai (an older contemporary of Riẓba) had forgotten to place an *eruv ḥaẓerot* for Mayence until after sunset, he ruled that he could do so then and announced his decision to those present in the synagogue. Although some scholar-students who were present wished to question his decision, he placed the *eruv*. A discussion between R. Shemariah and his students was held only on a subsequent day.[31] R. Isaac Or Zaruaʿ records that when he was a young student of R. Judah Sir Leon, "R. Judah was approached after services, in front of his home, while a group of students and homeowners were in his presence. R. Judah was asked a practical question concerning *notein taʿam lifegam* and he issued a permissive ruling."[32] No students offered, or were called upon for, their opinions.

A passage that perhaps captures the transition from the pre-Crusade period to the later one is found in *Sefer Raban*. In response to a case at hand, "all scholars of the generation, R. Jacob ha-Levi of Worms and his *yeshivah* and R. Isaac ha-Levi of Speyers and the members of his *yeshivah* wished to cancel the betrothal of the first [man]."[33] This situation occurred just after the First Crusade.[34] The twelfth-century shift had not yet fully taken hold; thus, opinions of the members of the academies were also noted. But the group is described as the "head of the academy and his school."[35]

We have already noted the evidence from twelfth- and thirteenth-century Provence for communal maintenance and support of major academies. In addition, the academies of Lunel, Béziers, Marseille, Montpellier, and Narbonne, while headed by great scholars, were known and identified in Provençal texts of the period primarily by the city in which they were located. It is also possible to trace (as but one example) at least four generations of scholars who headed the *yeshivah* at Narbonne from the late eleventh through the twelfth century.[36] Comparable institutional longevity is not found in Ashkenaz. As research by A. Grabois indicates, there existed in Provence, as compared to Ashkenaz, a more regulated elementary system as well, centered around the communally maintained *petites écoles*.[37] Moreover, one who held the title of *rosh yeshivah* in Provence was almost automatically appointed as the head or a member of the rabbinic tribunal in his city.[38]

A similar profile emerges for medieval Spain. Andalusian Jewry wished to distance itself to some extent from the Babylonian center, but the character of its indigenous academic institutions remained quite similar. While the arrival of great scholars from elsewhere turned Cordova and its sister city in North Africa, Kairawan, into centers of learning, they remained *centers* of learning, which in the Andalusian framework transcended the presence (or absence) of a particular scholar.[39]

The same is true for the leading *yeshivot* of Christian Spain. The academy at Lucena had been the seat of Talmudic scholarship in Moslem Spain for close to seventy years.[40] Following the flight of Jews from Andalusia in the middle of the twelfth century, descendants of its masters reopened the academy in Toledo. The leadership and development of the academy at Toledo can be traced over a period of more than 150 years.[41] The first stage begins with the family of Ri Megash arriving in Toledo to transplant the academy of Lucena (c. 1175) and reaches a successful conclusion with the ascendance of Ramah.[42] The second stage of development begins after the death of Ramah (1244) with the arrival of R. Yonah of Gerona and R. Moses ha-Kohen of Narbonne, followed later by R. Aharon ha-Levi (Ra'ah). The third stage is that of R. Asher b. Yeḥiel, who preserves the teachings of Ramah and is considered his successor in Toledo (c. 1325).[43]

In Moslem and Christian Spain the appointments of *roshei yeshivah* and communal rabbinic leaders and the regulation of these offices were in the hands of the community. The *ketav minui* and *ketav taqanta* found in the *Sefer ha-Shetarot* of R. Yehudah b. Barzilai of Barcelona were instruments for these procedures.[44] Payment for rabbis and heads of academies was connected to their appointments.[45] The professional rabbinate, whose members were often *roshei yeshivah* as well, developed much more quickly in Sefarad than in Ashkenaz. Despite the fact that the granting of *semikhah* may have been suspended in Spain between the times of Rif and Ri Megash, a professional rabbinate whose members (i.e., rabbis, judges, heads of academies) were officially appointed and funded by the communities was in existence in Sefarad throughout the Middle Ages.[46] The chronology of the development of the professional rabbinate in Ashkenaz has been discussed repeatedly.[47] Virtually all those who have addressed this issue agree that some type of formal relationship between the community and a rabbinic figure was established by the mid–fourteenth century, although several scholars place the beginning of these developments somewhat earlier.[48] The first bona fide evidence for rabbinic salaries comes from the end of the thirteenth century, but these sources deal with rabbis who served in outlying areas of Ashkenaz.[49] A communally appointed, salaried rabbinate in the major communities of Ashkenaz can be documented only at the end of the fourteenth, or beginning of the fifteenth, century.[50]

I have already noted with respect to the granting of tax exemptions and other privileges for scholars and the outright support of scholars that the communities of Christian Spain were much more receptive than their Franco-German counterparts.[51] Even the local study halls in Spain were more directly involved in service to their communities.[52]

In sum, the Ashkenazic communities were much less active than their Spanish counterparts in providing formal support for education and in fostering the careers of scholars, young and old. The academies of Ashkenaz were identified with the scholars who headed them, not with their communities. The communities did not appoint or even supervise the heads of the academies. These conclusions are consonant with our observations regarding the nature of elementary education in Ashkenaz. As we have demonstrated, there was no "system" of elementary education in Ashkenaz. The communities did not supervise the *melammedim* and made little effort to ensure that every child received an appropriate education. In the area of elementary education as well, Spanish Jewry maintained a more formal structure.

Ashkenazic Jewry had developed an outstanding system of communal government. Even if communal government in Spain was somewhat more developed, as Baer has posited, the Ashkenazic system, despite its different structure, was as effective as the Spanish one in providing essential religious and social welfare services for its residents.[53] One would expect that educational needs in particular would command the attention of the Ashkenazic communities. Yet these communities seem almost totally removed from the educational process.

Population shifts and general decentralization might provide a partial explanation. Jewish settlement in northern France was composed of a large number of small communities that were spread across the region.[54] It is to be expected that scholars would also be spread out and that focal points of scholarship would not be as concentrated as they were in pre-Crusade Germany and in Moslem and Christian Spain.[55] Indeed, the shift in Christian learning from the monasteries to the cathedral schools at the end of the eleventh century brought with it a transition similar to the one noted for Ashkenazic *yeshivot.* Scholars no longer flocked to the acknowledged monastic centers. Rather, they went where the masters were.[56] Thus, the school of Chartres, as R. W. Southern has noted, was only a leading school when an important master taught there.[57] But this geographic decentralization does not occur to the same extent in Germany after the First Crusade. Moreover, even if schools were not centralized, each local Jewish community should have been more active on its own behalf in providing and directing educational services.

The answer to this problem lies not so much in the logistics of education in Ashkenaz as in the educational philosophy of the society. The goal of education in Ashkenaz was to produce scholars. We will see in chapter 5 that the basic educational curriculum in Ashkenaz was structured with the hope that it might produce a young Rabbenu Tam. It was, above all, talmudocentric. As long as outstanding scholars were indeed being produced, the communities felt no acute need for an educational system with conventions and practices that would address the needs of ordinary men. The relative success of ad hoc Tosafist academies and the presence of scholars throughout the towns and cities of northern France and Germany eliminated much of the incentive for a communal effort to sponsor an educational system and to regulate the various educational levels and academic institutions. As for the support of scholars, there was no need to offer incentives, especially in light of the Talmudic restrictions placed on teaching or studying Torah for profit. Ashkenazic Jewry believed that scholarship would breed additional scholarship. As long as poor students could be aided in some fashion, the pristine notion that Torah must not be studied for any form of material gain prevailed.

The educational level of both laymen and upper-level students in Spain was generally lower than in Ashkenaz. Adults in Spain who showed some desire to study could very often not master even rudimentary Talmudic studies.[58] The claim advanced by G. Cohen and others, that there was a learned scholarly community in Moslem Spain prior to the arrival of R. Moses b. Ḥanokh, despite the low regard that Abraham Ibn Daud had for it, has been forcefully contested by I. Ta-Shema.[59] In the later period reactions and reflections concerning the penetration and diffusion of *Mishneh Torah* into Spain and Provence presume or confirm that the laity among Spanish Jewry were generally not very knowledgeable in Talmudic studies.[60] It was therefore necessary for the Spanish communities to be more involved in the regulation of education to ensure that acceptable levels of education were maintained. Responsibility for education could not be left to the individual student and his parents, as it was in Ashkenaz, because Spanish society was not as conducive to achieving a high degree of educational success. The primary goal of the educational process in Spain was to produce sufficiently educated laymen. Of course, some of the larger Spanish communities might have felt a greater responsibility to supply substantial educational facilities simply because of their size.

At the same time, the Spanish Jewish communities were interested in assuring the continuity of scholarship in their midst. There was a small but dedicated scholarly class in medieval Spain that was usually able to communicate effectively with the rest of society.[61] However, outstanding scholars who could train new students thoroughly were not found in abundance.[62] The communities and their members sought to ensure that the scholarly class would be perpetuated, so that it could continue to regulate matters of Jewish law and custom. Extensive means of support were necessary to allow capable students to develop and hone their abilities at the feet of qualified teachers.[63]

I. Ta-Shema has explained the difference between Ashkenaz and Spain with respect to the granting of tax exemptions to scholars in similar fashion.[64] It was precisely because the majority of people in each of its communities was not heavily involved in

Torah study that Spanish Jewry developed privileges for scholars and students to encourage and foster additional scholarship. In Ashkenazic society, where scholarship was perceived as the norm, scholarly privileges were not needed as an incentive and were therefore minimized. There were proportionally fewer scholars in Sepharad than in Ashkenaz, and it was therefore necessary to protect these scholars more.[65] In short, Spanish Jewish communities felt that it was necessary to develop formal structures to aid and protect their scholars and students, while Ashkenazic communities did not.[66]

J. Katz has argued that the weakness of the Ashkenazic system of communal government precipitated the need for the so-called Ashkenazic *semikhah.* Ashkenazic communities were not accustomed to appointing salaried officials but relied instead on learned individuals to perform rabbinic and judicial functions without compensation. In the late Middle Ages some of these functions became sources of income that led to financial and other abuses. As a result, formal ordination had to be instituted (or revitalized) in order to regulate and maintain the standards of the rabbinate. The Sefardic communities were able to avoid this problem because they had succeeded in developing, at an early stage of their history, a smoothly functioning communal organization that provided for the appointment of salaried rabbis from among those who had the appropriate background and training.[67]

In this instance as well, I suggest that the delay in implementation of a means to regulate rabbinic functionaries was not necessarily a mark of the Ashkenazic communal organization's weakness but of its lack of need. Until the Black Death, it was reasonable and efficient to rely on qualified volunteers to provide rabbinic services in Ashkenaz. Indeed, the formal Ashkenazic *semikhah* brought with it some vexing problems that were unknown to earlier generations.[68]

5

The Intellectual Milieu of the Tosafist Academies

HAVING ANALYZED THE economic theories and communal structures that affected educational practice in medieval Ashkenaz, I now turn to the inner life of the Ashkenazic academies. Because of the nature of the available sources, it is necessary to confine much of this phase of our investigation to the study halls or academies of the Tosafists. The massive literary productivity of the Tosafists, the great intellectual power these scholars displayed, and the fact that many members of Ashkenazic society were learned have created the impression that the Tosafist academies were relatively large institutions.[1] This impression is bolstered by passages in R. Menaḥem Ibn Zeraḥ's *Ẓedah la-Derekh* and R. Solomon Luria's *Yam shel Shelomoh* that describe the generation of Tosafist dialectic in groups numbering sixty or eighty students.[2]

On the other hand, the small size of the Ashkenazic communities in the twelfth and thirteenth centuries calls such large numbers into question.[3] Moreover, there are additional reasons to suspect that the numbers of students mentioned by R. Menaḥem Ibn Zeraḥ and R. Solomon Luria are exaggerated. As the *Ẓedah la-Derekh* text itself intimates, the number sixty may have been chosen because that is the approximate number of tractates in the Babylonian Talmud.[4] M. Breuer has recently studied the composition and size of study halls in Ashkenaz. He maintains that the

Tosafist academies did not consist of more than ten full-fledged students and were often smaller.[5] Even the seemingly large school and dormitory of R. Meir of Rothenburg probably did not contain more than fifteen students at any one time.[6]

While Breuer is correct in arguing that the Tosafist academies were relatively small, his specific conclusions must be modified. The critical factor in Breuer's computation is his assumption that the entire *yeshivah* of a particular teacher was housed in the bedrooms and contained in the dining area of the teacher's home. On the basis of the architecture of the period and various descriptive sources Breuer demonstrates that the eating and sleeping areas of the teacher's home could not support more than ten students in addition to family members.[7] Such calculations fail to account, however, for students who were either residents of the town themselves or who occupied rooms in the homes of other town residents. A passage in *Tosafot Qiddushin* explicitly distinguishes between students who dwell in the teacher's house and those who do not in regard to demonstrations of respect for their teacher when he enters the study hall.[8] Other contemporary sources refer to students who were boarded in the homes of other town residents.[9] While some married students left their wives at home in a faraway town or village and returned home only after a lengthy period, others lived in town with their wives and families, spending most of their time in the academy but returning home at night.[10] It is not possible to know exactly how many students lived outside the teacher's home in any given situation.[11] Assuming that all the students of a particular teacher studied together in his home even if they did not reside there, a large Tosafist academy could probably have consisted of as many as twenty-five students at any one time, but not much more than that.[12]

The great degree of intellectual freedom found in the *battei midrash* of the Tosafists has been amply documented. This degree of academic freedom has been attributed to the belief held by the Tosafists that truthful resolution of Talmudic contradictions and dilemmas is to be given the highest priority.[13] In light of the importance attached to academic freedom, academic ability should have been the most significant criterion in determining which scholars would become the heads of academies. Some scholars have indeed claimed that there was a fundamental difference in the hierarchy of Ashkenazic scholars in the pre-Crusade and Tosafist periods. In the pre-Crusade period good lineage (*yiḥus*) played a major role in determining who could ascend to leadership positions, both intellectual and communal, in the Rhineland communities. With the advent of the Crusades, this emphasis on lineage was downplayed and scholarly ability became the major criterion for leadership.[14]

If we look closely, however, at the leading Tosafists in northern France and Germany in the twelfth and thirteenth centuries, we find that they too came from a handful of families. While these families may or may not have been those of the pre-Crusade period, it is nevertheless clear that *yiḥus* still had a hand in determining intellectual leadership.[15] The leading Tosafists in northern France in the twelfth century (and the teachers of almost all French Tosafists of that century) were Rashbam, R. Tam, and Ri, all direct descendants of Rashi. The leading French Tosafist following Ri in the thirteenth century was R. Judah Sir Leon, another direct descendant. The most important Tosafists in twelfth-century Germany were Raban and Rabiah, grandfather and grandson. Other close familial relations also abound among the Tosafists. If sons-in-law are included, we have accounted for R. Yoel ha-Levi and many others. Of course, sons-in-law can be chosen for their abilities. In their case *yiḥus* and intellectual qualifications tend to merge.

The role of good lineage as a prerequisite for academic leadership might have had different connotations in the two periods. In the pre-Crusade period good lineage was an especially desirable societal value. It was important in terms of marriage and the distribution of priestly gifts in addition to its role in the realms of communal and intellectual leadership. In the Tosafist period the need for good lineage was somewhat more narrow. Leading scholars were those who had attained an appropriate level of intellectual achievement. Those starting out with *yiḥus* began much further ahead, so lineage continued to play a role in determining who would lead. It may well be that the significance of lineage in determining academic leadership in the Tosafist period is also related to the lack of an educational system in Ashkenaz documented earlier. Education was completely dependent on parental initiative. A child brought up in the home of a leading scholar would have a far better education on which to build, not to mention the likelihood of his inheriting a superior intelligence. The emphasis on lineage advocated by *Ḥasidei Ashkenaz* differed from the norm only because it demanded the restoration of good lineage to a full-fledged value, as had been the case in the pre-Crusade period.[16]

The Tosafists were clearly talmudocentric in orientation. While they had at their disposal a very full library of earlier Jewish literature,[17] the vast majority of their time was spent studying Talmud. Other halakhic or midrashic works were only introduced as a means of confirming or rejecting Talmudic interpretations.[18] In the galaxy of twelfth- and thirteenth-century European Jewish scholarship the Tosafists alone remained uninvolved in the study of Jewish philosophy.[19] To some extent this resulted from the fact that their contact with Christian scholarship was relatively limited. Compared to the leading Jewish scholars of Moslem lands, the Tosafists were societally and linguistically isolated from much of the culture around them. At the same time, mainstream Tosafists did not systematically engage in the study of Jewish mysticism either.[20]

Although somewhat conservative in terms of what they studied, the Tosafists were highly creative in terms of how they studied. Leading scholars such as R. Tam, Ri, Raban, and R. Yoel ha-Levi of Bonn were architects of a method of dialectical and critical study that constituted a revolution in Talmudic studies. The two basic components of this methodology (employed in varying degrees) are (1) the comparison of a Talmudic passage to any relevant Talmudic and rabbinic formulations with particular emphasis on the resolution of any contradictions and (2) the close, critical reading of the passage.[21] The precise nature and effects of this dialectic have been thoroughly described and need no repetition here. A brief chronology of the development of Tosafist dialectic is, however, in order.

Scholars have argued, since the early part of this century, about how the Tosafists came to develop their "new" methodology. Clearly, a form of critical dialectic had been an essential tool of the Amoraim themselves. Some have suggested that the creators of Tosafist methodology demonstrated their genius by returning to or reactivating the dialectic of Abbaye and Rava.[22] A. Grossman has recently demonstrated that the dialectical method found in works of R. Sasson, who taught at the academy of Worms in the last quarter of the eleventh century, adumbrates Tosafist dialectic.[23] Similarly, the commentary to *Nazir* that J. N. Epstein attributed to Rashi's son-in-law R. Meir (who studied in Worms and brought that methodology back to northern France) contains a small number of classic *tosafot*-type questions and responses.[24] More formal aspects of Tosafist methodology were developed around 1100. Rashbam wrote *tosafot* in the presence of Rashi; and the work of Riba, who studied in Mayence and perhaps with Rashi as well, reached R. Tam.[25] The question of how dialectic came to the academy at Worms remains. In any event, the contribution of the Tosafists lies in their rapid expansion and systematic development of this methodology and its application to halakhic decisions as well as to Talmudic interpretation.

E. E. Urbach has compared the Tosafists to the glossators who worked on Roman legal texts (especially the Code of Justinian) and to contemporary scholars of canon law.[26] Based primarily on studies of Kuttner and Kantorowicz, Urbach has delineated striking parallels between the methodologies of the Jewish and Christian scholars (which center on the resolution of divergent sources) and even between the terminologies that the two groups of scholars used.[27] While at times it appears that Urbach is prepared to argue that the developments in Christian scholarship influenced the parallel phenomena in Jewish circles, he resolutely refrains from doing so.[28] Urbach points to fundamental differences in the purposes and goals of the Jewish and Christians scholars as well as in the nature and significance of the texts on which they commented.

However, additional similarities between Jewish scholarship in western Europe in the eleventh and twelfth centuries and contemporary Christian scholarship must be taken into consideration. Until the beginning of the eleventh century the monastery was the seat of Christian scholarship. Monastic scholars mastered material related to biblical studies and canon law through intensive reading and repetition. The novice was encouraged, in effect, to memorize the literature as it was rather than to identify or reconcile contradictions posed by the various sources. The aim of the monastic program was the absorption of as much of Christian tradition as possible.[29] By the end of the tenth century cathedral schools such as the school at Chartres under Fulbert vied with the monasteries to become the centers of Christian learning. The competition continued and intensified in the mid–eleventh century; by 1100, the cathedral schools began to emerge victorious. These schools were fundamentally different from the monasteries in two ways. First, the reputation and significance of the cathedral school were associated not with its location (as with Cluny or Bec) but with the particular master who taught there at any given time.[30] The students who wandered to various locations following Peter Abelard and other famous masters were representative of these developments. Interestingly, these students were more inclined to identify themselves by noting with whom they studied rather than where they studied. Second, while the educational program in the urban schools *began* with the reading and expounding of a basic text (*lectio*), the goal of the process was to pose exploratory questions to clarify texts or doctrines and resolve conflicting passages or interpretations (*quaestio* and *disputatio*). Whether in biblical studies, canon law, or Christian theology, the juxtaposing of contradictory sources and the search for resolutions are at the center of the educational process.[31] The use of dialectic in this manner was a hallmark of the cathedral schools even before Peter Abelard. It was utilized by the canonist Bishop Ivo of Chartres (d. 1116) in his *Panormia* and even before that by Bernold of Constance.[32] Eleventh-century monastic theologians such as Anselm of Canterbury (d. 1109) and his teacher Lanfranc of Bec (who later became the Archbishop of Canterbury) also used these methods. By the end of the twelfth century a highly formalized system of dialectical study was in place.[33] Already at the beginning of that century monastic scholars such as Rupert of Deutz objected to this new methodology of learning and suggested that students return to the traditional ways of monastic study.[34]

Pre-Crusade scholarship in Ashkenaz bears some basic similarities to its monastic counterpart. It involved reading, and mastering as much earlier material as possible without creative attempts at reconciling differences between the sources. This is the nature of extant pre-Crusade rabbinic literature such as *Ma'aseh ha-Geonim,* as well as the works that comprise the *sifrut debei Rashi.*[35] Pre-Crusade scholarship was centered in the *yeshivot* of Mainz and

Worms. As I have demonstrated, these schools were identified by their locations and customs, not by the particular teachers who taught there.[36] In the beginning of the twelfth century, with the genesis of the Tosafist movement, all this changed. Dialectic, which began as a limited phenomenon in one Rhineland academy, won the day. Masters, not the reputation or the traditions of a school, attracted students and caused them to wander from France to Germany and back.

The chronology of the Christian developments predates the commensurate changes in Jewish circles by one generation. While I am not prepared to argue that dialectic was reintroduced to medieval Jewry via Christian scholars, it is possible that the Jewish interest in this methodology was fanned by its contemporary use in Christian circles. Urbach concludes that Jews did not have meaningful contact with Christian legal scholars or dialecticians, but this conclusion may also be questioned.

That Jews studied dialectic formally is doubtful. Even if they could read Latin,[37] there is no evidence that Jewish scholars were familiar with the Christian theological and legal literature in which dialectics were utilized. On the other hand, Jewish and Christian polemical literature attest to frequent discussions between Jewish and Christian clergy. Moreover, there was significant contact between twelfth-century Jewish and Christian biblical scholars.[38] While there is evidence that a number of twelfth-century Christian scholars could read Hebrew, the Christian exegetes indicate that they learned about the Jewish material and methodology orally.[39] E. Touitou and S. Kamin have argued that the exchange of ideas worked in reverse as well, with Jewish biblical scholars assimilating exegetical methodologies employed by the Christians.[40] There was nothing to preclude Jews from hearing from Christian scholars about the methods and forms of dialectic as well. If a circle with a fifty-mile radius is drawn around the leading cathedral schools of northern France (i.e., the schools of Laon, Chartres, Paris), one can find in that circle the locations of all the leading Tosafists of the period.[41] The concept of dialectic could certainly be grasped even in basic conversation and could be applied by Jewish scholars, just as Christian scholars could adapt Jewish *peshat* methodologies to which they were exposed. To be sure, Jewish and Christian biblical exegetes were working with a common text. But the method of dialectic was not totally foreign to the family of Rashi or to students of other pre-Crusade scholars. It was practiced in Worms, albeit on a much smaller scale.

The Bolognese canon lawyer Gratian may have studied dialectic with Abelard in France. In composing the *Concordia discordantium canonum* (*Decretum*), Gratian "compiled a comprehensive and fairly well arranged body of legal pronouncements, carefully grouped under legal headings of subject and topic and applied to them the *Sic et non* method of dialectic, giving also . . . a judgement on the issue and a brief discussion in which critical and legal principles were displayed."[42] Just as Gratian applied the theological dialectic that he learned in northern France to his legal studies, the early Tosafists might have applied the principles of dialectic that they gleaned from their contact with Christian scholars to their legal studies.

A passage in *Sefer Ḥasidim* is perhaps a reflection of this process. As we shall see, *Sefer Ḥasidim* objected to the overuse of dialectic by unqualified students. The importance of a balanced knowledge of Jewish law and custom, as distinct from exclusive preoccupation with novellas, was also stressed.[43] In one section the author of *Sefer Ḥasidim* writes that the study of Torah must be free from the influence of non-Torah disciplines, especially *dialeqtiqah shel goyim.*[44] Later in the section, *limmud shel niẓẓaḥon,* which I. Ta-Shema has noted describes quite accurately the *disputationes* held in the twelfth-century schools, is also censured.[45] This passage demonstrates conclusively that Jews were familiar with the existence of dialectic as a methodology of Christian scholarship. The passage, while it does not show close familiarity with this method nor prove Christian influence (although the author of *Sefer Ḥasidim* clearly considers such influence likely), nevertheless undercuts one of the basic arguments against such influence: Jews were certainly not ignorant of the Christian use of this methodology.[46]

The creative period of the Tosafists extended through the early thirteenth century, from R. Tam to R. Samson of Sens and from Raban to Rabiah. From the first quarter of the thirteenth century the degree of creativity lessened.[47] The steadily worsening position of Jews in Christian Europe (in addition to the fact that periods of creativity are usually brief and often give way to periods of consolidation) moved the focus of Jewish scholars away from the development of creative *ḥiddushim* and toward the compilation of halakhic norms and works that would guide the populace. The declining fortunes of Ashkenazic Jewry caused others to collect, edit, and sometimes embellish earlier *tosafot* texts.[48] Several leading scholars of the period bemoan, in very specific terms, not merely the exigencies of the times but the palpable shortcomings of their students.[49] In the face of increased persecution the Tosafist period ends circa 1300. A shift in methodology begun already at that time led to the subsequent development of the *pilpul* and *ḥilluq* methodologies that were to become prevalent in eastern Europe.[50]

Actually, a significant modification in Tosafist methodology can already be found in some *tosafot* texts composed in the mid–thirteenth century. Comments of Rashi, many quite lengthy, are reproduced in these texts in full. The primary aim of the texts seems to be to clarify and explain Rashi's comments and to offer a simple interpretation of the Talmudic text itself. Dialectical resolutions of conflicting Talmudic sources or comparisons of the passage at hand to other Talmudic passages are undertaken much less frequently than usual in these *tosafot.* Examples of such texts are the standard *tosafot* to *Qiddushin, Nazir, Arakhin,* and *Temurah; Tosafot R. Samson of Sens* to *Sotah;* and the so-called *Tosafot Rashba* to *Menaḥot.*[51]

E. E. Urbach and others have plausibly suggested that this development is to be attributed to the vicissitudes of the time. The trial of the Talmud and the accompanying loss of hundreds or perhaps thousands of Talmudic volumes as well as a measure of political and personal stability mandated this effort to provide additional Rashi texts, which included Rashi's citations from the Talmud itself. These texts would allow students to grasp more easily the correct interpretation of the Talmudic *sugya* at hand.[52]

Nevertheless, a crucial observation makes it difficult to accept this theory as the sole explanation. All of the Tosafot texts listed above were compared in the academy of the "brothers of Evreux,"[53] while other Tosafists of the same period do not appear to react in this manner to the shortage of books.[54] Indeed, S. W. Baron is skeptical about whether in fact the persecution of the

Talmud by the church led to a shortage in western Europe and whether the loss of the volumes in Paris had a significant impact upon Talmudic study.[55]

Consequently, a different factor may be suggested. The curtailing of comparative dialectic and the emphasis on simple, straightforward interpretation of the Talmudic text was undertaken primarily by Tosafists who were influenced by the ethical teachings and the educational critiques of the German Pietists. As recent scholarship has demonstrated, the German Pietists were gravely concerned about the overuse of dialectic and the development of dialectical *ḥiddushim* by unqualified students. The pietists wished to promote Talmudic studies that would more clearly direct the student in matters of *halakhah* and allow the student to master the Talmudic text at hand.[56] The unusual *tosafot* just described would make a major contribution toward achieving this aim. As I have suggested elsewhere, and I. Ta-Shema has more recently written, the brothers of Evreux composed their *tosafot* under the influence of the educational critique of the German Pietists.[57]

This contention is buttressed by the fact that another major characteristic particular to the academy at Evreux also corresponds precisely to the position of the German Pietists. The brothers of Evreux commented on virtually all the tractates of *Seder Qodashim,* an area that many Talmudists in Ashkenaz understandably ignored.[58] R. Shelomoh Luria, in the introduction to his *Yam shel Shelomoh,* cites a diatribe of R. Moses Taku against those whose Talmudic study was centered around unrestrained *pilpul.* In the course of his statement R. Moses complained that while Rabina and R. Ashi purposely did not redact any *gemara* on the two least practical orders of Mishnah to allow scholars to concentrate on understanding the remaining four orders, "we study only a portion of the remaining tractates."[59] The abbreviated curriculum of Talmudic studies that R. Moses described was apparently the norm not only in Ashkenaz but in other areas of medieval Europe as well.[60]

Although R. Moses had an ax to grind concerning the esoteric teachings of R. Yehudah he-Ḥasid, he might have found his Talmudic curriculum more acceptable, just as he concurred with the Pietists concerning the overuse of *pilpul.*[61] The German Pietists greatly valued the study of *Seder Qodashim* (as well as any other "unpopular" tractates) precisely because it was being ignored in many circles.[62] Members of their circle produced several significant commentaries on tractates in this order as well as all of the relatively few Ashkenazic commentaries on tractate *Sheqalim* in the Palestinian Talmud.[63] The concern shown by the German Pietists for the study of *Seder Qodashim,* running counter to the norm in the Tosafist period, may also reflect their well-documented desire to return to and imitate the curriculum of the pre-Crusade period. A significant commentary to this order was compiled in Mainz during the first half of the second century.[64]

In addition to these two major areas of correspondence between the academy at Evreux and German Pietism, there are several other indications of the influence of *Ḥasidei Ashkenaz* on R. Moses and R. Samuel of Evreux. Regarding proper intent in prayer, R. Moses of Evreux writes, "A person must remove all extraneous thoughts from his heart during prayer and direct his heart only to the source. He must consider every word before he expresses it.. . . . If he does this, his prayers will be acceptable before God."[65] Urbach has already noted that this formulation could well have been composed by a German Pietist.[66] Indeed, this passage is found in almost identical form at the end of a larger text attributed to R. Moses by both R. Aaron of Lunel in his *Orḥot Ḥayyim* and *Sefer Kol Bo.*[67] The text is described in *Kol Bo* as *devarim ha-mevi'im li-dei yir'at ha-ḥet*[68] *asher katav ha-Ram me-Evreux.* This text is appended to a treatise composed by R. Eleazar Roqeaḥ entitled *Sefer moreh ḥata'im/Sefer ha-kapparot.* Moreover, there are several close parallels between the earlier parts of the text (prior to the section on prayer, which is the largest component) and material in *Sefer Ḥasidim.* Of importance is the recommendation that on completion of Torah study one must assess whether the material that one has just studied has dimensions that can be fulfilled through religious practice (*im yesh bo davar she-tukhal le-kayyemo*).[69] *Torah lishmah* is defined by *Sefer Ḥasidim* as study for the sake of fulfilling the law.[70]

R. Samuel b. Shneur of Evreux also issued a statement lamenting the absence of proper *kavvanah* in prayer.[71] This formulation shows R. Samuel's frustration with the reality that his brother R.

Moses sought to correct. R. Samuel cites a liturgical interpretation "that he found written in the hand of R. Judah the Pious."[72] R. Samuel is called he-Ḥasid by his student R. Yedidyah b. Israel.[73] In late twelfth- and thirteenth-century Ashkenaz one who bore the title Ḥasid was not just a person who had achieved a high level of piety. Such an individual was usually connected in some way to the German Pietists.[74] Other students and family members produced liturgical commentaries and handbooks for both the congregation and the cantor, as well as *piyyutim.*[75] In this period, these activities, as well, were associated most often with *Ḥasidei Ashkenaz.*[76]

This hypothesis regarding the brothers of Evreux can be utilized to resolve difficulties concerning several works, most notably *Sefer ha-Yir'ah* (*Ḥayyei Olam*), whose attribution to Rabbenu Yonah of Gerona has been questioned.[77] The questions arose largely because these treatises appear to have been written by someone under the influence of German Pietism. R. Yonah studied at Evreux with both R. Moses and R. Samuel. It was there that R. Yonah came into contact with the teachings of the German Pietists.[78] Indeed, the only scholar cited by name in *Sefer ha-Yir'ah* is R. Samuel b. Shneur, who is referred to by the author as "my teacher."[79] The work is focused on issues of practical ethics and prayer, the two areas in the brothers of Evreux' teachings that independent evidence suggests were influenced by teachings of the German Pietists.

Two features of the manuscripts of *Sefer ha-Yir'ah* confirm this conclusion. A significant number of manuscript copyists copied this work (often called *Sefer Ḥayyei Olam* in the manuscripts) together with works of the German Pietists.[80] In addition, of the forty-three extant manuscripts of *Sefer ha-Yir'ah*/*Sefer Ḥayyei Olam* thirty-seven were written in Ashkenaz while only seven are Spanish.[81]

N. Bronznick has argued that *Sha'arei Avodah,* also attributed to R. Yonah, was not composed by him but was of Ashkenazic origin.[82] Bronznick notes, among other claims, that *Sha'arei Avodah* cites *midrashim,* as well as a *piyyut,* that were known only in Ashkenaz.[83] That R. Yonah is aware of Ashkenazic sources is no surprise given the time that he spent in the study hall at Evreux. Indeed, one of the works to which Bronznick refers, the *Midrash*

Mah Rabbu, is quoted almost exclusively in works by German Pietists. The *piyyut, Kevod Ot,* was written by R. Meir Sheliaḥ Ẓibbur. R. Meir was venerated in the literature of the Pietists as one who was expert in *sodot, midrashim, ve-ta'amim.*[84]

The process by which Pietistic teachings were transmitted to Talmudists in northern France remains unclear. A number of German Tosafists were apparently influenced by the spiritual and intellectual teachings of the German Pietists. They were, however, either Qalonymide relatives of R. Yehudah he-Ḥasid, residing mostly in Spires, or students (both direct and indirect) of R. Yehudah and R. Eleazar Roqeaḥ.[85] There is no evidence to suggest that the brothers of Evreux actually studied with R. Yehudah he-Ḥasid and R. Eleazar Roqeaḥ or received personal instruction from any other associates of the *Ḥasidei Ashkenaz,* and they rarely cite any of these figures. It is possible that the brothers of Evreux simply adopted a number of basic values, doctrines, and formulations of the Pietists that could be found in readily available, exoteric sources.[86] The only French Tosafist other than the brothers of Evreux who seems to have been connected to the German Pietists was R. Moses of Coucy.[87] In regard to Talmudic methodology and halakhic codification, R. Moses is very much in the mainstream of mid-thirteenth-century Tosafist thought.[88]

Why the heads of the study hall at Evreux should have chosen to embrace these teachings of the German Pietists is also not easily solved.[89] They may have reasoned that the serious declines that began to appear in their day, not only in terms of dialectic creativity and in the relationship between the Jews of northern France and their rulers but also in regard to general levels of Talmudic studies and religious observance, required a change in intellectual and religious values.[90] As H. Soloveitchik has described, R. Yehudah he-Ḥasid and R. Eleazar Roqeaḥ watched helplessly as many of the religious values of old Ashkenaz disappeared in the face of French Tosafist domination.[91] Perhaps in their own way the brothers of Evreux (and R. Moses of Coucy as well) constituted a French protest against parts of this trend. Nonetheless, the number of affinities between the academy at Evreux and German Pietism establish a strong probability that we are witnessing influence, not parallel development. For at least one *yeshivah* in thirteenth-century France the voice of the German Hasidim was no longer crying out in the wilderness.[92]

A curricular issue that remains to be discussed is the extent and nature of biblical studies in the academies of Ashkenaz. Tosafists noted that the practice in their day—to devote all of one's study time to Talmud—conflicted with the dictum of R. Joshua b. Ḥanina that one ought to devote equal study time to the three distinct disciplines of Scripture, Mishnah, and Gemara. R. Tam defends the contemporary practice by claiming that "through our [study of] Talmud we exempt ourselves." Since the Talmudic corpus contains material from the other disciplines, focusing on the Talmud exclusively would allow the scholar to be exposed to these disciplines while remaining firmly rooted in Talmudic study.[93] It is possible that Rabbenu Tam was simply trying to justify the fact that less time was being spent in the study of Scripture than Talmudic law mandates. But as R. Joseph Kimḥi wrote, R. Tam "did not make an effort at grammar . . . and did not occupy himself with Scripture [*higgayon*] because it is a virtue and not a virtue" (*Bava Meẓi'a* 33b).[94] Moreover, the view that the study of the Babylonian Talmud subsumes the necessary study of Scripture is already found in the Geonic period in a position of R. Natronai Gaon.[95]

In his ethical will, R. Yehudah b. ha-Rosh urges his children to set aside time to study biblical grammar and exegesis (*lilmod ha-pasuq be-diqduq u-perush*). R. Yehudah explains the reason for his suggestion: "Because I did not study this in my youth [*be-qatnuti*], since it was not usually taught in Ashkenaz, I was not able to teach it here [in Spain]."[96]

Neither formulation suggests that Ashkenazic Talmudists were unfamiliar with the biblical text. The statement of R. Tam indicates that most encounters with the biblical corpus in the academy transpired through the prism of Talmudic study. Study of the biblical text for its own sake was apparently not the norm in Ashkenaz. R. Yehudah was made aware, in his adopted Spanish homeland, of basic methodologies employed when biblical studies were pursued as a distinct discipline.[97] These methodologies were seemingly unknown (or at least untaught) in Ashkenaz. In order to determine more precisely the place of biblical studies in the Tosafist academies, it is necessary to review some recent research on the role of biblical studies in pre-Crusade Ashkenaz.

A. Grossman has argued that virtually all of the leading pre-Crusade scholars were intimately familiar with the biblical corpus and were involved in various aspects of biblical studies. Some of these scholars taught *miqra* to their students within the setting of the academies.[98] The evidence for these assertions is varied. Pre-Crusade scholars made extensive use of biblical texts in their Talmudic commentaries.[99] A thorough familiarity with the Bible was a prerequisite for the writing of *piyyutim,* an important aspect of pre-Crusade rabbinic culture.[100] Some scholars, most notably R. Gershom, issued halakhic rulings that were based principally on biblical verses.[101] While no full-fledged biblical commentaries were produced on an entire biblical book or section, the relatively large number of comments on biblical verses, the interest in biblical *massorah* and *nusaḥ,* as well as the use of Scripture in letters and other documents issued by pre-Crusade scholars, further attest to the prominent role that biblical studies must have played in the curriculum of pre-Crusade Ashkenaz.[102]

Many of the extant comments were made on verses outside of the Pentateuch or verses that are never cited or discussed by the Talmudic text. This would support the notion that comments on biblical verses were not made merely in the course of Talmudic lectures when a particular verse was cited by the Talmudic text but that there were separate lectures devoted to the biblical text itself.[103] Indeed, R. Yaʿakov b. Yaqar is referred to as a "teacher of Talmud and Scripture."[104] The comments on the biblical text made by pre-Crusade scholars are often devoted to the explication of difficult words and phrases within the verse, adumbrating the methodologies of Rashi, R. Yosef Qara, and Rashbam.[105]

Scholars have pointed to the two types of biblical commentaries produced in Ashkenaz during the Tosafist period as proof that heads of academies in the twelfth and thirteenth centuries also lectured on and interpreted biblical texts with their students. The first group consists of the so-called Tosafist commentaries to the Torah. These commentaries contain biblical interpretations attributed in many instances to leading Tosafists.[106] The largely anonymous authors or copyists will often indicate that they heard an explanation from "my teacher" or from a particular scholar, implying some sort of classroom setting. Tosafist biblical commentaries take several forms. First, there are collections or passages that simply reformulate or copy interpretations suggested in the course of Talmudic study, many of which appear in *tosafot,* and relate them to the text of the Pentateuch.[107] A second style of commentary consists of dialectical or critical analyses of Rashi's commentary to the Torah and, by extension, dialectical analysis of the biblical text itself. These analyses are essentially applications of Tosafist Talmudic methodology to the biblical or Rashi texts.[108] The standard literary styles used by the Talmudic *tosafot* to introduce a question (e.g., *im tomar, teimah*) and answer it (*yesh lomar, yesh omerim*) are ever present in the Tosafist biblical commentaries. It is possible that many of these verses together with Rashi's commentary were discussed in the course of Talmudic lectures.

There are, however, any number of verses in the Pentateuch interpreted by the Tosafist commentaries that have no moment in Talmudic literature.[109] Moreover, many of the works comment on almost every verse in a number of portions of the Torah, indicating that the biblical text itself was the object of study. It appears that the Tosafists and their students, following the Talmudic recommendation, reviewed or discussed (formally or informally) the weekly Torah portion.[110] R. Meshullam of Melun wrote to R. Tam concerning a contradiction raised by a student "when we were studying the portion [of *Meẓora*]."[111] Study of the weekly Torah portion, even if it took the form of a distinct lecture or academic session, employed the same dialectical method and form used for Talmudic studies. These discussions or lectures did not focus on comprehensive, intricate methods of literary or grammatical analysis and interpretation of the biblical text itself. When the contradiction was raised in R. Meshullam's study hall, the answer given was based on a Talmudic passage. Since the solution had possible halakhic implications, R. Meshullam hastens to add that "this is what we answered amongst ourselves [*bein yeshivatenu*] but we did not intend with this to offer a practical legal suggestion."

The presence of Rashi's commentary in these discussions does not alter their basic nature. A Talmudist with little interest in new pathways of scriptural interpretation could feel quite comfortable using Rashi's commentary. There is no doubt that the students of Rashi and their students made use of Rashi's commentary to the Torah even before it was ruled to be an acceptable substitute for the Aramaic Targum in reviewing the weekly portion.[112] While Rashi's commentary served as an important reference point for students of *peshat* in northern France, it was at the same time an excellent compendium of rabbinic and midrashic material as well.[113]

The other type of biblical commentary produced in northern France during the Tosafist period consists of the works of the *pashtanim* of northern France, such as Qara, Rashbam, Bekhor Shor, and Eliezer of Beaugency. These scholars commented extensively on biblical books that are not part of the Pentateuch, including books with little Talmudic or halakhic relevance.[114] Included in this enterprise are an intensive study of biblical grammar and syntax, the identification of literary devices found in Scripture, an understanding of biblical forms and style based on natural phenomena, an appreciation of the authors of various biblical books and their aims in writing them, and an effort to establish the correct text.

There are, however, several factors suggesting that this circle had no impact upon the curricula of the academies. The number of *peshat* exegetes known to us is quite small, and the majority of them come from two families. The lifetime of this circle was less than one hundred years, and its presence was limited to northern France. The first generation of northern French *pashtanim* studied in pre-Crusade Germany. Already in the pre-Crusade period, as has been noted, scholars wished to understand difficult words in the biblical text, as well as the "simple" meaning of biblical verses. Straightforward interpretations of verses are to be found even in comments of thirteenth-century Tosafists. Yet only in twelfth-century northern France is the search for *peshat* systematically undertaken by a handful of scholars. Recent research has further demonstrated the major role that Christian polemics played in the development of the study of *peshat*.[115] Tosafist masters' general lack of interest in contributing to Jewish polemical literature might have diminished their interest in the development of *peshat* methodology.[116]

M. Banitt has suggested that thirteenth-century Old French glosses to the biblical text and vernacular glosses to Rashi's commentary are evidence for the existence of a continuous vernacular translation of Scripture in both France and Germany. The groups of teachers that used these translations to teach the weekly Torah portion and *haftarah* in a rudimentary fashion to nonscholars were called *poterim.* An individual who taught Scripture at this basic level was called a *qara* or *naqdan.*[117] E. Touitou, building on the conclusion of M. Ahrend that *qara* (in the case of R. Yosef Qara) was a title akin to Professor of Bible[118] and on the suggestions of Banitt, has claimed that there was a cadre of Bible teachers in Ashkenaz who taught *peshat* interpretation of Scripture at an advanced level.[119] His textual proofs for the existence of these *ba'alei miqra* are a passage from Rashi's biblical commentary[120] (which Touitou himself notes is a paraphrase of a Talmudic formulation) and an exegetical passage from R. Avraham b. Azriel's *Arugat ha-Bosem.*[121] It should be noted further that R. Avraham b. Azriel was a dedicated student of R. Eleazar Roqeaḥ and the German Pietists, who, as we shall see, were more interested in biblical studies than was Ashkenazic society as a whole.

The weakness of these proofs aside, there can be no doubt that teachers of *peshat* did teach and discuss their interpretations and methodologies with groups of students.[122] However, there is no evidence that these lectures were connected in any way to the Tosafist academies. At most, some of the attendees may have been Tosafists. Indeed, among the known *pashtanim,* only Rashbam and Bekhor Shor were important Talmudists.[123] R. Yosef Qara studied in Worms (as well as in Mayence) and later in Troyes. He was involved in the transmission of Talmudic interpretations from Germany to France. But it appears that he was preoccupied in both regions with the study of Scripture, as his title implies.[124]

The biblical commentaries of the circle of *pashtanim* certainly do not reflect the normal give-and-take of the Tosafist academies. They are referred to, and structured as, the products of individual authors.[125] Even the addenda or responses of R. Yosef Qara and Rashbam to the comments of Rashi seem to be essentially literary and do not necessarily reflect classroom discussion.[126]

Rashbam's strong disclaimers about the relationship of his own

Torah commentary and Talmudic law highlight the difficulties that the Talmudist would encounter if he became involved in this type of exegesis. Indeed, Rashbam notes that most rabbinic scholars did not deal systematically with *miqra* because of the Talmudic dictum *ha-ʿoseq ba-miqra middah ve-einah middah.*[127] R. Yosef Qara calls attention to the fact that *baʿalei aggadah* and *baʿalei Talmud* will not appreciate an interpretation that runs counter to rabbinic exegesis.[128] The commentaries of R. Yosef Bekhor Shor are cited with great frequency by Tosafist commentaries, especially *Sefer ha-Gan.* Bekhor Shor's commentaries are replete with midrashic and Talmudic interpretations and analyses. They contain passages introduced by *im tomar/yesh lomar* in the style of the Tosafist commentaries, as well as interpretations using gematria.[129] R. Yosef's works certainly could convey the impression that he was interested in aspects of biblical interpretation other than *peshat.*[130] Generally, the *pashtanim* cited in so-called Tosafist commentaries appear as additional resources, not as methodological models.[131]

The vast majority of Tosafists did not accept the challenge of systematically searching for *peshat.* They adopted, instead, the position of R. Tam that there was no room for distinct classes or hours devoted to biblical studies in the academy curriculum. The verses that were talmudically relevant or that were read in the Torah were subject to Tosafist analysis, but even this analysis was talmudocentric. Urbach, in his *Baʿalei ha-Tosafot,* notes more than twenty Tosafists from whom comments on the Bible are extant. Most of these comments are related to legal issues and were probably made in the course of Talmudic lectures. Almost all are comments on the Pentateuch.[132] Riba, who commented on a verse in Ezekiel, studied in the pre-Crusade period.[133] R. Shmuel he-Ḥasid, who commented extensively on Chronicles, belonged to the German Pietists, whose unusual approach to biblical studies will be discussed shortly.[134] Comments that revolve around grammatical issues are invariably the product of early Tosafists who studied in pre-Crusade Germany.[135] There is also an interesting correlation between the French Tosafists who commented on or wrote *piyyutim* and those who authored *peshat* commentaries. The disappearance of *piyyut* composition and commentary in northern France coincides with the last of the *pashtanim.*[136] The comments of Rabiah that have survived consist entirely of gematria methodology or analyses of Rashi's commentary.[137] Only R. Moses of Coucy seems to have systematically commented on the Pentateuch itself.[138] His affinity to the German Pietists and his role as a *darshan* may explain his unique contribution.[139]

Profiat Duran (d. c. 1414) writes, "In this period, I note that Jewish scholars, even the greatest among them, show great disdain for biblical studies. It is enough for them to read the weekly portion [*shenayim miqra ve-eḥad Targum*] and still it is possible that if you ask them about a particular verse, they will not know where it is. They consider one who spends time doing biblical studies a fool; the Talmud is our mainstay. This disease is rampant in France and Germany in our generation, as it was in the preceding period. But in earlier generations it was not so. We see the glory of the Talmudists uplifted by . . . the great Rashi who delved into the meaning of Scripture [*he-ʿemiq be-havanat ha-miqra*] and wrote beautiful commentaries on it, including wonderful formulations about grammar and syntax."[140] Duran may have been exhibiting a degree of Sephardic bias in failing to mention any of the commentaries of the French *pashtanim.* Perhaps the small number and scope of these commentaries did not impress Duran. As their commentaries and halakic works indicate, Tosafists did know the content of the Bible, its Talmudic interpretation, and the commentaries of Rashi quite well. But the claim of Duran that Ashkenazic scholars subscribed to the notion *ha-Talmud hu ha-ʿiqqar* and did not systematically study the Bible other than in their review of the portion of the week was essentially accurate.[141]

6

Educational Theory and Practice in the Teachings of the German Pietists

THE *BOOK OF THE PIOUS* (*Sefer Ḥasidim*) is a particularly important source for the study of formal Jewish education in medieval Ashkenaz. Its importance lies in two areas. First, *Sefer Ḥasidim* provides corroboration or sometimes initial evidence for actual educational practices, as we have seen in the preceding chapters.[1] In addition, *Sefer Ḥasidim* reacts to the existing educational process by pointing out its deficiencies and offering guidance. As Y. Baer has written, "This work contains many suggestions for teachers and students. It is replete with material that describes life in the academies at that time."[2] The interest expressed in *Sefer Ḥasidim* in educational issues is perhaps part of a larger aim of this work. In the view of *Sefer Ḥasidim* a truly righteous person must involve himself in matters of importance to the community at large.[3]

Recent scholarship dealing with *Ḥasidei Ashkenaz* has focused on certain intellectual and communal reforms that were deemed necessary by the Pietists. An important component of the intellectual reforms is reflected in a critique of the unlimited use of dialectic. The Pietists felt that the unchecked use of the dialectical method among students of the Talmud would create and encourage haughty scholars whose studies were self-serving. As H. Soloveitchik has written, "The immortal accomplishments of the French and German Tosafists . . . should not however blind us to the genuine abuses that, in all probability, followed in their wake. And the remarks of *Sefer Ḥasidim* should be read in this light. They are less a criticism of *talmidei ḥakhamim* in general than a censure of certain contemporary phenomena."[4] Soloveitchik stresses that the goal of the German Pietists in their critique was, in addition, to restore the scholarly values of the Qalonymides to a place of importance in the intellectual tapestry of post-Crusade Ashkenaz. The German Pietists were aristocrats who sensed that they were in danger of being displaced. They wished to change the intellectual milieu of Ashkenaz back into one in which they were comfortable.[5]

I. Ta-Shema, while agreeing that the pietists sought to limit the power of the revolutionary ideas of the Tosafists regarding dialectic and Talmudic study, argues that the pietists sought, in addition, to create an ideal or utopian program of education for the entire Ashkenazic community. The sensitivity of the authors of *Sefer Ḥasidim* to manifestations of social inequality caused them to recognize the elements of competitiveness and arrogance inherent in Tosafist methodology. They therefore criticized this methodology and pointed out the negative effects it might have on the average student. But they went even further and formulated educational goals and plans. Concrete suggestions were made regarding curriculum, pedagogy, teacher-student relations, and the economics of education, so that both the more talented and the less talented students would be able to achieve success in their studies.[6] A cornerstone of this program was greater emphasis on practical halakhic study. Most students should spend their time engaged in the mastery of halakhic texts and in Talmudic study directed toward halakhic decision making rather than in Talmudic study aimed at the creation of dialectical or critical novellas.[7]

According to both Ta-Shema and Soloveitchik, the Pietists were not directing their comments against the Tosafists themselves but rather against the uncontrolled use of dialectic by those who were inspired by, or wished to imitate, the methodology of the Tosafists. *Sefer Ḥasidim* acknowledges that proper use of dialectic can yield worthwhile results.[8] Thus, the author of *Sefer Ḥasidim* expresses his concern in a situation where one teacher (*rav*) has access to a text of *tosafot* and another *rav* does not. The first teacher should share his *tosafot* text with his colleague.[9] However, use of dialectic by the unqualified student or teacher can weaken character. Sustained use of dialectic can lead the capable student to exhibit haughtiness, an unhealthy desire to emerge victorious, selfishness, a lack of intellectual honesty, or an air of intellectual superiority. In addition, the dialectical method can cause "such frustration in the hearts of mediocre students who are not as talented as their peers that they will eschew Torah study."[10] As a result, *Sefer Ḥasidim* recommends that a different, more salutary method of study be used,[11] a method that stresses the religious and ethical aspects of study rather than the intellectual.[12]

Another curricular issue that concerned the Pietists deeply was the place of biblical study in Ashkenaz, and here, too, they formulated a sharp attack on prevailing practices. This critique contains several components.[13] The first suggests that biblical studies should be given a much higher priority by older, accomplished students in Ashkenaz. A sample of this critique is found in a commentary of R. Eleazar Roqeaḥ to the pietistic leitmotif, Psalms 19:8 (*Torat ha-Shem temimah*). R. Eleazar insists that a penetrating scholar (*navon ha-maskil*) must be familiar with the entire biblical corpus for several reasons. First, numerous commandments are derived from, or explained in, the prophetic works. Second, knowledge of Scripture (and the Aramaic Targum) will allow the scholar to unlock "the secret of the Hebrew language . . . which in turn will yield the essence of life and the secret of the Torah." A scholar must have at least a passing familiarity with Scripture. If he does not, he will not know where verses cited in the Talmud come from and whether the Talmud is interpreting them simply or midrashically. Is the verse being used as a source of law or merely as secondary verification? Thus, "the Torah is faithful to the Talmud; it makes the fool wise."[14] The low priority given to biblical studies, especially the study of Nevi'im and Ketuvim, in the academies of Ashkenaz has been amply documented.[15]

Numerous similarities, in both style and content, between R. Eleazar's remarks and a passage in Abraham Ibn Ezra's *Yesod Mora* make it likely that the Ibn Ezra text was a source for the formulation of Roqeaḥ.[16] Ibn Ezra surveys typologically the different intellectual proclivities of Jewish scholars. His major argument is that a balance must be maintained. Scholars who study only Scripture, thinking that this exclusivity will lead them to the highest spiritual truths, are misleading themselves. The commandments are an essential component of the biblical corpus, and they can be fully understood only through study of the Talmud. Similarly, many scholars have studied only Talmud since their youth, ignoring biblical and grammatical studies in their belief that the Talmud provides all the knowledge that one must know to practice Judaism. A true scholar cannot be totally deficient in his knowledge of Scriptures (*req me-ḥokhmat ha-miqra*) because this lack of knowledge will diminish even his Talmudic expertise. He will not know from which biblical book a verse cited by the Talmud comes and whether the Talmud is interpreting this verse according to *peshat* or *derash*. He will not know how to read the verse properly, and the lack of grammatical knowledge will cause him to miss more subtle points about the verse of which the Talmudic authors were certainly aware.[17]

The underlying motives for the pietistic critique concerning biblical studies were virtually the same as the motives for the critique of dialectic. As we have seen, pre-Crusade Ashkenazic scholars made extensive use of biblical texts in their Talmudic commentaries and for a time issued halakhic rulings that were based principally on biblical verses.[18] There is evidence for lectures on biblical texts in the pre-Crusade academies.[19] Virtually all of the leading pre-Crusade scholars were intimately familiar with the biblical corpus and were involved in some aspect of biblical studies. The primacy of biblical study, then, is a value of pre-Crusade Ashkenaz that was subsequently neglected by normative Ashkenazic scholarship and is therefore stressed by the *Ḥasidei Ashkenaz*. Various pietistic texts proclaim the importance of being able to demonstrate "how the Talmud [= oral law] is derived from the Torah."[20]

Needless to say, biblical studies have pietistic utility as well. The use of the biblical text by the German Pietists and their followers as a source for ethical and pietistic material is well documented both in *Sefer Ḥasidim* itself and in other pietistic works.[21] Numerous passages within the so-called Tosafist commentaries to the Torah, not to mention the recently published commentaries of R. Yehudah he-Ḥasid and the commentary attributed to R. Eleazar

Roqeaḥ, are based on mystical, midrashic, and even *sensus literalis* biblical interpretations by the German Pietists.[22]

As we have demonstrated, Bible was taught in Ashkenaz on the elementary level. Pietists were concerned by the failure to utilize biblical study on this level as a source of moral instruction. From the earliest stage of the educational process, the study of the biblical text and even the teaching of reading itself could be used to awaken and encourage fear of God (*yir'at ha-Shem*) not only in the potential Pietist but also in the average Jewish child: "A student should have a teacher who knows [the subject matter]. When he teaches Scripture, the teacher must be able to make the student grasp religious issues such as respect for the Torah and awareness that God is the source of all sustenance. When the student grows older, he should be taught about divine reward and punishment."[23]

Also included in the Pietists' critique is the recommendation that biblical studies be promoted and valued as a discipline in which older nonscholars can participate. It is inappropriate to force a student who cannot master the study of Talmud to remain in that discipline.[24] At stake here was a fundamental educational argument between Ashkenazic society at large and the German Pietists. Ashkenazic society valued the scholar above all others. Reading and rudimentary biblical studies were taught to elementary-level students to give them the tools to advance in their studies and perhaps to impress upon them the value of study. The author of *Sefer Ḥasidim* recognized that not every student could be a scholar. He sought to dispel the notion prevalent in Ashkenazic society that one must aspire to study only Talmud. Thus, *Sefer Ḥasidim* suggests that students who cannot progress from biblical to Talmudic studies should be encouraged to remain engaged in study of the Bible.

In sum, the educational critique of the German Pietists regarding biblical studies was quite comprehensive. It addressed the absence of biblical studies on the higher level and sought to correct the ignorance of the average advanced-level Talmudic scholar in this discipline. It also sought to adjust the orientation of biblical studies on the lower level by emphasizing the value of the Bible for moral and religious instruction.

The German Pietists also felt that the study of Mishnah as a separate discipline ought to be part of the curriculum, as several passages in *Sefer Ḥasidim* and *Sefer Roqeaḥ* indicate.[25] Roqeaḥ refers several times in his biblical commentaries to *miqra,* Mishnah, and Talmud as the disciplines that comprise the totality of Torah.[26] R. Abraham b. Azriel, a student of the German Pietists, divides Jewish scholars into three categories: *ba'alei miqra, ba'alei Mishnah, ba'alei Talmud.*[27]

While the Pietists' position was not formulated as a full-fledged critique, it was another effort to revive pre-Crusade practice when the Mishnah itself, like the biblical verse, was used as a source of practical *halakhah.*[28] The promotion of Mishnah study as a separate discipline also had ramifications for the average student. The study of Mishnah was an important means of transmitting spiritual values and halakhic guidelines to the nonscholar. The absence of the study of Mishnah as a distinct entity in Ashkenaz is additional evidence for the lack of an educational system designed to train as broad a segment of the population as possible.[29]

The curricular and pedagogic reforms proposed by *Sefer Ḥasidim* can be best understood not merely as exhortations by the German Pietists to their own group, but as measures aimed at the educational weaknesses found in normative Ashkenazic society. Whether the Pietists intended, or had the ability, to implement any of their reforms is an issue that still has not been resolved; but these reforms are surely what they thought were needed in the realm of general Jewish educational practice. By suggesting a variety of reforms for educational practices in Ashkenaz, the Pietists were perhaps trying to ensure a supply of potential Pietists or at least to foster an intellectual environment that would be more hospitable to their way of thinking.

In addition to suggesting improvements in curriculum and pedagogy, *Sefer Ḥasidim* wished to heighten the sense of responsibility that individuals and communities felt toward dedicated scholars. In order to demonstrate this contention, I shall examine the positions of the German Pietists on several major issues concerning the economics of education and the relationship of the academies to their host cities (discussed earlier in a more general context).

The position of *Sefer Ḥasidim* on tax exemptions for scholars is somewhat enigmatic and has generated opposing viewpoints in recent scholarship. While such exemptions were not granted in practice in Ashkenaz, as we have seen, it appears that the German Pietists endorsed them. H. Soloveitchik writes that "the privileged economic position of the scholar is upheld by the Hasidim in stronger terms than those of the Talmud." The Ḥasidic position on tax exemptions, according to Soloveitchik, can be determined from section 807 in *Sefer Ḥasidim* (*Parma*) (*SḤP*).[30] In this passage, the concept of granting exemptions to scholars is adduced from Joseph's treatment of the land holdings of the Egyptian priests. If Pharaoh could make special economic provisions for his priests, Jewish communities can exempt scholars from taxes that are placed on the communities by local rulers. That *Ḥasidei Ashkenaz* were strongly committed to this ideal is seen from another text (attributed to Hasidic sources by R. Joseph Ibn Ezra), which portrays the strong punishment meted out to those who would not allow scholars in their community to be exempt from taxation. Two scholars who were financially well off (*'ashirim*) wanted to be exempt from paying taxes on the basis of the Talmudic law; and the entire community agreed except for two wealthy members (perhaps the two wealthiest members of the community), who insisted that the scholars' assets be evaluated and that they pay the appropriate amount of taxes. Within a month's time, just before Rosh Hashanah, these wealthy men died. A Hasid subsequently had a dream indicating that their deaths were due to their blockage of the efforts of those who wished to aid the Torah scholars by exempting them from the tax evaluation.[31]

On the face of it, Soloveitchik's analysis is contradicted by *SḤP* 1392, which recommends that a scholar share in the communal tax burden if he is able to do so. This section makes that point by relating the tale of a scholar who had a means of supporting himself and asked the community for an exemption because he studied all day. The scholar subsequently lost all his assets (after the exemption had been granted) and attributed the loss to his lack of involvement in the communal tax burden. Soloveitchik explains that this section does not contradict the Hasidic position as he had outlined it but rather modifies it. Any participation by scholars in the payment of taxes must be voluntary. The community is never advised to make scholarly participation obligatory. Only scholars who are able to should participate.

I. Ta-Shema argues, on the other hand, that *SḤP* 1493, which expressly limits tax exemptions to a scholar who studies literally day and night and has no other occupation or source of income, is to be taken as policy. Scholars who had any form of livelihood were not eligible to receive exemptions. As the *Sefer Ḥasidim* text asserts, "At the present time, since there is no scholarship without the pursuit of a livelihood, all [scholars] pay [taxes]." Moreover, even section 807 maintains that a tax exemption can be granted only to a scholar who studies day and night. According to Ta-Shema, the position taken in section 1392 depicts the reality in Ashkenaz. Scholars did pay taxes with the community since they invariably had a means of support or livelihood. The German Pietists were not interested in the proliferation of tax exemptions for scholars.[32]

Despite these strictures, a reexamination of the relevant texts leads to a reaffirmation of Soloveitchik's views. The essence of the Pietists' position, as expressed most clearly in section 807, is that members of a community have a responsibility to assist scholars who are engaged solely in study and therefore must exempt them from taxes: "If the ruler places a tax on the city, the residents of the city shall pay, but the scholars who study day and night shall not." The basic exemption as formulated in this passage is predicated on a scholar's dedication measured in terms of his commitment of time to study. It does not seem to depend on whether the scholar has assets or not. At the same time, pietistic thought required that each scholar evaluate whether he should accept or demand the largesse of the community. There are reports that R. Qalonymus, the wealthy father of the author of *Sefer Yiḥusei Tannaim va-Amoraim* and one with an affinity to the German Pietists, insisted on paying his share of taxes.[33] If a scholar's request for exemption is not appropriate, he will suffer the consequences, as the scholar himself notes in section 1392. Nevertheless, the community that he petitioned had granted his request; and in the view of *Sefer Ḥasidim* this was the correct action to be taken from the communal perspective, assuming that the scholar's claim proved legitimate.

In the pietistic text cited by R. Joseph Ibn Ezra, the reverse problem occurs. The two wealthy scholars petitioned the community for an exemption. The community as a whole (*kol ha-qahal*) wished to grant the exemption, but it was vetoed by two wealthy nonscholars. The text then describes the punishment received by the two nonscholars for not having done their civic duty. The term *'ashirim*—used to describe the scholars—need not be taken literally in the lexicon of the German Pietists. It simply indicates that these scholars had financial resources.[34] Even if they had certain means, they may still have been justified, after appropriate consideration, in seeking the exemption. But in any case the community must unanimously and unequivocally come to the aid of its bona fide, dedicated scholars. Anyone who interferes with the community in this enterprise will be held accountable. Thus, despite Ta-Shema, both this text and section 1392 reflect the position that certain scholars should be exempted from taxation even under the prevailing conditions in medieval Ashkenaz.[35]

Section 1493 begins with the Talmudic formulation of Reish Laqish that rabbinic scholars are exempt from taxes. The author of *Sefer Ḥasidim* adds that this exemption was to be granted to those who studied all the time. But according to Talmudic law if a scholar is also involved in business, he does not fall into the protected category and is not to be exempted. A problematic test case is then presented. The passage in question is a difficult one due to the abundance of pronouns whose antecedents are not clear. It seems likely that the request for exemption came from a father who was supporting his scholar-son. The father did not want to pay taxes because he claimed that he had no assets. All his assets were used to support his son. The community denied the father's request: "Since you are the one who deals with these assets (*nosei ve-notein*] you must pay taxes." The father perhaps assumed that the community would not tax him since he had given all his assets to his son and that his son would not be taxed for these assets because he was a dedicated scholar. The answer given to the father was that he and his son, when considered as a unit, were akin to the scholar who studied but was also involved in earning a livelihood.[36]

The section concludes with the observation that since nowadays (as opposed to the Talmudic period) there is unfortunately no scholar who is not involved in earning some form of livelihood, the actual practice in Ashkenazic communities is that scholars do pay taxes. This practice has been amply documented by Ta-Shema. But

Sefer Ḥasidim adds one phrase emphasizing that this communal policy, despite its basis in Talmudic law, is not right. All scholars must pay taxes now simply because they do not have the power to change the policy of the communities (*ein yadam teqeifah ʿal ha-ẓibbur*). It is one thing to make the father pay in the case in question, since he deals extensively with his funds on behalf of his son. But *Sefer Ḥasidim,* in this final expression of pique or frustration, is arguing that because the exigencies of the day force even the most dedicated scholars to become involved to some extent in securing their own livelihoods (unless they too have agents to manage all their financial affairs), tax exemptions should not be limited to those who have no pursuit other than the study of Torah. This position is consistent with what emerges from the other pietisitc sources that I have analyzed.[37] Even a scholar who devotes a small amount of time to business should be exempted from sharing in the communal tax burden if he is properly dedicated.[38]

In expressing their position concerning the granting of tax exemptions to scholars, the Pietists wished to introduce practices that were found only in some Spanish communities. While their reasons were somewhat different and no influence in either direction need be inferred, the German Pietists took a position most similar to the one that R. Meir ha-Levi Abulafia and R. Asher b. Yeḥiel wished to implement in Spain. If a scholar is totally dedicated to his studies but must devote some time to another pursuit in order to earn a livelihood, he is nonetheless entitled to a tax exemption because his dedication, given the realities of the times, has remained complete. The assets that a scholar has or the livelihood that he must earn are not automatic reasons for the community to withhold an exemption. The scholar ought to be exempt, as Ramah wrote, "not because of his poverty but because of his Torah." In the view of *Sefer Ḥasidim,* the scholar contributes to the spiritual well-being of the community and thus the community must be prepared to exempt him.[39]

Providing additional sustenance for dedicated scholars is also implicit in the attitudes of the German Pietists concerning the support of teachers. *Sefer Ḥasidim* readily allows the teacher of Talmud to be compensated through the means of *sekhar battalah:* "It is permitted to teach youngsters [*qetanim*] and receive compensation but not older students [*gedolim*]. . . . If a person has another position, he may be compensated for the teaching of Torah in place of the other salary that he must forfeit."[40] Perhaps the unqualified endorsement of *sekhar battalah* was another way for the Pietists to try to give scholars an advantage in Ashkenazic society, where even this method of payment was sometimes shunned.

We have noted that the scholar who studied or taught Torah in Ashkenaz was never paid a salary by his community. Approbation for communal funding of a religious functionary is to be found in an halakhic ruling of R. Yehudah he-Ḥasid. The ruling of R. Yehudah is no longer extant; but his position can be established from a response of R. Eliezer of Bohemia, who took issue with it. R. Eliezer wrote to R. Yehudah that if local religious functionaries in the outlying areas of Ashkenaz were to be retained, it was crucial that they be permitted to receive the occasional donations of individuals, for example, those offered at Purim. R. Yehudah had apparently ruled (in cases where the individuals who used the services of a local religious functionary could not afford to compensate him through the payment of *sekhar battalah*) that the functionary should be paid out of communal funds rather than out of occasional private donations.[41] Private support was a denigration of the office involved, but a public salary was acceptable.[42]

The appropriateness of paying scholars in order to retain their services is perhaps evident in a section of *Sefer Ḥasidim* that has been referred to as the depiction of the ideal of Torah study in this work.[43] The initial thrust of the passage is to confirm the primacy of accurate halakic information as a goal of Torah study. King David spared no effort to consult with leading halakhists and scholars to ascertain and standardize the law. Next, this section notes that King David honored scholars even more than he did the wealthy. He provided for the scholars in a tangible fashion so that they would be able to study freely. David wanted to have these scholars available at all times to advise him. Therefore, "he prepared their livelihood."

The German Pietists vigorously recommended another means of support for scholars, which did have basis in Talmudic law. Just as Zevulun assumed the burden of supporting Yissakhar in his studies, it was appropriate for individuals to undertake the support of scholars under similar conditions. *Sefer Ḥasidim* offers numerous suggestions on how and when to offer this type of support:

> If one person is not a scholar [*ben Torah*] and is not dedicated to study and his brother is a scholar, it is better for the unlearned brother to be involved in business in order to support his brother so that he can study. And if one brother is wealthy but is not a scholar and is forgetful and the other brother is a scholar—if the scholar says to the wealthy brother, "Give me funds so that I can generate revenue," and the wealthy brother wishes to sustain his scholarly brother, he should not give the scholar the money [to invest but provide for him] so that the scholar will not deviate from his studies.[44]

Or, in a more complicated variation,

> Two friends or two brothers or father and son who have a business that one can take care of, thereby allowing the other to study [exclusively]—if one of the parties forgets everything that he learns and the other one remembers, the forgetful one should manage the business and the one who remembers should study. But if the one who remembers wastes time and the one who forgets is more dedicated [to his study], the more dedicated one should study Torah.[45]

Such arrangements had to be taken seriously by both sides. If there is a poor scholar who cannot study because he has to make a living and a rich person agrees to sustain him for half the reward for his study, the arrangement is only effective if the rich man lives up to his commitment. Similarly, if the scholar is lazy, his partner receives a greater share of the reward.[46]

The Pietists attempted to increase communal interest in the educational process and to promote centers of study other than the elite Tosafist academies. *Sefer Ḥasidim* exhibits great interest in the further development of local schools or classes. These local classes were already in existence but, as I have noted, had little to do with the local community in terms of regulation or formal support, just as the more recognized Tosafist academies had no formal connection to their host community but came or went as the masters did.[47] *Sefer Ḥasidim* urges two teachers who teach Talmud in one city or town to cooperate so that students of varying abilities can progress both academically and socially. *Sefer Ḥasidim* confronts anew the issue of whether one should continue to study locally or go away to pursue additional educational opportunities, and it proposes criteria to aid in the decision. We learn from the advice of a pietistic *ḥakham* to some concerned parents that the hometown is to be favored when parental guidance has led to a positive commitment to observance and exposure to a larger city and other peer groups may cause the loss of certain values. This holds true even if the level of scholarship in the larger locale is higher than that of the hometown.[48]

Sefer Ḥasidim cautions that if one feels he cannot learn in his hometown because of certain pressures, he must be very careful not to pull away other students with him when he seeks to study elsewhere.[49] The aim of *Sefer Ḥasidim* is not so much to promote the importance of the hometown per se as it is to develop respectability and responsibility for communal schools. Indeed, the author of *Sefer Ḥasidim* and R. Eleazar Roqeaḥ are not perturbed by scholars' going away to study if the trip will prove educationally productive. They do not seek to eradicate the phenomenon of wandering students.[50] They are simply trying to build up the hometown as a center of learning for all its residents. Thus, *Sefer Ḥasidim* bears no animus toward the student who for the sake of his achievement wants to leave town. His leaving, however, should not cause a dissolution of the hometown class, which is serving others well. The concerns of the Pietists in this matter seem to be quite similar to those expressed by R. Yonah. Commenting on the verse in Proverbs "The eyes of the fool are toward the [faraway] corner of the earth," R. Yonah describes the fool as one who "does not want to learn from the people of his hometown who possess knowledge but who says instead, 'I yearn to go to a certain place where there are wise, well-known scholars and I will study Torah from them.' Perhaps he will not be able to reach his destination and he will find himself devoid of knowledge, as the Rabbis taught, 'Let not a person say, when I have time I will study, lest he not have time.' " R. Yonah goes on to argue that it is the complete haughtiness of this fool that prevents him from learning from all others, including those in his town.[51]

Sefer Ḥasidim makes no distinction at all between well-known Tosafist academies and study halls directed by lesser scholars. The head of a study group or academy is never described as more than a *rav* who maintains a house of study in a city or town. He is never identified on the basis of his intellectual capabilities or the size and importance of his following.[52] All scholars in *Sefer Ḥasidim* are referred to anonymously. This convention undoubtedly reflects the notion found in *Sefer Ḥasidim* that anonymous authorship is to be valued as a guard against intellectual haughtiness.[53] Indeed, this view may also be seen as another aspect of the attempt made by the German Pietists to restore the intellectual values of pre-Crusade Ashkenaz. The German Pietists wished to return not only to the methodology of learning of pre-Crusade days but to the reserved posture that characterized the students engaged in this type of learning. As I have demonstrated, academies in the pre-Crusade period were known mostly by their location, not by the outstanding scholars who studied in them.[54]

The German Pietists reacted to many aspects of the educational practices of Ashkenazic society in the high Middle Ages. They were especially concerned with the lack of an educational system that could serve both scholars and nonscholars.[55] Existing educational practices, which were most conducive to the development of scholars and least conducive to the development of the religious observances of each student, were in need of modification. The Pietists also attempted to reinsert into the curriculum methodologies and disciplines from the earlier period in Ashkenaz that they felt were more useful and spiritually productive. The loss of these practices and concepts was, in their eyes, detrimental to Ashkenazic Jewry as a whole. Not wishing to diminish scholarly productivity but rather to increase it, the Pietists demanded that qualified scholars receive appropriate incentives and aid from their communities. In sum, the German Pietists suggested innovative and perceptive ways to increase the availability and effectiveness of normative Torah education throughout the Ashkenazic communities so that Pietist, scholar, and layman would be best equipped to know and serve their Maker.

Appendix A
The Origin and Orientation of *Sefer Ḥuqqei ha-Torah*

Sefer Ḥuqqei ha-Torah (*SḤH*) is a detailed treatise describing a bilevel educational system. Problems in education on both the elementary and advanced levels are identified and addressed. The most novel provision of this document calls for the establishment of quasi-monastic study halls for *perushim,* accomplished students who would remain totally immersed in their studies for a period of seven years. A linear transcription of the S*ḤH* text is presented below.[1]

Since the publication of *SḤH* by M. Güdemann in 1880,[2] scholars have argued about the date, provenance, and purpose of the work.[3] All the attempts to identify the place and time in which *SḤH* originated employed essentially two methods. The first was to focus on terms or phrases in the text that either ruled out or suggested a particular location. For example, since the text refers to a certain custom as *minhag Ẓarefat* (line 68), it is likely that the text was not composed in northern France.[4] On the other hand, since the text refers to unspecified Geonim as the originators of certain practices and also refers to practices of R. Saʿadiah Gaon and the Babylonian exilarch, it is possible that the text was of Babylonian origin.[5]

Another method employed by scholars was to identify institutions within the text. The *midrash ha-gadol,*[6] which was to be maintained by the surrounding communities, is akin to the *yeshivot* of southern France as described by Benjamin of Tudela in his travelogue, *Mas'at Binyamin.*[7] N. Golb has tried to show that the *midrash ha-gadol* existed in northern France, one such school being located in Rouen.[8] G. Scholem and I. Twersky have identified the text as Provençal based on the claim that the *perushim* who studied in the *midrash ha-gadol* were a prototype of Provençal scholars in the twelfth century.[9]

Complicating the effort to ascertain the provenance of *SḤH* is the question first raised by Y. Loeb in 1881 in his review of Güdemann's book as to whether *SḤH* was actually in effect in some community or whether it was simply a utopian suggestion.[10] S. Baron wrote that "[*SḤH*] doubtless originated in one of the northern communities under the impact of Provençal mysticism or of German-Jewish Pietism of the school of Judah the Pious and Eleazar of Worms. This view was arrived at because of the unique statutes of the work, for which we have no record of their practice." Statutes such as the consecration of the sons of Kohanim and Leviyim for Torah study and the mandate for a permanent group through which the community could fulfill its obligation to study were "expressions of pious wishes but were never formally enacted by any communal authority."[11]

If the document is in fact of Provençal origin, it is likely that the document was actually in effect or at least represented active institutions and practices. The educational organization outlined in *SḤH* on both the elementary and advanced levels is quite similar to that of Provence in the twelfth and thirteenth centuries.[12] If, however, *SḤH* is of Ashkenazic origin, the document was probably a theoretical blueprint. As I have noted, there was nothing in Ashkenaz comparable to the highly organized and communally funded educational institutions of *SḤH.*[13]

While all attempts to identify with certainty the origins of *SḤH* may prove fruitless, I suggest that the connection between *SḤH* and the German Pietists merits further investigation. I. Twersky has succintly summarized the essential provisions of *SḤH* as follows:

> It strives, by a variety of stipulations and suggestions, to achieve maximum learning on the part of the student and maximum dedication on the part of the teacher. It operates with such progres-

> sive notions as determining the occupational aptitude of students, arranging small groups in order to enable individual attention, grading the classes in order not to stifle individual progress. The teacher is urged to encourage free debate and discussion among students, arrange periodic reviews . . . utilize the vernacular in order to facilitate comprehension. Above all, he is warned against insincerity and is exhorted to be totally committed to his noble profession.[14]

Several of these measures are suggested by the author of *Sefer Ḥasidim* in order to maximize the educational achievements of every student. For example, a great concern of the German Pietists was that students of different abilities were not separated within the educational process of Ashkenaz. Such insensitivity could keep the brighter student from developing fully and would certainly cause the weaker student to become frustrated. The core of this strong critique is expressed in the following sections of *Sefer Ḥasidim:*

> One person should not do a kindness for another where a transgression will result. . . . If B's sons are ill-qualified and lazy and will disturb and deter the sons of A, A should not allow the sons of B to study with his sons [even though B cannot afford a tutor for his sons]. One who tutors youngsters and finds some to be more perspicacious than the others, so that the two groups cannot learn together and the brighter students need their own tutor, should not remain silent . . . even though he will lose money if he splits his class. Educate the child in his own way (Proverbs 22:6). If a students appears to have aptitude for the study of the Pentateuch but not for the study of Talmud, do not force him to study Talmud. . . . 'At age fifteen, [begin] the study of Talmud (Avot 5:21).' This teaches that if a father sees that by this age his son cannot study Talmud, he should be taught laws and midrash and reading [Scripture].[15]

SḤH insists in six distinct passages (lines 40–41, 86–87, 108, 115, 141, 200) that teachers not allow their own affairs to cause distractions while they are teaching. Thus, the *melammed* could not assume any additional employment, nor could the academy head engage in conversation when it was time for him to teach.

There are five sections in *Sefer Ḥasidim* expressing the same concerns in similar terms.[16]

SḤH advises that academy heads should not conduct their classes in their own homes but rather in the dormitory of the *perushim,* lest they remain constantly in the presence of their wives. The academy heads should remain with the *perushim* for the entire week and return to their homes on Friday. After the Sabbath they should return to the abode of the *perushim.* This procedure was to be followed so that the academy heads could avoid sexual thoughts while they taught (lines 102–10). In *Sefer Ḥasidim,* the *rav* is advised to set up a *beit midrash* on the far side of his home. This arrangement is suggested to prevent the students from gazing at the female members of the household as they enter and leave the home. If this precaution is not taken, "their Torah study will be accomplished while sinning." While the section in *Sefer Ḥasidim* is designed to shield the students from sexual thoughts and the section in *SḤH* seeks to protect the teacher, the problem addressed and the unique solution offered are essentially the same. Indeed the arrangement in *Sefer Ḥasidim* will also prevent the academy head from constantly being in his wife's presence, just as the separate dormitory for the students in *SḤH* will prevent them from gazing at women.[17]

At the beginning of a section on Torah study the author of *Sefer Ḥasidim* writes,

> Scripture states, 'The Torah of God is without blemish, it restores souls (Psalms 19:8)." When is the Torah without blemish? When it restore souls. When does it restores souls? When it is without blemish. Moses blessed the sons of Levi and the Kohanim that they should go and study Torah and not return to their homes until they have studied enough so that they could answer all questions. As the verse states, '[the Levite] . . . will not recognize his parents or his brothers or his sons (Deuteronomy 33:9)' since for so many years he has remained with his teacher. 'For they have followed Your words and Your covenant they have kept.' They will remain [with their teachers] until 'They shall teach Your statutes to Jacob and your Torah to Israel.' (Deuteronomy 33:10)—until they learn enough so that they can resolve all doubts.[18]

SḤH is, to my knowledge, the only other medieval text that utilizes Deuteronomy 33:10 in this fashion (lines 6–14). The sons of the priests and Levites who are consecrated as youngsters to study Torah and who become *perushim,* separated from everyone including their families for seven years while they study (lines 15–31), fit the image described by the author of *Sefer Ḥasidim.*

Another possible key to the origin of *SḤH* that has not been probed sufficiently lies in the practices and phrases that appear to be similar to monastic ideals. The *perushim,* who are chosen originally through some form of parental consecration, ensconce themselves in their fortresses of study away from all worldly temptations. They devote all of their time to the holy work of God (*melekhet shamayim*)[19] and serve as representatives of the rest of the community in this endeavor. It is possible that *SḤH* represents an attempt to recast the discipline and devotion of monastic education, which was certainly known to, and perhaps admired by, Jews, in a form compatible with Jewish practice and values.[20]

Sefer Ḥuqqei ha-Torah

1 זה ספר חקי התורה הקדמונים לכבוד התלמידים והרבנים אשר (196 א)
2 גבלו ראשונים: אלה החקים והמשפטים והתורות. להבין ולהורות.
3 אמרות ה׳ אמרות טהורות. אשר תקנו אנשי שכל הראשונים. יראי
4 השם בהסכמת הגאונים. על אודות התורה להכין אותה ולסעדה. להרבותה
5 בישראל וביהודה. ויקבלום בני יעקב איש תם. לחק עולם לדורותם:
6 החק הראשון. על הכהנים והלוים להבדיל אחד מבניהם להקדישו
7 לתלמוד תורה. ואפי׳ בעודו בבטן אמו. כי כן מצוים מהר סיני דכ׳
8 כי נתונים נתונים המה לי כלום מבטן אמם. וכת׳ יורו משפטיך
9 ליעקב. ונא׳ ואת עמי יורה דעה. ונא׳ כי שפתי כהן ישמרו דעת.
10 וכן זקני ישראל כמו כן יבדילו מבניהם כי כן הפריש יעקב וכ׳
11 וכל אשר תתן לי עשר אעשרנו לך בשתי מעשרות הכתוב מדבר במעשר
12 ממון ובמעשר בנים. וכן אמר יחזקאל ובניהם אשר ילדו לי העבירו
13 להם לאכלה מלמד שהיו מקדשין מבניהם לתלמוד תורה מבטן אמם.
14 ילדו לי פי׳ לשמי:
15 חק שני לקבוע מדרש לפרושים המקבלים עליהם עול תורה אצל בית
16 הכנסת. ואותו בית נקרא מדרש גדול כי כאשר מעמידים חזנים
17 להוציא רבים ידי חובתם מן התפלה כך מעמידין תלמידים קבועים
18 להגות בתורה בלי הפסק להוציא רבים ידי חובתם מתלמוד תורה ולא
19 תהיה מלאכת שמים נסוגה אחורנית. פרושים הם תלמידים המקדשים
20 לתלמוד תורה ונקראין בלשון המשנה פרושים ובלשון מקרא נזירים

(196 ב) 21 שנ׳ ואקים מבניכם לנביאים ומבחוריכם לנזירים. והפרישות מביאה

22 לידי טהרה שנ׳ והתקדשתם והייתם קדושים ואו׳ וקדשו וטהרו:

23 חק שלישי על הפרושים שלא יצאו מן הבית עד ז׳ שנים ושמה יאכלו

24 וישתו ושמה ישכבו ואל ידברו במדרש דברים בטלים. ואין חכמה

25 נכללת בתלמיד הנכנס ויוצא לבד במי שממית עצמו באהלי תורה שנא׳

26 זאת התורה אדם כי ימות באהל. וכל המספר בדברים בטלים בבתי

27 כנסיות ובבתי מדרשות עובר בעשה שנ׳ ומקדשי תיראו וכאשר יקדיש

28 אדם אחד מנכסיו לשמים כך יקדיש אחד מבניו לתלמוד תורה. ואם

29 יצאו הפרושים מן המדרש קודם ז׳ שנים יפרעו קנס ידוע. וסמך

30 לדבר ותופשי התורה לא ידעוני. מלמד שהיו אוסרין עצמן לדעת

31 חקי האלקים ותורותיו:

32 חק רביעי לגבות מכל ישר׳ יב״פ (שיטים) בשנה לעזרת המקדש במקום

33 מחצית השקל שהיו אבותיו מביאין לעבודת בית המקדש ולצורך הקרבנות

34 כן אנחנו חייבין להביא נדבה לעזרת המקדש מדי שנה בשנה לפרנס

35 התלמידים ולפרוע הרבנים והמתרגמנים ולקנות ספרים. וכאשר

36 הקרבנות מביאין שלום בעולם כך התלמידים חכמ׳ שנ׳ וכל בניך

37 למודי ה׳ וג׳ ונא׳ שלום רב לאהבי תורתך ואין למו מכשול וג׳:

38 חק חמישי להעמיד משגיח על התלמידים לתת שיעור על תלמודם

39 ולראות פקחות הנער׳ ועצלנותם כי המלמדים דומים לפועלים השאפים

40 תמיד כי ינטו צללי ערב. וזה המנהג כשר לקיים והייתם נקיים מה׳

41 ומישראל. על כן המלמדים לא ילמדו בבתיהם רק בבית מדרש לשם מצוה.

42 ושם הבית נקרא מדרש קטן.וזה המשגיח נקרא למלמדים. ואם (יראה)
43 המשגיח בתוך הנערים נער קשה ואטום יביאהו לאביו ויאמ׳ לו השם
44 יזכה בנך למעשים טובים כי לתלמוד תורה הוא קשה מאד פן ילכו
45 הנערים הפקחים בשבילו אחורנית ולא יקח מעותיו בחנם פך יחשב
46 כגזלן. ושמא ילך הנער אצל מלמד אחר ויצליח שם לפניו:
47 חק ששי שלא יקבלו המלמדים יותר מעשרה תינוקות בענין אחד ואע״פ
48 שאמ׳ חכמ׳ כ״ה דווק׳ בארץ ישר׳ דאוירא מחכים ובזמן שישר׳ שרוין
49 על אדמת׳ וידם תקיפה כי נפש החפשית היא גבוהה וחזקה וזכה וצלולה
50 ויכולה לקבל שכל ומדע על שאינה משועבדת לזולתה
(197 א) 51 ונפש אשר משועבדת היא שפלה וחלשה ויבישה ואינה יכולה
52 לקבל שכל ומדע על שהיא משועבדת לאדנים קשים ועזי פנים
53 וכל יגיעה ועמלה הולך לאיש אשר לא עמל בו. טרודה בהתמד
54 בעבודות קשות ומפילין עליה אימה ופחד והחמה מסלקת החכמה
55 על כן נזהרו המלמדים שלא לקבל לפניהם למעלה מעשרה תינוקות.
56 וסמך לדבר אלקים נצב בעדת אל ועדה עשרה כדילפינן מבכל
57 המקום אשר אזכיר את שמי אבוא אליך אבוא בגי׳ עשרה וכאשר
58 עשו חכמים חיזוק וסייג לדברי תורה כן עשו הגאונים סייג
59 בכל דברי חכמים:
60 חק שביעי על המלמ׳ שלא ילמדו הנערים בעל פה כי אם במכתב
61 למען ילעיזו להם התרגום על המכתב כמ׳ שלועזין העברי להיות
62 נוחין בגרסת הלמוד ולהכניסם בהלכה ותרגם אונקלוס התורה
63 בלשון ארמית מפני בני בבל שהיו מדברים בה כדי להשמיע תורה

64 להם בלשונם וכן פי׳ רב סעדיה גאון זצ״ל התורה בלשון ערבי

65 כדי שיבינו מפני שלא היו מבינים בלשון הקודש. ונהגו חכמים

66 תלמידי ראש גולה לקרא הסדר בשבת שנים מקרא ואחד תרגום

67 להשמיע לנשים ולעמי הארץ דברי תורה אולי יכנס היראה בלבם.

68 וכן מנהג צרפתים לקרא הסדר בשבת שנים מקרא ואחד לעז

69 כלשון בני המדינה:

70 חק שמיני ללמד לנערים תרגום בלעז על המכתב למען ירוצו בגרסת

71 התלמוד ויהיו נוחים להכנס בהלכה. ולא יצטרכו המלמדים לטרוח

72 על התנוקות אלא בסוגיא ולא במשמעות מתוך שהורגלו במשמעות התרגום:

73 חק תשיעי על המלמדים להרגיל הנערים לשאל זה מזה בכל יום לעת

74 ערב שיתחדדו ויהיו מפולפלים ויתגדל בהם הדעת שנ׳ ברזל בברזל

75 יחד ואיש יחד גת פני רעהו. ועל כן יתביישו זה מזה הנערים על

76 שלא ידעו להשיב זה לזה כהוגן מאימת המלמד:

77 חק עשירי על המלמדים להחזיר לנערים בששי בשבת מה שלמדו בשבוע

78 זה ומה שלמדו בשבוע שעבר. ובראש חדש יחזרו מה שלמדו בחדש

79 זה ובחדש שעבר. בתשרי יחזרו מה שלמדו בקיץ. ובניסן יחזרו

80 מה שלמדו בחורף. פן ישכחו דבר ויהיו זכרנים יותר. וכן שנינו

81 השוכח פרק אחד או (197 ב) הלכה אחת עובר בשני לאוין על

82 השמר לך ושמר נפשך מאד פן תשכח את הדברים אשר ראו עיניך ופן

83 יסורו מלבבך כל ימי חייך והודעתם לבניך:

84 חק אחד עשר על המלמדים ללמד הנערים בלילי חורף מראש חדש

85 מרחשון עד ראש חדש ניסן רביעית הלילה כי ימי החרף קטנים

86 הם וכל נער ונער יתן חלקו לשכן המאור:
87 חק שנים עשר על המלמדים שלא יעשו שום מלאכה ולא סופרות
88 במעמד תלמודם פן יבטלו מתלמודם ולא יוכלו למלאות חקם. ויהיו
89 נקיים מאמונתם שהם חייבים לעשות מלאכת שמים באמונה. ומשפט
90 עסק המלמדים כפי חכמתם ועל פי השוטרים הממונים על עבודתם.
91 סליק:
92 תקנו קדמונים ז״ל לקנות בית המדרש אצל בית הכנסת לחבר
93 שניהם יחד מקום לתפלה ומקום לתלמוד על פי מדרש ילכו מחיל
94 לחיל יראת אלקים בציון. והיו (ב)מקומות הפרושים בשכירות
95 וכל פרוש ופרוש יתן חלקו בשכירות הבית כאשר הם נותנים
96 בשכירות הרב והמתורגמן ואותו הבית קנוי מהקדש הקהל אך
97 בשכירות הוא עומד לפרושים ולעשירים והשכירות לראש הישיבה
98 או לפרוע המתורגמן:
99 ועוד תקנו לקבוע מדרש לפרושים בעיר שעיקרה במלכות וכל הקהלות
100 אשר סביבותיה תשלחנה נדבות בכל שנה ושנה לעזרת המדרש לפרנס
101 את התלמידים ולפרוע את הרבנים והמתורגמנין ואת(ו) (ה)מדרש נקרא
102 מדרש (גדול) אשר ממנו יוצא חקים ומשפטים בישר׳:
103 ועוד תקנו על ראשי ישיבות שלא יקבעו בית המדרש בבתיהם רק
104 בבתי הפרושים פן יהיו מצויין אצל נשותיהם תמיד. ויעמדו
105 שם כל ימי השבוע ובערב שבת יחזרו לביתם ושמחים עם נשותיהם
106 ואנשי ביתם. ובמוצאי שבת חוזרין בבתי הפרושין והיו להם חליפות
107 שמלות האחד לובש בבתיהם והאחד לשרת בקדש בבית המדרש. וכל זה
108 פן יהרסו בערות דבר ויבאו לידי קרי ורצונם לדבר דברי תורה

109 בטהרה וראשי ישיבות לא יקבלו לפניהם בעלי בתים לפי שאין תלמודם

110 עיקר מפני מחשבות עסקיהם לבד תלמידים שאין להם עול בית כדי

111 שיחא לחם עסק למדרש. ויעמדו מתורגמין לתרגם ההלכה פעמים או

112 שלש עד שתהא שגורה בפיהם:

113 ועוד תקנו ראשי ישיבה בלתי שרים. פי׳ אם יהיה לפני ראש הישיבה

114 ארבעים תלמידים יעמידו לפניו ארבעה מתורגמנין

(198 א)

115 אחד לעשרה תלמידים ובצאת ראש הישיבה בבקר מבית הכנסת יבא בבית

116 המדרש בלי הפסק פי׳ שלא ידבר בינתים. ויפרש ההלכה כמשמועתה:

117 תקנו קדמונים ז״ל להקדיש הבן הבכור בעודו בבטן אמו וסמך למנהג

118 בטרם אצרך בבטן ידעתיך ובטרם תצא מרחם הקדשתיך. וזה פירוש

119 אשר קדש ידיד מבטן זה היה אברהם דדרשינן ידיעה כת׳ לגבי ירמיה

120 בטרם אצרך בבטן ידעתיך. ולגבי אברהם כת׳ כי ידעתיו למען וגו׳

121 כלומר כבר מה להלן נקדש בבטן אף כאן נקדש בבטן ומקבל עליו

122 ואומ׳ אם תלד אשתי זכר יהי קדש לה׳ ובתורתו יהגה יומם ולילה:

123 והיה ביום השמיני אחר שנכנס לברית מילה מושיבין הילד עלי

124 מצעות וחומש התורה על ראשו ויברכוהו זקני הקהל או ראש ישיבה

125 וכן יברכוהו ויתן לך האלקים מטל השמים עד מברכיך ברוך ויסמוך

126 ראש הישיבה ידו עליו ועל החומש ויאמ׳ ילמד זה מה שכתוב בזה ג״פ

127 יקיים זה מה שכתוב בזה ג״פ. תהיה תורת ה׳ בפיך. לא ימוש ספר

128 התורה הזה מפיך וג׳ ויעשה האב משתה ושמחה על הברית ועל הפרישות

129 דכ׳ שם גבי חנה וישב שם עד עולם:

130 ועוד תקנו על המלמדים יהיה מלמד חשוב מקבץ עד ק׳ תלמידים נערים

131 ללמדם תורה ולוקח בשכירותו ק׳ ליטרין ומשכיר להם י׳ מלמדים
132 בשמנים ליטרין ועשרים ליטרין הנותרים יהיו לחלקו. ולא ילמד הוא
133 שום נער. אך יהיה הוא שוטר המשגיח על המלמדים לתת להם שיעור על
134 תלמודם ומשכיר להם בית גדול ללמד בחדרים ובעליות וכל נער ונער
135 יתן חלקו בשכירות הבית וזה הבית נקרא מדרש קטן וישבו שבע שנים
136 (ב׳ שנים) חומש. וב׳ שנים נביאים וכתובים. וג׳ שנים מסכתות
137 קטנות וילכו בבית אביהם בלילות ויצאו מלפני המלמד וילכו לבית
138 המדרש הגדול העומד אצל בית הכנסת ללמוד מסכתות גדולות לפני
139 ראש ישיבה וישבו עמו ז׳ שנים כחק הפרושים:
140 ועוד תקנו ראשי ישיבה בלתי שרים פי׳ אם יהיה לפני ראש הישיבה
141 מ׳ תלמידים יעמידו לפניו ד׳ מתורגמנין אחד לעשרה תלמידין.
142 ובצאת ראש הישיבה בבקר מבית הכנסת יבא בבית המדרש בלי הפסק
143 ויפרש ההלכה והמתרג׳ יקבלו שטתו על ראשון ראשון ועל אחרון
144 אחרון וכשישלים הרב מלפרש יצאו המתורגמנין והתלמידים מלפניו:
145 וילכו בחדריהם ועליותיהן (198 ב) וכל מתרגם ומתרגם יבאו
146 לפניו עשרה תלמיד׳ המוטלים עליו ויחזר ההלכה לתלמידיו
147 פעמ׳ וילכו לאכל וכאשר יעבדו מעל שלחנם יחזרו בהלכה פעם
148 שלישית וישובו וישבו לפני הרב. והרב יפרש להם (ה)הלכה אחרת
149 ויצאו מלפניו כמשפט הבקר ויחזרו ההלכה פעמים. ואם יש להם שהות
150 ביום יחזרו ההלכה של בקר וההלכה של ערב ביחד. ויעמד החק הזה
151 מניסן ועד תשרי. ובחרף כמו כן יפרש הרב שחרית כאשר בארנו.

152 ופעם אחרת בצאתו מבית הכנסת בלילה ויצאו מלפניו ויחזרו ההלכה

153 פעמים טרם יאכלו. ואחר גמר השלחן יחזרו ההלכה פעם שלישית

154 ויחזרו הלכת בקר והלכת ערב ביחד וילכו לישן. ואם ירצו

155 התלמידים לחזור תלמודם כל הלילה הרשות בידם. אמרו חכמים ז״ל

156 אין רנה של תורה אלא בלילה שנ׳ יומם יצוה ה׳ חסדו ובלילה שירה

157 עמי ואו׳ נותן זמירות בלילה:

158 ועוד תקנו חכמ׳ אצל זקני העדה לעסק בשבת במלאכת הקדש לדרש

159 תורת האלקים להסיר מכשול ולהרים המוקש כדי שיהיו נזכרים

160 מדברי אלקים חיים. וכן דרשו חכמ׳ ז״ל ששת ימים תעבד ועשית כל

161 מלאכתך ויום השביעי שבת לה׳ אלקיך פי׳ לשם ה׳ כי לשון מנוחה

162 שייך אצל אדם שהוא עייף ויגע מעסקיו. וזאת המדה אינה אצל הבורא

163 י״ש דכ׳ לא ייעף ולא ייגע ואין חקר לתבונתו. על כן פי׳ לה׳

164 לשם ה׳ לעסוק במלאכת הקדש לדרש בתורת האלקים ולהרים מכשול

165 מתוך הקהל ולהרבות זכות וצדק עליהם להדריכם בדרך ישר. וכן

166 משפט הגדולים הקרובים למלכות לעסוק בעבודת המלך בששת ימי המעשה

167 וביום השביעי יעסקו בתורה ויזכרו דברי אלקים חיים לקיים כמ׳

168 שנ׳ למען תהיה תורת ה׳ בפיך לכל הפחות יום אחד בשבוע ונאמ׳

169 לא ימוש ספר התורה הזה מפיך והגית בו יומם ולילה:

170 כיצד מלמדים את הנערים וכיצד נותנין למלמדים שיעור עלי תלמודם:

171 אמ׳ חכמ׳ ז״ל בן חמש למקרא. אדם נותן בנו לתלמוד תורה ביד המלמד

172 בר״ח ניסן שהוא כשר לכל דבר כאשר אמ׳ חכמ׳ ז״ל מוציא אסירים

173 בכושרות זה ניסן שהוא כשר לכל דבר לא קר ולא חם. ואו׳ למלמד

174 בפיר׳ שיעור התלמוד יוודע לך שתלמד לבני בזה החדש הכרת האותיות

175 ובחדש השני הניקוד ובחדש השלישי צירוף האותיות במלות ומכאן

176 ואילך יבא טהור ויעסוק בטהרות בספר ויקרא. ואם לאו תתפרע כפועל

177 בטל ובכל חדש וחדש (199 א) תוסיף לבני אם ילמוד בני החדש הזה

178 חצי סדר בחדש אחר יגמור הסדר ובתמוז ועד תשרי ילמוד הסדר עברי שלם

179 בכל שבוע ומתשרי ועד ניסן לעז. והיא שנת ששי לנער. ובשנה השנית

180 שהיא שנת שביעי לנער ילמוד תרגום במכתב ולא על פה. וילעיז

181 התרגום כמו העברי ובשמיני ובתשיעי נביאים וכתובים:

182 אמ׳ חכמים בן עשר למשנה אז יכניסו הנער בגמרא מסכת ברכות ומסכתות

183 קטנות בסדר מועד ג׳ שנים. ובשנה רביעית קדש לה׳ שהיא י״ג לנער:

184 אמ׳ חכמ׳ בן י״ג למצוות וסמך לדבריהם עם זו יצרתי לי תהלתי יספרו

185 ז״ו בגי׳ י״ג פי׳ כאשר יגיעו עמי למניין זו אז תהלתי יספרו וראויין

186 הם להמנות במניין העדה ולהתפלל וראויין הם להפקד במניין הפרושים

187 ויקח האב את בנו הפרוש וימשיכהו בדברים טובים אשריך שזכית

188 למלאכת הקדש ויכניסהו אל בית הקבוע לפרושים וחובת הפרישות אינה

189 חל על הנער עד שיגיע לי״ו שנה ויביאו אותו לפני ראש הישיבה ויסמוך

190 ידיו עליו לאמר זה קדש לה׳ ויאמ׳ לבנו אני מצוך הנה את אשר תאכל

191 בביתי כי לתלמוד תורה הקדשתיך וישב שם ז׳ שנים ללמד מסכתות גדולות:

192 גם אמ׳ חכמ׳ לא המדרש עיקר אלא המעשה. ועוד אחד המרבה

193 ואחד הממעיט ובלבד שיכוין לבו לשמים. פי׳ דרשו חכמ׳

194 אלה הדברים על ההמון כדי להמשיכם אל האמונה ואל היראה.

195 וסמך לדבריהם ועתה ישראל מה ה׳ אלקיך שואל מעמך כי אם

196 ליראה וגו׳ מפני שהעם רודפים במלאכתן על כן דיי להם בקבלת האמונה.
197 אבל הפרושים יכולים להתחתן בשתים במדרש ובמעשה וגם ראשי
198 ראשי ישיבות יתנו שיעור לתלמודם סדר מועד לב׳ שנים. סדר נשים
199 לב׳ שנים. סדר נזיקין לב׳ שנים. סדר קדשים לב׳ שנים. והכל
200 מתלמוד גמרא. בין יהיו קבועים למדרש הפשט בין יהיו קבועים
201 למדרש התוספות. ואל יתעכבו ראשי ישיבות בתפלת השחר בבית
202 הכנסת עד גמר תפלה רק עד קדושה רבא מפני שיהיה שהות לתלמידים
203 לחזור תלמודם: סליק ספר חקי התורה: בריך רחמנא דסייען:

Appendix B
The Ashkenazic Educational Initiation Ceremony

Five texts describe, in varying degrees of detail, a ceremony conducted in Ashkenaz during the Tosafist period that might be termed "an initiation of the child into a life of study."[1] In the ceremony described in these texts the prospective student is brought either to the synagogue or to the teacher's home (which, as has been noted, served as a classroom in this period). In the presence of the scholar-teacher the child is given a "lesson" in the recitation of the Hebrew alphabet and some verses. The various texts note many attendant customs, such as coating the letters with honey and instructing the child to lick the honey off or covering the child on the way to the ceremony. In most cases the customs were designed to imitate, in some way, the giving of the Torah at Mount Sinai. The texts present the components of the ceremony in a different order, with slightly different emphases and with different reasons and proof texts for some of the practices. These differences are not terribly significant, although they may shed light on the relationship of the texts.

The precise content of the ceremony and the time of its occurrence are difficult to establish. Nonetheless, it is clear that some form of the ceremony was in vogue throughout the twelfth and thirteenth centuries. The author of *Sefer Assufot,* a student of R. Eleazar Roqeaḥ, describes it in almost exactly the same way as his teacher. There are two addenda: one is an opinion of R. Yehudah he-Ḥasid that letters should not be written on the cakes given to the children since the letters would become erased through the eating and digestion process; the other is the inclusion in the recitation of a brief mystical formula and a short explanation for why the child is told to recite the alphabet both forward and backward.[2] From the comment of R. Yehudah it is apparent that the ceremony was in use, at least in his region.[3] In addition, R. Meir of Rothenburg responded to two questions concerning the appropriateness of certain aspects of the ceremony.[4] A twelfth-century text refers to the ceremony and one of its components.[5] No leading scholars are mentioned in any of the texts. In the second section of the Hamburg 152 text the brother of R. Meir of Rothenburg, R. Abraham, responds to questions on the nature of the ceremony. The questions and answers are virtually identical to those found in the *Maḥzor Vitry* text.

The purpose of the ceremony, its relationship to other medieval Jewish and general educational initiation ceremonies, and its possible connection to pre-Crusade or mystical teachings require further investigation.[6]

Notes

Abbreviations

The following abbreviations are used in the notes.

AHR	*American Historical Review*
AJS	*Association for Jewish Studies*
B.B.	*Bava Batra*
B.M.	*Bava Meẓiʿa*
B.Q.	*Bava Qamma*
BT	Babylonian Talmud
HUCA	*Hebrew Union College Annual*
JJS	*Journal of Jewish Studies*
JQR	*Jewish Quarterly Review*
MGWJ	*Monatsschrift für Geschichte und Wissenschaft des Judentums*
MT	Moses b. Maimon, *Mishneh Torah*
PAAJR	*Proceedings of the American Academy for Jewish Research*
PBT	G. Paré, A. Brunet, and P. Tremblay, *La renaissance du XIIème siècle: les écoles et l'enseignement* (Paris, 1933)
PT	Palestinian Talmud
REJ	*Revue des études juives*
RMB	R. Meir of Rothenburg, *Responsa* (Berlin, 1891)
RMC	R. Meir of Rothenburg, *Responsa* (Cremona, 1557)
RML	R. Meir of Rothenburg, *Responsa* (Lemberg, 1860)
RMP	R. Meir of Rothenburg, *Responsa* (Prague [Budapest], 1895)

SḤB *Sefer Ḥasidim,* Bologna ms., ed. R. Margaliot (Jerusalem, 1957)
SḤH *Sefer Ḥuqqei ha-Torah* (see Appendix A)
SḤP *Sefer Ḥasidim,* Parma ms., ed. J. Wistinetski (Frankfurt, 1924)
SḤR *Sefer Ḥasidim,* Rome ms., ed. M. Hershler, *Genuzot* 1 (1984): 125–62

Notes to Chapter 1

1. Perhaps the best known of the studies of the 1930s is J. W. Thompson's *The Literacy of the Laity in the Middle Ages* (Berkeley, 1939). See esp. pp. 95–100, 130–46, 157, 196. For other studies of the period, see J. T. Rosenthal, "English Education since 1970—So Near and Yet So Far," *History of Education Quarterly* 22(1982): 508, n. 2.
2. See M. T. Clanchy, *From Memory to Written Record: England, 1066–1307* (Cambridge, 1979); B. A. Hanawalt, "Medieval Literacy," *History of Education Quarterly* 21 (1981): 370–71; and the literature collected by Rosenthal, "English Education" 508–9, nn. 5–7. For a quantitative measure of the growth of literacy among the laity in the late medieval period, see J. H. Moran, "Literacy and Education in Northern England, 1350–1500," *Northern History* 17 (1981): 1–23. Moran argues for an increase in literacy from 15 percent to 30 percent. See below, n. 27.
3. N. Orme, *From Childhood to Chivalry* (New York, 1984), 144–56.
4. To some extent the old notion that literacy in the medieval period was to be found only among the clergy was fostered by the fact that literacy was originally evaluated in terms of knowledge of Latin. See Hanawalt, "Medieval Literacy," 368.
5. A Landgraf, ed. *Commentarius Cantabrigienis in Epistolas Pauli e Schola Petri Abelardi* (Notre Dame, 1937), 2:434, trans. in B. Smalley, *The Study of the Bible in the Middle Ages* (Oxford, 1952), 78. See also R. W. Southern, *Medieval Humanism and Other Studies* (New York, 1970), 11. On the implications of this statement for the interaction of Jewish and Christian scholars, see A. Grabois, "The Hebraica Veritas and Jewish-Christian Intellectual Relations in the Twelfth Century," *Speculum* 50 (1975): 633. Cf. R. Joseph Kimḥi, *Sefer Ha-Berit,* ed. F. Talmage (Jerusalem, 1974), 26:

   והם היהודים והיהודיות הצנועות בכלל מעשיהם ובניהם מקטנם
   ועד גדולם מגדלים אותם בלימוד תורתם.

Note that although this assessment comes from the Jew (*ma'amin*), the Christian (*min*) agrees to it (p. 27). See J. Rembaum, "Re-evaluation of a Medieval Polemical Manuscript," *AJS Review* 5 (1980): 86–88.

6. R. Chazan, *Medieval Jewry in Northern France* (Baltimore, 1973), 20, 52. Cf. L. Rabinowitz, *The Social Life of the Jews of Northern France,* 2d ed. (New York, 1972), 213–20 and S. Stampfer, "Yediʿat Qero u-Khetov Eẓel Yehudei Mizraḥ Eiropah bi-Tequfah ha-Ḥadashah," in *Temurot be-Historiyah ha-Yehudit be-Et ha-Ḥadashah,* ed. S. Almog et al. (Jerusalem, 1988), 459–62. For a comparison of the educational levels in Ashkenaz and Sepharad, see I. Ta-Shema, "Shipput ʿIvri u-Mishpat ʿIvri ba-Me'ot ha-11-12 bi-Sefarad," *Shenaton ha-Mishpat ha-ʿIvri* 1 (1974): 353–54. On illiteracy within Spanish Jewry, see below, chap. 4, n. 60. On the use by Jews of the vernacular in the educational process, see M. Güdemann, *Ha-Torah veha-Ḥayyim Bimei ha-Beinayim be-Ẓarefat ve-Ashkenaz* (Warsaw, 1897; repr. Tel Aviv, 1968), 38; I. Twersky, "Toledot ha-Ḥinnukh," in *Encyclopedia Ḥinnukhit* (Jerusalem, 1964), 4:260 and M. Banitt, "L'étude des glossaires bibliques des Juifs de France au moyen âge." *Proceedings of the Israel Academy of Sciences and Humanities* 2 (1967): 188–210; idem, "Les Poterim," *REJ* 125 (1966): 21–33.
7. See, e.g., the lavish praise heaped on the scholars of northern France in this regard by (1) the anonymous author of the gloss to Ibn Daud's *Sefer ha-Qabbalah* written c. 1195 in Provence (see J. Cohen, "The Nasi of Narbonne," *AJS Review* 2 [1977]: 55–56) and published in A. Zuckerman, *A Jewish Princedom in Feudal France* [New York, 1972], p. 386); (2) Ramban, in his crucial letter to the rabbis of this area during the Maimonidean controversy in 1232 (C. Chavel, ed., *Kitvei Ramban* [Jerusalem, 1968], 1:336–37; cf. Ramban's introduction to the treatise *Dinna de-Garmi* and R. Solomon Luria's introduction to *Yam shel Shelomoh*); (3) Ha-Meiri (c. 1300), in the introduction to his commentary on *Avot,* ed. B. Perag (Jerusalem, 1974), 56.
8. L. Thorndyke, "Elementary and Secondary Education in the Middle Ages," *Speculum* 15 (1940): 403, and the literature cited there in n. 3.
9. M. Güdemann, *Geschichte des Erziehungswesens und der Cultur der abendländischen Juden während des Mittelalters* (Vienna, 1880) 1:50–51. Cf. J. H. Mundy, *Europe in the High Middle Ages* (London, 1979), 84–85. Güdemann's source for the existence of separate communal funds for education, R. Nissim b. Reuben (*Responsa of Ran* [Warsaw, 1882], no. 84), is describing the institutions of fourteenth-century Perpignan. See below, chap. 3, n. 64. Rabinowitz (*Social Life,* 217)

also maintains that there were formal elementary schools whose teachers were paid by the community.

10. Güdemann, *Geschichte,* 117–18. The quotation is from R. Samson b. Ẓadoq, *Sefer Tashbeẓ* (Warsaw, 1876), no. 533, citing a ruling of R. Samuel of Bamburg. Cf. J. Wistinetski, ed., *Sefer Ḥasidim,* (Jerusalem, 1924), sec. 862 (hereafter *SḤP* from ms. [Parma] De Rossi 1133, on which the text is based).
11. This conclusion may be reached from a careful reading of E. E. Urbach's *Ba'alei ha-Tosafot* (hereafter Urbach), 4th ed. (Jerusalem, 1980). It is stated explicitly by H. Soloveitchik, "Three Themes in the Sefer Ḥasidim," *AJS Review* 1 (1976): 340. On the ramifications for higher education in Ashkenaz, see below, chap. 5.
12. See Urbach, 1:45, 58–61, 229, 253–54, 485–86. On the role of *yiḥus* in the structure of the Tosafist academies, see below, chap. 5.
13. See V. Aptowitzer, *Mavo le-Sefer Rabiah,* 5–6, based on Aptowitzer, ed. *Sefer Rabiah,* 2d ed. (Jerusalem, 1964), 2:562. See also S. Albeck, introduction to *Sefer Raban* (New York, 1958), and Urbach, 1:379.
14. See Aptowitzer, *Mavo,* 6 and I. A. Agus, *R. Meir of Rothenburg* (New York, 1947), 1:7–8. This view relies in part on a text in which R. Meir (who could not have been born before 1212–15 according to Aptowitzer and Agus) states that while he studied with R. Isaac as a child (*keshehayiti tinoq*), R. Isaac consulted with Rabiah concerning the laws of mourning:

> זכורני כשהייתי תינוק והייתי בווירצבורג והציקותי מים על ידי הרב ר׳ יצחק מווין, באה אלינו נכרית אחת ואמרה לר׳ יוסף . . . שנפטרה אחותו ושאלו להראבי״ה כדת מה לעשות והשיב לו להתאבל.

(*Sefer Mordekhai* to *Mo'ed Qatan,* no. 925; cf. *Haggahot Maimuniyyot* to *Hilkhot Aveilut* 7:6). According to both scholars, Rabiah died before 1225. Urbach (2:523–25) maintains, however, that R. Meir was born after 1220. He argues that other texts indicate that R. Isaac Or Zarua' had consulted Rabiah on the laws of mourning prior to the time that R. Meir studied with R. Isaac and that R. Isaac merely reported to R. Meir (in the quotation reproduced above) the results of that earlier consultation. Furthermore, the term *tinoq,* used by R. Meir to describe his status when he studied with R. Isaac, can refer to a young man in his twenties and need not refer to a preteen or teenage student. But Urbach (2:526) agrees that R. Meir was in Paris at the burning of the Talmud (1242) and that he had studied in Wurzburg, first with R. Isaac Or Zarua' and then with R. Samuel b. Menaḥem, before he traveled to France to continue his studies. It is clear that R. Meir began to study with at least some of his teachers in France before the burning of the Talmud (e.g., R. Ezra of Moncontour, who according to Urbach [1:336–37] could not have been alive in 1242). It is also probable that he studied with R. Judah b. Moses ha-Kohen of Mayence before he reached France; see Agus, *R. Meir,* 9. Since R. Meir remained for only a short time in France following the burning of the Talmud (Urbach, 2:528, n. 33), it is likely that he began to study with R. Yeḥiel of Paris and R. Samuel of Falaise before 1242 as well. We know that R. Meir spent extended periods of time studying with some of his teachers (e.g., R. Isaac Or Zaruaʿ; see Urbach 2:525). Given the various locations and teachers that R. Meir reached before 1242, it is quite possible—even taking Urbach's assumptions into account—that he began to study with R. Isaac Or Zaruaʿ while still in his early teens. Note that Urbach's proofs (2:525, n. 17*) for the use of *tinoq* (as opposed to *naʿar* or *yeled*) as a term describing a young man in his twenties are quite weak. Cf. G. Duby, *The Chivalrous Society* (Berkeley, 1977), 112–22.

15. For R. Judah Sir Leon, see the biographical details in Urbach, 1:321. He is, by age sixteen, an active member of the *beit midrash* of Ri and R. Elḥanan, to whom he was closely related. Judging from the amount of the material that he cites from these two scholars and the deaths of R. Elḥanan in 1184 and Ri around 1190, R. Judah reached Dampierre before age fifteen. R. Elijah of London studied with R. Samson of Sens; see M. Saks's introduction to his edition of *Perushei R. Eliyyahu mi-London u-Pesaqav* (Jerusalem, 1956), 14. Cf. Urbach, 2:500 and C. Roth's "*Toledot Rabbenu Eliyyahu*" in Saks, *Perushei R. Eliyyahu,* 29, n. 50. R. Samson emigrated to Israel in 1211. It is virtually impossible that R. Elijah was born before 1195, since he reportedly expressed an interest to travel to France in 1280 and died in 1284 (Roth, "*Toledot*", p. 41). For R. Samuel b. Elḥanan b. ha-Ri, see above, n. 12.
16. See M. Breuer, "Toward the Investigation of the Typology of the Western Yeshivot in the Middle Ages" [Hebrew], in *Studies in the History of Jewish Society in the Middle Ages and in the Modern Period,* ed. E. Etkes and T. Salmon (Jerusalem, 1980), 53–54 and the sources cited by Breuer in nn. 57–60. The phenomenon is attested to in Ashkenazic academies in the pre-Crusade and post-1348 periods as well.
17. See Soloveitchik, "Three Themes," 339–42 and I. A. Agus, "Morei ha-Talmud ve-Talmideihem ba-Ḥevrah ha-Yehudit be-Germanyah" in *Samuel Belkin Memorial Volume,* ed. H. Leaf and M. Carmilly (New York, 1981), 138–41.
18. See S. Eidelberg, ed., *Teshuvot Rabbenu Gershom* (New York, 1955), no. 71; the responsum of R. Yehudah ha-Kohen published by A.

Grossman in *'Alei Sefer* 1 (1975): 33; R. Meir b. Barukh, *Responsa* (Cremona, 1557), no. 125 (hereafter *RMC*) and (Prague, 1895) no. 833 (hereafter *RMP*); *Sefer Mordekhai* to *Bava Meẓi'a*, no. 346; *SḤP*, sec. 801. Note the special stipulations in *RMC*, nos. 3 and 310. Cf. *Tosafot Bava Meẓi'a* 66a, s.v. *u-Minyumei amar asmakhta la qanya*. See also the ruling of Maharam concerning the hiring of a tutor on the Sabbath cited in a Cambridge manuscript of *Sefer Tashbeẓ*, Add. 667, 1, fol. 117b. (On the manuscript, see J. Leveen, "A Maḥzor of the School of Rashi," *REJ* 125 [1966]: 127, 138.) See S. Gross, "Toledot ha-Ḥinnukh, Derakhav u-Mosdotav be-Yahadut Ashkenaz ve-Ẓarefat ba-Shanim 950–1350," (Master's thesis, Bar-Ilan University, 1982), 25–26.

19. Responsum of R. Joseph Tob Elem in ms. Oxford, Bodl. 1298, fol. 40b; *RMP*, 434–35; responsum of R. Gershom in J. Mueller, *Teshuvot Ḥakhmei Ẓarefat ve-Lothaire* (New York, 1958), no. 99.
20. *Haggahot Maimuniyyot* to *Hilkhot Talmud Torah* 1:1. Cf. R. Meir of Rothenburg, *Teshuvot, Pesaqim, u-Minhagim*, ed. I. Z. Kahana, (Jerusalem, 1957–60), 2:255.
21. See L. Finkelstein, *Jewish Self-Government in the Middle Ages* (New York, 1924), 168–69.
22. *Ketubot* 50a. A father must continue to oversee his son's education from ages six through twelve.
23. S. Rosenthal, ed., *Sefer ha-Yashar*, no. 31. A similar ruling is attributed to Ri in *Sefer Mordekhai* to *Sanhedrin*, no. 705. Cf. *Sefer Ḥasidim* (ms. Rome 285), p. 141, no. 51 (hereafter *SḤR;* pagination follows the partial transcription by M. Hershler in *Genuzot* 1 [1984]). Undoubtedly, some fathers did undertake to teach their own sons, possibly even past the elementary level. See *SḤP*, secs. 127, 751, 967, 1469, and *SḤR*, 152, no. 104. Cf. below, n. 98.
24. *SḤP*, sec. 822. Cf. sec. 671 (*ve-ḥeleq ha-maskirim melammedim lilmod* [*le-limmud*?] *'aniyim ke-ḥeleq ha-lomdim*), 630, 751, and *Sefer Miẓvot Gadol, 'aseh* 12.
25. Pope Alexander III's canon promulgated at the Third Lateran Council in 1179 is recorded in *Decretales Gregorii Papae IX* (Paris, 1601), 5:5:1 (= J. D. Mansi, *Sacrorum conciliorum collectio*, vol. 2 [Florence, 1778, repr. 1961], cols. 227–28). The text of the canon and a translation are furnished in H. J. Schroeder, *Disciplinary Decrees of the General Councils* (St. Louis, 1937), 229, 556.
26. Mansi, *Sacrorum consiliorum collectio*, cols. 999–1000. See N. Orme, *English Schools in the Middle Ages* (London, 1973), 174–76. The repetition of the basic proviso for elementary education in 1215 is

perhaps an indication that the canon of 1179 was being ignored. See G. Pare, A. Brunet, and P. Tremblay, *La renaissance du XIIe siècle: Les écoles et l'enseignment* (Paris, 1933) 81 (hereafter PBT). Cf. B. Tierney, *Medieval Poor Law* (Berkeley, 1959), 19–20; Thorndyke, "Elementary and Secondary Education," 401–2; A. F. Leach, *The Schools of Medieval England* (London, 1915), 133; R. W. Southern, *The Making of the Middle Ages* (New Haven, 1953), 194.

27. See Thorndyke, "Elementary and Secondary Education," 406 and the literature cited there in n. 2. See also F. B. Artz, *The Mind of the Middle Ages,* 3d ed. (Chicago, 1980), 311–12. These schools were not under church auspices. See PBT, 82, n. 1, and C. W. Previté-Orton, ed., *The Cambridge History of the Middle Ages* (London, 1936), 8:692–94. Cf. J. Le Goff, *Time, Work and Culture in the Middle Ages* (Chicago, 1980), 120.

28. See *SḤP,* sec. 109 (with the last line clarified by R. Margalioth, ed., *Sefer Ḥasidim* [Jerusalem, 1957], sec. 644 [hereafter *SḤB* from the Bologna ms. the text is based on]):

> וזה כפרתך אל תלך בדרך אתם יותר ועל כל אות ואות שיצא מפיהם צריך או תענית או מעות לעניים שאין להם במה להשכיר מלמדים לבניהם ותגרום שילמדו מה שהחטאת אתה אותם שלא ידעו ללמוד כגון קטנים.

Cf. I. Marcus, *Piety and Society* (Leiden, 1981), 95. See also *SḤP,* secs. 762–63 concerning the importance of reviewing lessons with poor students who have no one else to help them. On the use of word games as an educational device during this period, see M. M. Mc-Laughlin, "Survivors and Surrogates: Children and Parents from the Ninth to the Thirteenth Centuries," in *The History of Childhood,* ed. L. DeMause (New York, 1974), 125.

29. See Isaac b. Moses, *Sefer Or Zarua', Pisqei Bava Meẓi'a* (Zhitomir, 1862), sec. 181 (hereafter *Sefer Or Zarua', Pisqei B. M.*). R. Eliezer of Toul, a student of Ri, was hired by one of the lay leaders of the German community of Boppard as a private tutor. See Urbach, 1:335. See also M. Brann and A. Freimann, *Germania Judaica* (Frankfurt, 1917), 1:62. R. Gershom served as a tutor for a short period of time (*hayah sakhur la-talmidim*) but the level of the students, the subject matter taught, and at what stage in his career is not clear. See S. Eidelberg, ed., *Teshuvot Rabbenu Gershom,* 169 and nn. 1–3 and A. Grossman, *Ḥakhmei Ashkenaz ha-Rishonim* (Jerusalem, 1981), 116. Cf. F. E. Talmage, *David Kimḥi: The Man and the Commentaries* Cambridge, 1975), 14–15; B. Septimus, *Hispano-Jewish Culture in Transition* (Cam-

bridge, 1982), 124, n. 76; R. Isaac Al-Fasi, *Responsa* (Pittsburgh, 1954), no. 223; and Solomon Ibn Adret, *Responsa* (Bnei Brak, 1958), vol. 1, no. 1042.

30. See R. Solomon Luria, *Responsa* (Lemberg, 1859), no. 36. The statement of R. Tam was recorded in a gloss of R. Isaac of Corbeil to chap. 3 of *Bava Batra,* based on a *tosafot* text from chap. 2.

31. It is easiest to catalog these responsa according to the chronological order of the respondents: (1) Eidelberg, *Teshuvot Rabbenu Gershom,* nos. 71–73; (2) R. Joseph Tob Elem, ms. Bodl. 1208, fol. 40b; (3) R. Yehudah ha-Kohen, responsum published by A. Grossman in *ʿAlei Sefer* 1 (1975): 33; (4) Rabbenu Tam, *Sefer Ha-Yashar,* ed. S. Rosenthal (Berlin, 1898), nos. 31, 71; (5) R. Yoel ha-Levi in *Sefer Or Zaruaʿ, Pisqei B. M.,* no. 243 (cf. ms. Bodl. 637, fol. 276r); (6) Ri, in *RMP,* no. 477 = *Sefer Or Zaruaʿ, Pisqei B. M.,* no. 242; (7) R. Samson of Sens in *RMP,* nos. 385–87 and *Teshuvot Maimuniyyot* to *Sefer Qinyan,* no. 30; (8) R. Joseph of Clisson in *Teshuvot Maimuniyyot* to *Sefer Qinyan,* no. 31; (9) various teachers of R. Meir of Rothenburg in *RMC,* no. 191; *RML* (Lemberg, 1860), no. 157; and *RMB* (Berlin, 1891, ed. M. Bloch), no. 17; (10) R. Meir of Rothenburg, *RMC,* nos. 23, 125; 191 (= *RMP,* no. 138 and *RMB,* no. 157); *RMB,* p. 276, no. 55; *RMP,* nos. 37, 85, 250, 385, 434–35, 488, 667, 833; in *Mordekhai Bava Meẓiʿa* (*Mord. B.M.*), no. 282 and several rulings in *Mord. B. M.,* 343–46 and *Mordekhai Bava Batra* (*Mord. B.B.*), no. 621. (11) R. Ḥayyim Or Zaruaʿ, *Responsa* (Leipzig, 1860), nos. 66, 167. See also S. Ehrenreich, ed., *Sefer Raban* (New York 1958) [end of *B. M.,* chap. 5], 204d; the Raban text published by S. E. Stern in *Ẓefunot* 1:2 (1988): 11; I. A. Agus, *Teshuvot Baʿalei ha-Tosafot* (New York, 1954), 198; R. Samson b. Ẓadoq, *Sefer Tashbeẓ* (Warsaw, 1876) no. 528 and *Haggahot R. Pereẓ,* ad loc.; (*Haggahot*) *Mord. B.M.* no. 457; *Or Zaruaʿ, B.M.* no. 188; and S. Assaf, *Meqorot le-Toledot ha-Ḥinnukh be-Yisrael* (Tel Aviv, 1930), vol. 1, nos. 12, 13.

32. See S. Safrai, "Elementary Education in the Talmudic Period," in *Jewish Society through the Ages,* ed. H. H. Ben-Sasson and S. Ettinger (New York, 1969), 150–52.

33. See S. D. Goitein, *Sidrei Ḥinnukh* (Jerusalem, 1962), 77–90. For Spain, see Assaf, *Meqorot,* vol. 2, nos. 37, 38 (esp. entry 9), 40 (esp. entries 1, 5), 58 (esp. entry 3) and vol. 4, nos. 7 (esp. entry 2), 18; Isaac al-Fasi, *Responsa,* no. 223; Rashba, *Responsa,* vol. 1, no. 1157; and see below, nn. 37–38. Despite Y. Baer's contention (*A History of the Jews in Christian Spain,* (Philadelphia, 1961), 1:236) that "we hear very little during this period of the appointment of teachers for all the

children of the community," the Spanish references are significant when compared with the total absence of such appointments in Ashkenaz. Cf. I. Sonne, "On Baer and His Philosophy of History," *Jewish Social Studies* 9 (1947): 63. See also A. A. Neuman, *The Jews in Spain* (Philadelphia, 1942), 2:65–66 and A. Levine, *Free Enterprise and Jewish Law* (New York, 1980), 154. There is one reference to a *melammed* in Ashkenaz who taught all the children of a community, but it is certainly peripheral to our discussion. R. Eliezer of Bohemia, in a responsum written in response to a ruling of R. Yehudah he-Ḥasid (*Sefer Or Zarua*ʿ, vol. 1, no. 113), notes that in the outlying areas of Ashkenaz, in central and eastern Europe, the small communities sometimes hired a jack-of-all-trades who served as cantor and judge and *melammed* and was guaranteed a certain income. This source is also important for tracing the development of salaried communal functionaries in Ashkenaz. See below, chap. 4, n. 49 and chap. 6, n. 41.

34. R. Meir ha-Levi, *Yad Ramah le-Bava Batra* (Warsaw, 1887), chap. 2, no. 58:

> ושמעינן מינה דמחייבינן ציבורא אותוביה מקרי דרדקי בכל מאתא
> . . . והכי נמי מסתברא מדקתני התקין יהושע בן גמלא מושיבין
> מלמדי תינוקות ואי דלא יהבינן ליה אגרא מציבורא מאי שידהו
> מושיבין. אלא לאו דיהבינן ליה אגרא מדציבורא והכין עדיף כי היכי
> דלילפו בני עניים כבני עשירים.

See below, n. 50, and *Nimmuqei Yosef* to *Bava Batra* 21, s.v. *le-tinoqot shel beit rabban.*

35. Cited in Assaf, *Meqorot,* vol. 2, no. 41.
36. Meir of Rothenburg, *Teshuvot, Pesaqim, u-Minhagim,* vol. 1 no. 24. See also *RMB,* 320 (= *RMP,* no. 865). Cf. I. A. Agus, "Ha-Shilton ha-Aẓma'i shel ha-Qehillah ha-Yehudit Bimei ha-Beinayim," *Talpiyyot* 6 (1953): 109.
37. See Finkelstein, *Jewish Self-Government,* 59–61, 220, 247–49. The Mayence ordinance reads

> ובמה שאין מספיקים במה שנותנים למלמדים של התנוקות שאין
> מספיק ההקדש שאין להם כל כך, יקחו משאר הקדשות שהניחו נוחי
> נפש עבור נשמתן ויתנו למלמדים אם לא פירש השכיב מרע לצורך
> מה והמותר יתנו במקום שרוצים הקהל.

The Speyers ordinance reads,

> ובמקום שאין מספיקים במה שנותנים ללמד
> תנוקות יקחו ממה שמניחין לזכור נשמתן למלמדים אם לא פירש וכו׳.

38. Perhaps the ordinance was intended, in part, to provide tutors for orphans. The term *heqdesh* in the Mayence ordinance clearly refers to monies given to the community as charity. See *Sefer Or Zarua'*, *Hilkhot Ẓedaqah,* no. 30; *RML,* nos. 234, 425, 478–79; and *Tosafot B.B.* 8b, s.v. *u-leshanot.* On the varying connotations of this term in Ashkenaz, Provence, and Spain, see the sources collected in B. Z. Dinur, *Yisrael ba-Golah* (Jerusalem, 1966), 2:381–83, 385–89 and Y. Y. Yuval, *Rabbanim ve-Rabbanut be-Germanyah,* 1350–1500 (Ph.D. diss., Hebrew University, 1985), 187, n. 26. See also *SḤP,* 41, 273, 356–57; *SḤR,* 141, no. 51; R. Asher b. Yeḥiel, *Responsa* (Venice, 1607) 6:2, 13:4; R. Nissim b. Reuben Gerondi, *Responsa,* (Constantinople, 1548) no. 75; L. A. Feldman, *The Life and Times of Nissim b. Reuben Gerondi* (Ph.D. diss., Columbia University, 1968), 41, n. 2; D. Fink, "The Corporate Status of *Heqdesh* in Early Sefardic Responsa," in *Jewish Law Association Studies,* (Chico, 1985), 1:17–24; and Goitein, *Sidrei Ḥinnukh,* 39, 91, 96.
39. Responsum of R. Yehudah ha-Kohen, published from two manuscripts by A. Grossman in *'Alei Sefer* 1 (1975): 33:

    ראובן שהכניס בנו לבית הספר לפני שמעון ופסק עמו לתת שכר כך וכך והביא בנו לבית שמעון והביא ספרו ללמד לו וגם חביריו הביאו ג"כ ספריהם והיו מניחים אותם במקום המיוחד להם.

    and *SḤP,* no. 764:

    אמרו עליו [על זקן אחד] שהיה רגיל במקום שהתינוקות היו רגילים ללכת לבית רבן, היה מחלק להם פירות ואגוזים כדי שיעסקו בתורה. וכשעומדים מבית רבן היה נותן להם פירות ואגוזים ושואל להם מה היו לומדים והם עוסקים בתורה.

    (See the text published by M. Hershler in *Genuzot* 2 (1985): 179–80.) Cf. *SḤR,* 155, no. 119; and *SḤP,* 367, sec. 1512:

    שנים היו בעיר אחד צדיק ואחד רשע כשגדלו וכשהיו קטנים והלכו לבית הספר למקום רבם ללמוד.

    For rooms rented to the *melammed,* see *Mord. B.B.*, 468:

    ראובן שהשכיר בית לשמעון . . . אם רוצה שמעון למלאת הבית דיורין הרשות בידו להרבות מלמדים וסופרים ושכירין ותושבין.

    See the next note.
40. See *Tosafot 'Eruvin,* 72a, s.v. *u-modin* and J. Wilman, ed. *Tosafot R. Perez̦* (New York, 1981), s.v. *u-modin; Sefer Or Zarua',* 2:46a (*Hilkhot 'Eruvin,* no. 172 = *Haggahot Maimuniyyot* to *Hilkhot 'Eruvin* 4:7[2];

Tosafot Qiddushin 59a, s.v. *'ani; RMP,* no. 37; *SḤP,* sec. 1073, 1497, 1500. See also Gross, "Toledot ha-Ḥinnukh," 46–49.

41. See the initiation ceremonies (discussed more fully in App. B) in S. Hurwitz, ed., *Maḥzor Vitry,* (Jerusalem, 1963), 628, and *Sefer Roqeaḥ, Hilkhot Shavu'ot,* (Venice, 1549), no. 296. See also *SḤP,* sec. 462 and Rashi, *Berakhot* 17a, s.v. *le-vei kenishta.* Cf. I. Twersky, "Toledot ha-Ḥinnukh," 257. The lack of communal supervision even in situations where the parents could have especially benefited from it is evident in *SḤP,* sec. 821 and Maharam's ruling cited in *Mord. B.B.,* no. 621. Cf. *SḤB,* sec. 139.
42. See S. Luce, "Catalog des documents du tresor des chartres," *REJ* 2 (1886): 33–34, 47, 50–53, 56–57, 66; A. Grabois, "Écoles et structures sociales des communautés juives," in *Gli Ebrei nell'alto medioevo,* (Spoleto, 1980), 937–62; idem, "Les écoles de Narbonne au XIIIe siècle," in *Juifs et Judaisme de Languedoc,* (Toulouse, 1977), 141–57; B. Z. Benedikt, "R. Moshe b. Yosef," *Tarbiz* 19 (1948): 20–21. See also the description of Radaq cited in Assaf, *Meqorot,* 2:33; and cf. Talmage, *David Kimḥi* 14–16.
43. *REJ* 2:42. Cf. *REJ* 2:17–18. B. Blumenkranz and N. Golb had an ongoing debate concerning the existence of separate buildings for academies in Ashkenaz. The literature is collected and reviewed by Blumenkranz in *Art et archéologie des Juifs en France médiévale* (Paris, 1980), 277–303. See also N. Golb, "Nature et destination du monument hebraique découvert a rouen," *PAAJR* 48 (1981): 155–61. Blumenkranz held that all *scholae* were synagogues and that all academic activities took place in them. See also D. Bertin, "Deux constructions juives du XIIe siècle," *Archives Juives* 12 (1976): 55–60.

    The reference to *ḥadarim* in Paris c. 1240 (Assaf, *Meqorot,* 4:4) can easily refer to rooms used as *battei midrash;* see below, chap. 4, n. 18. There are references after 1348 to *chambres* in Germany. These were quarters-synagogues for older students that perhaps served also as schoolrooms for younger students (ibid., n. 5 and M. Breuer, *Ha-Yeshivah ha-Ashkenazit be-Shilhei Yemei ha-Beinayim* (Ph.D. diss., Hebrew University, 1967), 47.
44. See S. Salfeld, *Das Martyrologium des Nürnberger Memorbuches* (Berlin, 1898), 8, 16, 37, 213.
45. Rabbenu Tam, *Sefer Ha-Yashar,* no. 71. Cf. *Mord. B.M.,* 77a.
46. See Rashi, *B.B.,* 21a, s.v. *sofer mata* and *Tosafot,* s.v. *sofer mata.* Cf. Rashi, *Sanhedrin,* 17b, s.v. *beit din makkin ve-ḥovshin* and *Yad Ramah,* s.v. *kammah yehe ba-'ir;* and Rashi, *B.B.,* 8b s.v. *melamdei tinnoqot. Sefer Ḥuqqei ha-Torah* (see App. A) refers to a more orga-

nized system for elementary education, which included supervising the teacher or teachers. Student aptitude and progress were measured and evaluated. In one version the parents of the students paid to maintain the arrangement, while in another it would seem that some communal funding was also available. The *melammedim* all taught in a study hall, rather than in their own homes. However, questions concerning the origin of the document and whether it was ever in effect render it most difficult to consider as a source for educational realia in Ashkenaz. See chap. 4, n. 2 and App. A. Cf. Twersky, "Toledot ha-Ḥinnukh," 257, and I. A. Agus, *The Heroic Age of Franco-German Jewry* (New York, 1969), 318. The supervising *maqrei dardeqei* in Worms (Assaf, *Meqorot,* 4:13) is mentioned in a 1387 text, which Assaf mistakenly appended to a text from the 1340s. In general, a much greater degree of scholarly organization on all levels permeated Ashkenaz in the period following the Black Death. See Breuer, *Ha-Yeshivah Ha-Ashkenazit,* 9–10, 33–37 and below, chap. 3, n. 72.

47. On Jewish communal size in northern France, see S. Albeck, "Yaḥaso shel Rabbenu Tam li-Veʿayot Zemanno," *Zion* 19 (1954): 104–5; S. W. Baron, "Rashi and the Community of Troyes," in *Rashi Anniversary Volume,* ed. H. L. Ginsberg (New York, 1941), 58–62; B. Blumenkranz, "Quartiers juifs en France (XIIe, XIIIe, XIVe siècles)," *Melanges de philosophie et de litterature juives* 3–5 (1958–62): 77–86. For Germany through the period of the First Crusade, see Grossman, *Ḥakhmei Ashkenaz ha-Rishonim,* 6–9. See also *Teshuvot Geonei Mizraḥ u-Maʿarav* (Berlin, 1888), no. 165 and B. Altmann in *PAAJR* 10 (1946): 57.

48. S. Z. Ehrenreich, ed., *Sefer Raban,* (New York, 1958), 209, col. 4; *Sefer Mordekhai, B.B.* no. 512. The manuscript from which B. Pozna published parts 3 and 4 of the *Sefer Or Zaruaʿ* (*Pisqei B.Q., B.M., B.B., Sanhedrin, Avodah Zarah*) in 1887 in Frankfurt (ms. British Museum Or. 2860) contains a lacuna at this point in *B.B.* It is the only known ms. for this section. See Urbach, 1:440. However, in the *Simmanei Or Zaruaʿ* (ms. Vatican 148, fol. 93v–94r) the same selectivity that has been noted in *Sefer Raban* and *Sefer Mordekhai* is apparent. It is also significant that *Tosafot B.B.,* 21a, s.v. *sakh maqrei dardeqei* explains that until twenty-five students are enrolled, no member or members of the community can force the others to hire a teacher. This interpretation runs counter to all Spanish commentaries, which mandate the hiring of one teacher until the twenty-five-student mark is reached. See B. Menat, ed., *Ḥiddushei ha-Ritba* (Jerusalem, 1975), p. 54. As we shall see later, Ashkenazic halakhic commentators do deal with the

hiring of teachers in connection with *sugyot* in *B.M.*, 76–78, Talmudic sections dealing primarily with the laws for individuals who hire workers. Most Spanish commentaries are silent there regarding the hiring of teachers. Cf. A. Halpern, ed., *Ḥiddushei ha-Ritba* (London, 1962), 173; *Tur Yoreh De'ah,* sec. 245; and *Beit Yosef,* ad loc.

49. See *Mishneh Torah, Hilkhot Talmud Torah* 2:5–6; chap. 2 in its entirety is a halakhic paraphrase of the Talmudic *sugya.*

50. See R. Meir's collection of responsa, *Or Ẓaddiqim* (Warsaw, 1902), no. 241. The questioner, apparently an authority in his own right, suggested that funds for *melammedei tinoqot,* in smaller towns and villages where the individuals who required the services of the *melammed* could not afford to pay the entire cost, be raised by imposing a tax on the entire community in accordance with the ruling of R. Yehoshua' ben Gamla. While Ramah does not necessarily endorse this plan in his answer, his description of the communities' responsibilities when it comes to hiring *melammedim* is parallel to his comment in *Yad Ramah* (quoted above, n. 34). Cf. R. Yeruḥam b. Meshullam, *Toledot Adam ve-Ḥavvah* 2:1; *Sefer Mesharim,* 29:3. In R. Samson b. Zemaḥ Duran, *Responsa,* vol. 3, no. 153 the position of the *melammed* is defined by the *sugya* in *Bava Batra.* See also vol. 1, no. 64 and E. Shochetman, "Dinei Ḥinnukh ba-Mishpat ha-Ivri 'al Pi Meqorot ha-Talmudiyim ve-Sifrut ha-Posqim shel Yemei ha-Beinayim" (Master's thesis, Hebrew University, 1969), 30–39.

51. See Eidelberg, *Teshuvot Rabbenu Gershom,* no. 71. The *melammed* claims that the hirer brought him into the household to teach the hirer's three sons. The hirer promised to bring in other students who were his son's peers so that the total income of the teacher would be the tutition paid by ten students. Rabbenu Gershom ruled that the father was not liable to pay the sum for ten students (who did not materialize), since his promise was mere talk, designed to interest and lure the teacher. Rashi, describing a supervising teacher and his subordinates in his commentary to *B.B.*, uses a class size of ten as a point of reference. We have already noted (above, n. 46) that it is unlikely that this comment of Rashi reflects actual educational practice in Ashkenaz.

52. Ashkenazic communities in Eastern Europe had developed by the sixteenth century a fairly well organized system for elementary education. See Assaf, *Meqorot,* vol. 1, nos. 45, 50, 51 and Ramo's gloss to *Ḥoshen Mishpat,* 163:3. Cf. A. F. Kleinberger, *The Educational Theory of Maharal of Prague* (in Hebrew) (Jerusalem, 1962), 19–29; E. Roth, *Sefer Taqqanot Nikolsburg* (Jerusalem, 1961), 79–83; and J. Katz, *Tradition and Crisis* (New York, 1961), 187–90. For western

Europe, see the "Worms Memorbucher" published by A. Berliner in *Qovez ʿal Yad* 3 (1886).
53. *RMC,* no. 310.
54. *RMP,* no. 488. Cf. *SHP,* sec 827, 820.
55. *RMB,* no. 55, p. 276.
56. Salfeld, *Martyrologium, 38:*

ר׳ ברוך ב״ר יחיאל הכהן והנער המלמד למלין ב״ר ברוך.

Breuer (*Ha-Yeshivah ha-Ashkenazit,* 46–47) notes that a number of yeshiva students in fifteenth-century Germany earned money tutoring. Evidence for this practice in the pre-Crusade period is found in a responsum of R. Gershom. See Eidelberg, *Teshuvot Rabbenu Gershom,* no. 71, p. 165. Cf. Tam, *Sefer ha-Yashar,* no. 31 and below, chapter 3, n. 55.
57. *Nedarim* 37a. Cf. I Lange, ed., *Perushei ha-Torah le-R. Ḥayyim Paltiel.* (Jerusalem, 1981), p. 573 (comment to Deut. 4:5) and *Perush Baʿal ha-Turim,* Deut. 4:5. See below, chapter 3, nn. 2, 3.
58. *Sefer Or Zaruaʿ, Pisqei Bava Meẓiʿa,* nos. 245–46; *Mordekhai, Bava Meẓiʿa,* no. 343.
59. *Sefer Miẓvot Qatan,* no. 106.
60. See below, chap. 3, n. 13.
61. See above, n. 51 and S. Gross, "Toledot ha-Ḥinnukh," 28.
62. Virtually all of the questions related to *melammedim* extant in Ashkenazic responsa literature indicate that the tutor was responsible for one or two students per half year or per year. See above, n. 31, and esp. *RMP,* nos. 434–35. Although responsa literature reflects difficult situations rather than the norm, the uniform number of students in the background information of the questions bespeaks the reality of the times. Cf. I. A. Agus, *Urban Civilization in Pre-Crusade Europe* (New York, 1965), 2:730–36 and S. Gross, "Toledot ha-Ḥinnukh," 29–32.
63. R. Meir b. Barukh, *RML,* no. 131:

מלמד ומשרת וסופר הנהיגו רבותי לפטור עד ב׳ זקוקים . . . מידהו עני שיש לו יותר מזקוק ומלמד ומשרת וסופר יותר מב׳ זקוקים . . . צריך ליתן מס על הכל.

64. See I. A. Agus, *Teshuvot Baʿalei ha-Tosafot,* no. 103; E. Shochetman, "Dinei Ḥinnukh," 97–101; S. Gross, "Toledot ha-Ḥinnukh," 52–53. Privileges for scholars in Ashkenaz are discussed below, chap. 3.
65. *RMC,* no. 198. See also *RMP,* no. 541.
66. See above, nn. 39–40 and Gross, "Toledot ha-Ḥinnukh," 27.
67. *Mordekhai, Bava Batra,* no. 468. On the economic conditions of this

period and their impact on Jewish occupations, see S. Albeck, "Yaḥaso shel R. Tam li-Veʿayot Zemanno," *Zion* 19 (1954): 104.

68. *Mordekhai Bava Batra,* 468; *Responsa of R. Ḥayyim Or Zaruaʿ,* no. 66. R. Eliezer of Toul, who was apparently a very successful and well-situated tutor, had problems collecting his salary. See *Sefer Or Zaruaʿ, Bava Meẓiʿa,* no. 181 and E. E. Urbach, *Baʿalei ha-Tosafot,* 1:335–36. Cf. *SḤP,* sec. 821.
69. *RMP,* 37; *Mordekhai Ketubot,* 232; and *B.B.,* 674.
70. See *Responsa of R. Gershom,* ed. S. Eidelberg, no. 72 and *Sefer Or Zaruaʿ, Bava Meẓiʿa,* no. 246. Cf. *Tosafot Pesaḥim,* 49b, s.v. *lo maẓa bat.* See also S. Gross, "Toledot ha-Ḥinnukh," 49–52.
71. *Sefer Or Zaruaʿ B.M.,* no. 242; *RMP,* no. 477 in the name of *rabbanei Ẓarefat.* Cf. S. Gross, "Toledot ha-Ḥinnukh," 61–63.
72. *Sefer Raban* to *B.B.,* 21, ed. S. Z. Auerbach (repr. Jerusalem, 1975), 209c–d.
73. *Tosafot Qiddushin,* 59a, s.v. *ʿani ha-mehappekh.* On the identification of R. Isaac as R. Isaac of Evreux, see Urbach, *Baʿalei ha-Tosafot,* 2:632–33.
74. The position of R. Isaac of Corbeil is found in *Responsa of R. Solomon Luria,* no. 36 (repr. Jerusalem, 1969), fol. 116.
75. *Ketubot* 63a.
76. *Tosafot, Ketubot* 63a, s.v. *be-omer eni zan.*
77. *Commentary of R. Asher b. Yeḥiel* to *Ketubot,* chap. 5, sec. 32.
78. See above, n. 40. For *melammedim* who were paid to teach a certain book of the Bible and received payment when that task was completed see below, n. 94. Note that Urbach explained the positions of R. Tam and R. Elijah as reflections of the different values assigned to various forms of labor in the two regions of northern France in which they lived (*Baʿalei ha-Tosafot,* 1:122–23). This type of explanation was criticized by J. Katz in his review of Urbach's book in *Qiryat Sefer* 31 (1956): 11. My explanation is along the lines of that of Katz's.
79. See above, n. 63, and *Tosafot Qiddushin* 17a, s.v. *ḥalah shalosh.*
80. *Tosafot R. Pereẓ, Bava Meẓiʿa,* 77a, s.v. *savar lah kavvateh be-ḥada.*
81. *Tosafot Bava Qamma,* 85b, s.v. *roʾin oto.* Cf. E. Shochetman, "Dinei Ḥinnukh," 52–76.
82. See above, n. 44.
83. See *Teshuvot Rabbenu Gershom,* no. 72. R. Gershom charges *melammedei tinoqot* with the responsibility of working diligently and faithfully since they are performing *melekhet shamayim.* Later in the same responsum, R. Gershom must address himself to the question of whether a *melammed* may moonlight as a scribe to supplement his

income. Cf. S. Gross, "Toledot ha-Ḥinnukh," 54–60. *Tosafot R. Pereẓ* (above, n. 80) also used the phrase *melekhet shamayim* to describe the role of the *melammed*.

84. *Sefer Roqeaḥ* (repr. Jerusalem, 1967), p. 11. For the length of the *melammed*'s teaching term, see the sources in B. Dinur, *Yisrael ba-Golah,* vol. 2, pt. 6, pp. 37–38.
85. See below, chap. 2, n. 43.
86. *SḤP,* 820.
87. See App. B.
88. See chaps. 5 and 6.
89. M. Breuer, "Min'u Beneikhem min ha-Higgayon," in *Sefer Zikkaron le–R. David Ochs* (Ramat Gan, 1978), 249–50. Breuer assumes that the formulation of R. Tam justifying the study of Talmud exclusively and the critique of R. Yehudah b. ha-Rosh that he missed studying the Bible *be-diqduq ube-ferush . . . lefi shebeqatnuti lo lamadti oto ki lo hurgelu lelammedo be-Ashkenaz*" apply to the rudimentary study of Bible on the elementary level as well as to the study of Bible by older students. Nothing can be proven regarding elementary education from the formulation of R. Tam. Moreover, R. Yehudah did not claim that Scripture was not being taught at all in Ashkenaz. His objection was that the grammatical, lexicographic, and exegetical nuances of the biblical verses were not taught. For a full discussion of these sources, see chapter 5, nn. 93–97.
90. See, e.g., *Teshuvot Rabbenu Gershom,* ed. S. Eidelberg, no. 71, p. 166.
91. See M. Banitt, "L'étude des glossaires bibliques des Juifs en france au moyen âge," *Proceedings of the Israel Academy of Sciences and Humanities* 2 (1967): 195.
92. *Sefer Or Zarua',* vol. 1, *Hilkhot Qeri'at Shema, no. 12.*
93. See chap. 6, n. 21.
94. See *Sefer Or Zarua', Pisqei Bava Meẓi'a,* no. 242. Such a *melammed,* according to Ri, has the status of a *qablan,* not a *sakhir.* See also *RMP,* no. 477.
95. *Teshuvot Rabbenu Gershom,* ed. S. Eidelberg, no. 71. Cf. *Sefer Ḥuqqei ha-Torah* (below, App. A), lines 60–72, 134–35, 170–80.
96. See above, n. 31.
97. See J. H. Mundy, *Europe in the High Middle Ages,* 464–65; PBT, 22–23.
98. It is possible that some parents kept a *melammed* for their son even after the child was old enough to enter the more advanced phases of the educational process. There is reference, for example, to a father-in-law

who agreed to provide a tutor for his new son-in-law. See *RMP,* no. 251. Cf. *Responsa of R. Hayyim Or Zarua',* no. 167, and above, n. 23. Cf. *Sefer Ḥuqqei ha-Torah,* (below, App. A), lines 129–38.

Notes to Chapter 2

1. The book was published in Paris by Librairie Plon. A second edition was published in 1972 containing a new introduction by Ariès in which he responded to some of the critiques of his first edition.
2. The work was translated by R. Baldick and published in New York by Vintage Books. All page references are to this edition.
3. P. Ariès, *Centuries of Childhood,* 9–10, 128–29. Cf. D. Hunt, *Parents and Children in History* (New York, 1970), 34 (hereafter simply Ariès).
4. Ariès, 33–34, 43–50, 91–92. Cf. D. Wrong's review of Ariès's work in *Scientific American* 208 (1963): 182.
5. Ariès, 129–31. Cf. L. Stone, *The Family, Sex and Marriage in England, 1500–1800* (London, 1977), 112–14. Like Ariès, Stone wished to demonstrate shifts in attitude toward childhood in European society (in Stone's case, specifically English society) as the Middle Ages gave way to the early modern period. Ariès, however, spends more time discussing attitudes toward childhood in the medieval period to sharpen his comparisons. Stone's conclusions ultimately dovetail with Ariès's conclusions both in terms of the nature of the shifts and the time table. Stone was more sensitive than Ariès in distinguishing between the attitudes of the upper and lower strata of society. See below, n. 12.
6. Ibid., 100–2, 113–21.
7. Ibid., 27–29, 128.
8. Ibid., 38–40.
9. L. White, "Technology Assessment from the Stance of a Medieval Historian," *American Historical Review* 79 (1974): 9–10. Cf. Stone, *Family, Sex, and Marriage,* 105–7, 113. For the change in attitude beginning with the late seventeenth century, see pp. 246–48.
10. Ariès 140, 145–54.
11. Ibid., 315–24, 365–69, 411–13. Upper-class or upper-middle-class children were sent to a boarding school or to live with a tutor in order to acquire an education. Lower down the social scale, children were sent to the homes of others to begin work as apprentices, domestic servants, or laborers. See Stone, *Family, Sex, and Marriage,* 107, 109–11.

12. Ibid., esp. 405–7. L. K. Berkner ("Recent Research on the History of the Family in Europe," *Journal of Marriage and the Family* 35 [1973]: 395–96) notes correctly that Ariès's examples are based almost exclusively on sources reflecting the attitudes of the aristocracy and upper classes in European society. Attitudes of the lower classes toward children and childhood would probably be less enlightened. As will be shown, it is appropriate to compare attitudes toward children in Jewish society to the attitudes of the upper class in general society.
13. U. T. Holmes, "Medieval Childhood," *Journal of Social History* 2 (1968): 164–72. Cf. M. McLaughlin, "Survivors and Surrogates" (see chap. 1, n. 28). While McLaughlin refers only once to Ariès in a note to her article (p. 102, n. 4), it is obvious that the material she assembles is designed to conflict with some of Ariès's conclusions. A more direct attack is mounted by L. Demause, "The Evolution of Childhood," in *The History of Childhood,* ed. Demause (New York, 1974), 1–73. See also A. Wilson, "The Infancy of the History of Childhood," *History and Theory* 19 (1980): 132–53.
14. William Marshal was an English statesman who lived in the latter half of the twelfth century (1146–1219). His biography was written in the thirteenth century by a biographer who was old enough to remember some aspects of William's life. The details of his childhood may have been supplied by family members. See J. Crosland, *William the Marshall: The Last Great Feudal General* (London, 1962), 8–10. Crosland characterizes the childhood portion of the biography as "ringing true." For background on William's being taken as a hostage (as a guarantee for a truce between Stephen and William's father Marshal John), see pp. 19–20. Interestingly, while King Stephen displays a very positive attitude toward childhood (as Holmes notes), John himself is unconcerned that his son's life is in danger while he is held captive. John says, "What does it matter? I possess the anvil and hammer with which to produce many more." See below, n. 21.
15. Chrétien de Troyes was a contemporary of William. This reference is from his *Conte du Graal.* See Holmes, "Medieval Childhood," 166, n. 11.
16. Hunt, *Parents and Children,* 39–44.
17. I. H. Forsythe, "Children in Early Medieval Art, Ninth through Twelfth Centuries," *History of Childhood Quarterly* 4 (1976–77): 31–70. See also, in the same volume, L. Demaitre, "The Idea of Childhood and Childcare in the Medical Writings of the Middle Ages," 461–90.
18. *History of Childhood,* ed. L. DeMause (New York, 1974), 101–81.

This volume led to the creation of the *History of Childhood Quarterly.* The nascence of this periodical is itself an indication of the revitalized interest of scholars in childhood in history. Following the publication of vol. 4, the periodical was renamed the *Journal of Psycho-History.* For additional bibliography, see *History of Education Quarterly* 26 (1986): 95–96, nn. 1, 2.

19. See McLaughlin, "Survivors and Surrogates," esp. 117–18, 127, 132.
20. Ibid., 135–39. Bartholomaeus Anglicus taught theology at the University of Paris and c. 1225 joined the Franciscan order. His views on childhood are found in his oft-printed encyclopedia, *De proprietatibus rerum.* In this work Bartholomew cites the views of Greek, Jewish, and Arabic scholars on medical and scientific subjects. Vincent's *De eruditione filiorum nobilum* was written at the request of Queen Margaret, wife of St. Louis. It was edited by A. Steiner in 1928. See also A. L. Gabriel, *The Educational Ideas of Vincent of Beauvais* (South Bend, 1962).
21. McLaughlin, "Survivors and Surrogates," 111–12, 120–21. Thus, there is evidence for royal and church legislation to prevent the "overlaying" of infants by their parents. Cf. Stone, *Family, Sex, and Marriage,* 474 and E. Shorter, *The Making of the Modern Family* (New York, 1975), 168–75.
22. E. Kanarfogel, "Attitudes toward Children and Childhood in Medieval Jewish Society," in *Approaches to Judaism in Medieval Times,* ed. D. Blumenthal (Chico, 1985), 2:1–34. Cf. K. Stow, "The Jewish Family in the Rhineland in the Middle Ages," *AHR* 92 (1987): 1085–1110 and I. Ta-Shema in *Zion* 53 (1988): 353. The bulk of Ariès's sources are from France and England, with other areas in western Europe represented as well. For Jewish attitudes toward childhood in Arab and Mediterranean Moslem lands, see S. D. Goitein, *A Mediterranean Society,* vol. 3, *The Family,* pp. 229–50. Goitein devotes an entire section to depicting the nuclear family as described in the texts of the Cairo Geniza. There is also a piece on the value of children to parents. On the whole, this section seeks to collect and broadly categorize the material.
23. The commentary was edited by M. Kasher and Y. Blacherowitz as part of their *Perushei Rishonim le-Massekhet Avot* (Jerusalem, 1974). M. Saperstein, who has worked extensively with this commentary, has noted the many discrepancies between the printed edition and the manuscript (Escorial Library of Madrid, Hebrew ms. G.IV.3). See M. Saperstein, *Decoding the Rabbis* (Cambridge, MA, 1980), 221, n. 2. I have checked the manuscript version of the passage analyzed here

(fol. 14r–v) and the discrepancies are minor. In the printed edition the passage is found on p. 63.

24. Saperstein, *Decoding the Rabbis,* 21, n. 1, and in greater detail, idem, “R. Isaac b. Yeda'yah: A Forgotten Commentary on the Aggadah,” *REJ* 138 (1979): 17–45.
25. The Hebrew reads,

    שינה של שחרית ויין צהרים ושיחת ילדים מוציאין את האדם מן העולם.

26. ויערב לאב כל אשר ידבר אם טוב אם רע.
27. כי כן טבע האדם להיות האב והאם משתדלים כשהם קטנים מן הגדול היודע לבחור בטוב ומאוס ברע ואינו צריך עוד למינקת.
28. R. Isaac is certainly not preaching against parental love; he is merely arguing that the effects of this great attraction must be controlled. Cf. the comments of R. Yonah and R. Baḥya b. Asher. See *Perushei R. Yonah 'al Massekhet Avot,* ed. M. Kasher and Y. Blacherowitz (Jerusalem, 1969), 45: “The conversation of children—this pleasure [שעשוע] tugs at the hearts of people because of their love for the children, and the study of Torah is thereby vitiated.” See also *Kitvei R. Baḥya,* ed. C. B. Chavel (Jerusalem, 1970), 580: “Constant conversation with them will lead one to frivolity . . . because their words tug at the heart and people are drawn to them.”
29. J. Shatzmiller, “Doctors and Medical Practice in Germany around the Year 1200: The Evidence of Sefer Ḥasidim,” *Journal of Jewish Studies* 33 (1983): 583–94. On the richness of *Sefer Ḥasidim* as a source for family life within the larger Ashkenazic society, see esp. p. 584. See now E. Yassif, “Ha-Sippur ha-Exemplari be-Sefer Ḥasidim,” *Tarbiz* 57 (1988): 253–54.
30. At the same time, it must be noted that just as Ariès (pp. 25–26) and Holmes, “Medieval Childhood,” 165 have shown that the terms for “small child,” “young child,” “adolescent,” etc. in medieval French and other Romance languages were often interchanged, we find in medieval Hebrew instances of a twenty-year-old being called a *yeled* or a two-year-old being referred to as a *na'ar.* See above, chap. 1, n. 14. See also *Responsa of Maharil* (Cracow, 1881), no. 96. This interchangeability does show, to some extent, that the ages and stages of childhood were not as fixed then as they are today. In the case of *Sefer Ḥasidim* the context in most cases will aid in making judgments.
31. *SḤP,* sec. 432.
32. *SḤP,* sec. 770. See also sec. 815.

33. *SḤP,* secs. 102–3. See also secs. 13 (p. 12) 301, and 960 (p. 236). I do not think that the sensitive appreciation of childhood in these sections is necessarily at odds with the attitude expressed in 857, that a truly wicked youth deserves to receive a particularly harsh punishment. Positive parental attitudes toward childhood do not dictate that the child (young adult) who strays must be held near at all costs.
34. Cf. Rashi's commentary to *Avodah Zarah,* 17a, s.v. *avi ha-dai hu,* where Rashi justifies 'Ula's custom of kissing his sisters following synagogue services: "He would see the way of people when they leave the synagogue to immediately kiss their father and mother or an important person on his leg or on his hand (as a sign of giving honor)." In light of the sources cited below, this text may also reflect historical reality.
35. *Sefer ha-Orah,* ed. S. Buber, vol. 2, no. 133, p. 221 and *Sefer Issur ve-Heter,* ed. Freiman (repr. Jerusalem, 1973), no. 127: "Once a child [*tinoq*] was sitting on the shoulders of my teacher [*rebbi*] in the synagogue. When it came time to recite the Shema, he instructed that the child be removed from him because the average child is unclean [*setam tinoq ba-ashpah*] and it is not proper to recite Shema near the child." *Shibbolei ha-Leqet* (ed. S. Buber, end of sec. 15, p. 8) identifies the teacher as R. Isaac b. Judah (z"l). The child, according to this text, was sitting on R. Isaac's lap.
36. Other synagogue customs of this period, such as the reading of certain verses of the Book of Esther in a loud voice and the drowning out of Haman's name, are explained by medieval halakhists as customs initiated to make the young children happy and thereby retain their interest. Several customs at the Passover Seder also developed for this reason. See *Sefer Or Zarua',* vol. 2, *Hilkhot Shabbat,* sec. 68; *Haggahot Maimuniyyot* to *Hilkhot Megillah,* end; and the sources cited in M. Güdemann, *Ha-Torah veha-Ḥayyim,* 90, nn. 4–6 and in D. Goldschmidt, *The Haggadah: Its Sources and its History* (in Hebrew) (Jerusalem, 1960), 11, nn. 7–9. Cf. Ariès, 125–26. Ariès and others included additional types of evidence in their evaluations of the attitude of parents to children. These may not be as crucial or as indicative for Jewish society, but they are nevertheless worth noting. There is ample evidence for Jewish children playing with toys and other games in this period. See L. Rabinowitz, *The History of the Jews in Northern France* (repr. New York, 1972), 225–26. The evidence must be evaluated (in light of the argument of Ariès and Holmes, referred to above) to determine whether adults' playing with the same toys and games renders this material insignificant.

37. R. Eleazar's elegy is found in A. Habermann, *Sefer Gezerot Ashkenaz ve-Ẓarefat,* 166–67.
38. Ariès, 128.
39. *Haggahot R. Pereẓ* to *Sefer Ammudei Golah* (Kappust, 1820; repr. Jerusalem, 1979), fol. 3a. Cf. *SHP,* sec. 12. The observation about the derivation of breast milk is undoubtedly based on the formulation in Bekhorot 6b, *dam ne-ʿeqar ve-naʿaseh ḥalav.* Cf. Baḥya Ibn Paquda, *Ḥovot ha-Levavot, Shaʿar ha-Beḥinah,* (Warsaw, 1865), chap. 5 p. 118. A similar observation is made by Bartholomew of England (see McLaughlin, "Survivors and Surrogates," 115, n. 59, and above, n. 30). In Christian sources the notion that the mother's milk is blood frothed white is found as early as the second century in the writings of Clement of Alexandria. See Clement of Alexandria, *The Instructor,* Ante-Nicene Christian Library, vol. 4 (Edinburgh, 1867), 141. See also C. W. Bynum, *Jesus As Mother: Studies in the Spirituality of the High Middle Ages* (Berkeley, 1982), 132.
40. This text was published and edited by A. M. Habermann in *Qoveẓ ʿal Yad* 11 (=n.s. 1) (1936): 47–88. The relevant section is on p. 82.
41. Meiri's comment to Psalms 22:6 reads as follows: "This [verse] is a suggestion to educate one's son in deportment and ethics according to the child's way, i.e., according to the child's age, a five-year-old according to his way and a ten-year-old according to his way."
42. *Ẓedah la-Derekh* (repr. Jerusalem, 1977), art. 1, prin. 3, chap. 14, p. 32a. R. Menaḥem's father fled from France in 1306 and settled in Navarre, where Menaḥem was born c. 1310. R. Menaḥem later studied in Toledo with R. Yehudah, son of R. Asher b. Yeḥiel (Rosh).
43. See M. Güdemann, *Ha-Torah veha-Ḥayyim,* 89–90. Most medieval Jewish halakists and exegetes maintained that formal education should begin at age six or seven, as was the practice in Christian Europe (Cf. L. Demaitre, *Doctor Bernard de Gordon* [Toronto, 1980], 11–12). The Talmudic sources on which their formulations were based are not in uniform agreement; see *M. Avot* 5:21, *B.B.* 21a, and *Ketubot* 50a. Cf. *Midrash Tanḥuma,* ed. S. Buber, (Vilna, 1895), 3:79. See *Mishneh Torah, Hilkhot Talmud Torah* 1:6, 2:2; Rashi and R. Yonah to *Avot,* 5:21; the Ashkenazic *Avot* commentary in ms. Bodl. 388, fol. 109v; the *Avot* commentary in *Maḥzor Vitry,* ed. S. Hurwitz, pp. 549–50; *Daʿat Zeqenim, Paʿaneaḥ Raza* to Leviticus 19:23; *Perush R. Eleazar Roqeaḥ ʿal ha-Torah,* ed. S. Kanevsky, Leviticus, p. 266, Numbers, p. 33; R. Yehudah b. Qalonymus, *Yiḥusei Tannaim va-Amoraim* in ms. Oxford 2199 (cited in Assaf, *Meqorot,* 4:2). Cf. M. Brill, "Gil ha-Yeled be-Kenisato le-Beit ha-Sefer," *Tarbiz* 9 (1937): 354 and Shochetman,

"Dinei Ḥinnukh," 23–29. Several sources maintain that formal education should begin at age five. See *Tosafot Ketubot,* 50a, s.v. *ve-safei le; B.B.,* 21a, s.v. *be-bazir mi-bar; Orḥot Ḥayyim,* ed. M. Schlesinger (Berlin, 1902), 2:25; ms. Hamburg 152, fol. 86r; *SḤB,* 1140. While this position may have been proposed as a resolution of divergent Talmudic sources, it is possible that some Ashkenazic scholars favored an earlier start of formal education. This would be consistent with the belief that a child's moral education should not be put off until the child reaches a more "teachable" age. See *Sefer Ḥuqqei ha-Torah* in Assaf, *Meqorot,* 1:15; Yehudah Ibn Abbas, *Yair Netiv* in Assaf, *Meqorot,* 2:29; and Ha-Meiri to *B.B.* 21a and *Avot,* ed. B. Perag, p. 101.

44. See chap. 1, n. 5.
45. Chapter 1, nn. 39–40.
46. See above, nn. 11, 13. Cf. *Teshuvot Rabbenu Gershom,* ed. S. Eidelberg, no. 71, pp. 165–66.
47. See, e.g., the Ashkenazic initiation ceremony as recorded in *Maḥzor Vitry,* ed. S. Hurwitz, p. 628.
48. Student groups tended to be heterogeneous, with no real attempt made to differentiate between levels or even different ages. See I. Ta-Shema, "Miẓvat Talmud Torah ki-Ve'ayah Ḥevratit Datit be-Sefer Ḥasidim," *Bar Ilan* 14–15 (1977): 110–11. The educational process was very much goal-oriented. The true scholar would acquire the skills, tools and incidental knowledge needed on his own. Even the initiation ceremony children underwent (see App. B) indicated that their education was part of the attempt to produce scholars, not a personalized experience for them. See M. Breuer, "Ha-Yeshivah ha-Ashkenazit shel Yemei ha-Beinayim," in *Ḥinnukh ha-Adam ve-Yi'udo,* ed. World Conference for Jewish Thought, vols. 9–10 (Jerusalem, 1967), 142–43. Cf. *Maḥzor Vitry,* 628, sec. 507 (end) and *SḤB,* sec. 946.
49. *SḤP,* secs. 820, 822–23, 827.
50. *Sefer Ḥuqqei ha-Torah* in Assaf, *Meqorot,* 1:10–11.
51. *SḤP,* sec. 160. Cf. *SḤP* sec. 820, and Ariès, 100–127. In counseling that tutors for young children be hired not only on the basis of their grasp of the material to be taught but also for their ability to use the material to teach religious values, the author of *Sefer Ḥasidim* describes the nature of a young child's intellect in this way: "A child's intellect [*libbo,* perh. "capacity for understanding"], is like the intellect of an adult who is dreaming. Dreamers are under the impression that all [that they are dreaming] is true. So too children—they assume that all your words are true until they are indoctrinated by bad people." See also *SḤP,* sec. 683.

52. *SḤP,* secs 795–96, 824–25.
53. *SḤP,* secs. 748–49, 830, 1496.
54. I. Ta-Shema, "Qavvim le-Ofyah shel Sifrut ha-Halakhah be-Ashkenaz ba-Me'ot ha-13/14," *'Alei Sefer* 4 (1977): 32. See also Ta-Shema in *Bar Ilan* 14–15 (1977): 107–9.

Notes to Chapter 3

1. In his seminal work, *Ba'alei ha-Tosafot: Toledoteihem, Ḥibbureihem ve-Shittatam,* E. E. Urbach touches briefly on sources that relate to these issues but does not present a coherent picture. See J. Katz's review of the first edition of Urbach's book in *Kiryat Sefer* 31 (1956): 9–16. M. Breuer has discussed these topics as they concern the *yeshivot* of Ashkenaz in the late middle ages. See his *Ha-Yeshivah ha-Ashkenazit be-Shilhei Yemei ha-Beinayim* (Ph.D. diss., Hebrew University, 1967), chap. 3. More recently, he has focused on aspects of the relationship between academies and their communities in Europe in the high Middle Ages. See Breuer, "Le-Ḥeqer ha-Tippologiyah shel Yeshivot ha-Ma'arav Bimei ha-Beinayim," in *Studies in Jewish Society in the Medieval and Early Modern Periods,* ed. E. Etkes and Y. Salmon (Jerusalem, 1980), 45–55. N. Golb has also advanced several theories about the communal nature of the academies in Ashkenaz and Provence. See below, chap. 4, n. 1.
2. BT *Nedarim* 37a, PT *Nedarim* 4:3 (fol. 11b), based on God's words in Deuteronomy 4:5: "Behold I have taught you statutes and laws [*ḥuqqim u-mishpatim*]. . . . Just as I have [taught you] gratis, so you [must teach] gratis." The PT text excludes the teaching of Scripture from this restriction since this discipline is not included in the description *ḥuqqim u-mishpatim.* The BT source allows teachers of Scripture to receive payment because Scripture is usually taught to young children; see the commentaries of Rashi and R. Nissim of Gerona, *Nedarim* 37a. The Amora Rav explains that one who teaches Scripture to young children is compensated not for the teaching of Torah per se but rather for watching the child and ensuring his safety (*sekhar shimmur*). R. Yoḥanan held that this teacher is paid because he teaches the child how to vocalize and chant the verses of Scripture, which is not the same as Torah study (*sekhar pissuq te'amim*). Ostensibly, R. Yoḥanan would permit one who teaches Scripture to someone

who is old enough to take care of himself and does not require *shimmur* to receive compensation while Rav would not. See the commentary of R. Nissim, s.v. *ve-R. Yoḥanan amar* and note his reference to Maimonides, *Mishneh Torah, Hilkhot Nedarim* 6:7. Cf. R. Menaḥem ha-Meiri, *Beit ha-Beḥirah* to *Nedarim* 37a.

3. The concept of *sekhar battalah* is not introduced in the BT passage. It is, however, implicit in several *sugyot* allowing certain judges and teachers of various temple rites to be paid for their services; see BT *Ketubot* 105a–106a, and below, n. 13. Cf. *Sifrei* to Deuteronomy 8:1, ed. L. Finkelstein, 2d ed. (New York, 1969), sec. 48, p. 111 and *Mishnah Bekhorot* 4:5.
4. *Tosafot Bekhorot* 29a, s.v. *mah ani be-ḥinnam. Tosafot* also permits the teacher of young children to receive payment based on BT *Nedarim* 37a. Cf. Rashi, *Qiddushin* 58b s.v. *bi-sekhar* and *Tosafot* s.v. *memav; SḤP,* sec. 1496. R. Asher b. Yeḥiel, in his commentary to *Nedarim* 37a, attributes these rulings to Ri. See also R. Asher's commentary to *Bekhorot* 29a (4:6); Urbach, 2:667–69; and R. Yeruḥam, *Sefer Toledot Adam ve-Ḥavvah* 2:1 (Venice, 1553), fol. 17a.
5. *Sefer Miẓvot Qatan,* no. 106. R. Isaac bases his ruling on the position of Rav (above, n. 2) that the teacher of young children can be compensated. He assumes that any teacher who has to work hard to ensure that his students learn and progress is performing a kind of *shimmur* and thus may receive compensation. Cf. *Shir ha-Shirim Rabbah* to the phrase in chap. 8, verse 12, *ha-'elef lekha Shelomoh.* See also Y. Lange, "Pisqei R. Yiẓḥaq mi-Corbeil,"*Ha-Ma'ayan* 16 (1976): 99–100.
6. *Maḥzor Vitry,* ed. S. Hurwitz, pp. 471–72. On the identity of the author of this commentary, see I. Ta-Shema in *Qiryat Sefer* 42 (1977): 507–8.
7. *Maḥzor Vitry,* 524 (in a comment to the statement of the Tanna R. Ẓadoq in *Avot* 4:7, אל תעשם קרדום לאכל מהם):

   > הוי מלמד אותה לאחרים ולא תטול שכר עליה ואל תעש עצמך כפועל הנשכר לחטוב עצים בקרדומו . . . ואת אשר נהגו ליטול שכר שסמכו על מה שמצינו באגדה שאין זה אלא שכר ביטול. אבל שכר תורה אין כל בריה יכול לשער. ומ"מ מלמדי תינוקות של בית רבן מותרין . . . שאין נוטלים אלא שכר שימור.

8. *Sefer Rabiah,* ed. V. Aptowitzer, 1:452 and idem, *Mavo la-Rabiah,* 15–16. See also *Piyyutei R. Simeon bar Isaac,* ed. A. Habermann (Jerusalem, 1938), 186:

   > עושי מלאכה ומתאבקים בעפרה ואין נהנים בכבודה ולא בכתרה ולא יעשוה קרדום ולא עטרה.

See also R. Eleazar Roqeaḥ, *Commentary to Deuteronomy,* ed. S. Kanevsky (Bnei Brak, 1981), 171.

9. See H. H. Ben-Sasson, *Toledot ʿAm Yisrael,* (Tel Aviv, 1969), 2:79–80; M. Breuer, *Rabbanut Ashkenaz Bimei ha-Beinayim* (Jerusalem, 1976), 19, Aptowitzer, *Mavo la-Rabiah,* 338; and M. Frank, *Qehillot Ashkenaz u-Vattei Dineihen* (Tel Aviv, 1937), 22–25. On Rashbam, see Urbach, 1:46. On R. Tam, see E. E. Urbach, *Baʿalei ha-Tosafot,* 1:62. R. Tam may have been a vintner. Cf. H. Soloveitchik, "Can Halakhic Texts Talk History?" *AJS Review* 3 (1978): 172, n. 54; *Sefer ha-Yashar* (responsa), ed. S. Rosenthal, p. 31; I. A. Agus, *R. Meir of Rothenburg* (New York, 1947), 1:25.
10. See *Tosafot Berakhot* 11b, s.v. *she-kevar niftar* and *Tosafot R. Judah Sir Leon,* ed. N. Saks (Jerusalem, 1969), s.v. *mishe-qara.* See also *Tosafot Yeshanim* to *Yoma* 85b, s.v. *teshuvah* and *Maḥzor Vitry,* pp. 494–95. Cf. *Sefer Tashbeẓ,* no. 193; *Siddur Ḥasidei Ashkenaz,* ed. M. Hershler (Jerusalem, 1972), 32, 54, 151.
11. As Ben-Sasson, noted (*Toledot ʿAm Yisrael*) moneylending would be an obvious choice. See R. Joseph b. Moshe, *Leqet Yosher* (Berlin, 1903), 118–19; Breuer, *Rabbanut Ashkenaz,* 19; and cf. *SḤP,* sec 765.
12. See G. Paré, A. Brunet, and P. Tremblay, *La renaissance du XIIème siècle,* 75–82; G. Post, K. Giocarinis, and R. Kay, "The Medieval Heritage of a Humanistic Ideal: *Scientia donum dei est, unde vendi non potest,*"*Traditio* 11 (1955): 197–210; J. Le Goff, *Time, Work, and Culture in the Middle Ages* (Chicago, 1980), 64, 120; J. W. Baldwin, *Masters, Princes, and Merchants* (Princeton, 1970), 1:117–20, 125–30; L. K. Little, *Religious Poverty and the Profit Economy in Medieval Europe* (Ithaca, 1978), 33, 173, 176–78; N. Orme, *English Schools in the Middle Ages* (London, 1973), 118–19, 157–58; and A. Murray, *Reason and Society in the Middle Ages* (Oxford, 1978), 228–30.
13. The views of Ri and R. Tam (*Tosafot Ketubot,* 105a, s.v. *gozrei gezerot*) were formulated to solve problems of Talmudic interpretation and do not reflect actual educational practices in medieval Ashkenaz. Cf. R. Joel Sirkes, *Bayit Ḥadash* to *Tur Ḥoshen Mishpat* 9, s.v. *vekatav.* On the identification of Ri as "my teacher" found in the printed text, see Urbach, 2:626. The position of Ri is cited in the *Shittah Mequbbeẓet* as *leshon Rashi mahadura qamma.*
14. The responsum of R. Meir of Rothenburg (*RMP,* no. 942)—which according to Yuval (*Rabbanim ve-Rabbanut be-Germanyah* [see chap. 1, n. 38], 13, n. 16), deals with an early example of an academic salary—probably refers to the salary of a member of the nascent professional rabbinate in Ashkenaz; see below, chapter 4, n. 48.

15. *Teshuvot Rabbenu Gershom,* ed. S. Eidelberg (New York, 1955), no. 68. R. Gershom is pleased with the fact that this scholar does not earn his livelihood from teaching Talmud. Cf. A. Grossman, *Ḥakhmei Ashkenaz ha-Rishonim,* 411. See also *Teshuvot Rabbenu Gershom,* no. 73, and Grossman, p. 116.
16. On the use of *melekhet shamayim* in this context, see *Sefer Ḥuqqei ha-Torah* (below, App. A), line 19; *Tosafot R. Pereẓ* to *B.M.* 77a, s.v. *savar lah;* I. Twersky, *Rabad of Posquières,* 2d ed. (Philadelphia, 1980), xx–xxi and idem, *Introduction to the Code of Maimonides* (New Haven, 1980), 170–75.
17. See the ruling attributed to R. Isaac Or Zaruaʿ by three later sources (*Responsa of R. Jacob Weil,* no. 151; *Terumat ha-Deshen,* no. 342; and *Haggahot Asheri* to *B.B.* 2:12), as well as *Sefer Or Zaruaʿ, Hilkhot Ẓedaqah,* no. 26. Yuval (*Rabbanim ve-Rabbanut,* 12–13) plausibly assumes that R. Isaac is reflecting relevant Talmudic texts or paraphrasing Rashi's interpretations of them rather than describing the realia of his own day. See also Rashi to *Shabbat* 114a, s.v. *le-mitraḥ be-rifteh;* M. Breuer, *Rabbanut Ashkenaz,* 19; and cf. Y. Handelsman, "Hashkafotav shel Rabiah ʿal Darkhei Hanhagat ha-Qehillot," *Zion* 48 (1983): 28–30.
18. See *SḤP,* secs. 807, 1493, and below, chap. 6.
19. I. Ta-Shema, "Al Petur Talmidei Ḥakhamim me-Missim Bimei ha-Beinayim," in *ʿIyyunim be-Sifrut Ḥazal, ba-Miqra, uve-Toledot Yisrael,* ed. Y. D. Gilat et al. (Ramat Gan, 1982), 316–19.
20. See A. Grossman, *Ḥakhmei Ashkenaz ha-Rishonim,* 411–14 and D. Berger's review, "Ḥeqer Rabbanut Ashkenaz ha-Qedumah," *Tarbiz* 53 (1984): 482.
21. Ta-Shema begins his analysis of the Ashkenazic position on tax exemptions for scholars with a citation from *Terumat ha-Deshen* and comments that the absence of any earlier literature on this issue is in itself noteworthy. See also Y. Dinari, *Ḥakhmei Ashkenaz be-Shilhei Yemei ha-Beinayim* (Jerusalem, 1983), 25–26. The attempt by some halakists to permit tax exemptions for scholars in the post-1348 period is significant in light of steps taken in other areas that seemed to be an attempt to limit the prestige of scholars at that time (ibid., 19–22). Breuer (*Ha-Yeshivah ha-Ashkenazit,* 11) claims that tax exemptions were granted to scholars in fifteenth-century Ashkenaz in order to provide additional financial benefits for heads of academies; see below, n. 60.
22. On the identity of R. Ḥayyim Paltiel, see Y. Lange in *ʿAlei Sefer* 8 (1980): 140–46.

23. See *RML,* no. 424. There are two additional sources indicating that leading scholars paid taxes in thirteenth-century Ashkenaz; see Ta-Shema, "Al Petur," 318. On the methods used for computation and enforcement of the payment of taxes in medieval Ashkenaz, see Y. Baer, "Ha-Yesodot veha-Hatḥalot shel Irgun ha-Qehillah ha-Yehudit Bimei ha-Beinayim," *Zion* 15 (1950): 33–34 and B. Altmann in *PAAJR* 10 (1940): 57.
24. See B. Septimus, "Kings, Angels, or Beggars: Tax Law and Spirituality in a Hispano-Jewish Responsum," in *Studies in Medieval Jewish History and Literature,* ed. I. Twersky (Cambridge, 1984), 2:317–19 (hereafter Septimus, "Tax Law"). See also below, n. 34.
25. See Maimonides' *Commentary to the Mishnah* on *Avot* 4:7, ed. J. Kafaḥ, p. 441; *MT Talmud Torah* 3:9–11; and *Iggerot ha-Rambam,* ed. J. Kafaḥ, p. 134. Cf. I. Twersky, *Introduction to the Code of Maimonides* (New Haven, 1980), 5, n. 6 and 81–83.
26. See *Sefer Ha-Qabbalah,* trans. G. D. Cohen, pp. 74–77. A similar role was played in twelfth-century Provence by R. Meshullam b. Jacob of Lunel. See Twersky, *Rabad of Posquières,* 14.
27. *Sefer ha-Qabbalah,* 66, 70–71, 77, 80, 83; see also M. Steinschneider in *He-Ḥaluẓ* 2 (1853): 61, and A. A. Neuman, *The Jews of Spain,* 2:64–65.
28. See Ya'akov b. Asher, *Arba'ah Turim, Ḥoshen Mishpat,* no. 9. See also R. Yehudah's *Sefer ha-Shetarot,* ed. S. Z. H. Halberstam (Berlin, 1898), 131–32.
29. Cf. Septimus, "Tax Law." 316, 321; idem, "Piety and Power in Thirteenth-Century Catalonia," in *Studies in Medieval Jewish History and Literature,* ed. I. Twersky (Cambridge, 1979), 1:218–20.
30. See *Yerushalmi Ḥagigah* 1:7. This passage is alluded to by Rabbenu Yonah. See below, n. 32.
31. R. Yonah of Gerona, *Perush R. Yonah Gerondi 'al Mishlei* (repr. Tel Aviv, 1963) 14:4 (p. 69). Cf. A. Shrock, *R. Jonah b. Abraham* (New York, 1948), 137.
32. *Iggeret ha-Teshuvah,* ed. B. Zilber (Bnai Brak, 1968), 22–23. *Sefer Orḥot Ḥayyim* (vol. 1, *Hilkhot Talmud Torah,* sec. 10) cites this passage in the name of R. Yonah as legal precedent.
33. *Perush 'al Mishle* 10:15 (p. 41).
34. See *Sefer Derashot u-Ferushei R. Yonah 'al ha-Torah,* ed. S. Yerushalmi (Jerusalem, 1980), 106, 207–8, 216; and see now I. Ta-Shema, "Ḥasidut Ashkenaz bi-Sefarad: Rabbenu Yonah Gerondi— ha-Ish u-Fo'alo," in *Galut Aḥar Golah* (Jerusalem, 1988), 188–91.
35. See my "Compensation for the Study of Torah in Medieval Rabbinic

Thought," in *Of Scholars, Savants, and Their Texts,* ed. R. Link-Salinger and R. Herrera (New York, 1989), 135–37.

36. See Septimus, "Tax Law," 316, n. 27.
37. R. Yonah's position is cited by R. Yeruḥam b. Meshullam, *Toledot Adam ve-Ḥavvah* (Venice, 1553), 2:1, fol. 17a.
38. See Ramban in *Shittah Mequbbeẓet* to *Bava Batra* 8a, s.v. *ha-kol* (end). See also R. Asher b. Yeḥiel to *Bekhorot* 4:5, and Ritva to *Nedarim* 37a.
39. See *Yad Ramah* to *Bava Batra* 21a (2:58), and Ramah's collection of responsa, *Or Ẓaddiqim,* no. 241. Cf. Septimus, *Hispano-Jewish Culture in Transition* (Cambridge, 1982), 12, 112, and 124, n. 76; idem, "Tax Law," 315–16; and my "Compensation for the Study of Torah," 137–38.
40. Septimus, "Tax Law," 327.
41. Ibid., 322–23; I. Ta-Shema, "Al Petur Talmidei Ḥakhamin me-Missim Bimei ha-Beinayim," 313–14; and E. E. Urbach, "She'elot u-Teshuvot ha-Rosh be-Kitvei Yad uvi-Defusim," *Shenaton ha-Mishpat ha-ʿIvri* 2 (1975): 141–42.
42. See the case addressed by Ramah in Septimus, "Tax Law," 309–13; and see Ta-Shema, "Al Petur," 315–16. Note that Ri Megash, Rif (and perhaps Ramban, also) favored more restrictive requirements for exemption. See Septimus, "Tax Law," 314 and 323, n. 48 and Ta-Shema, "Al Petur," 313.
43. Maimonides refers to these rabbinic figures in formulating his position against subsidized, professionalized scholarship (above, n. 25).
44. Note that the term *toratan ummanutan* was not used in Ashkenazic parlance to connote scholars entitled to support for full-time study, as was the case in Sepharad. Rather, it was used to describe a scholar totally devoted to Torah study and unconcerned with earning a livelihood either because of unlimited financial resources from some livelihood requiring no attention or because he did not care about being destitute. See R. Israel Isserlein, *Terumat ha-Deshen,* no. 342. Cf. Y. Dinari, *Ḥakhmei Ashkenaz be-Shilhei Yemei ha-Beinayim,* 26. This term could also refer to a scholar who studied only Talmud and did not engage in the study of any other discipline. See Yehudah ibn Tibbon in the introduction to his translation of *Ḥovot ha-Levavot* (repr. Jersualem, 1969), 6. He mentions scholars in Christian lands (*Ereẓ Edom* = Ashkenazic scholars) who do not study any disciplines other than Torah and Talmud because *toratan ummanutan.*
45. See *RMB,* nos. 234, 237 and *SḤP,* secs. 400–401, 1599, 1601; I. Agus, *Teshuvot Baʿalei ha-Tosafot,* no. 91; *Teshuvot Maimuniyyot Qinyan,*

no. 27; *Sefer Or Zarua'*, 1:113 (responsa). See also L. Landman, *The Cantor: An Historic Perspective* (New York, 1972), 21–27. Payment of rabbis in Ashkenaz did not begin until the fifteenth century. The development of a paid, professionalized rabbinate occurs much earlier in Spain. See below, chapter 4, n. 46.

46. See R. Isaac bar Sheshet, *Responsa,* no. 202. Y. Y. Yuval (*Rabbanim ve-Rabbanut,* 377–78) has determined that the earliest use of this privilege in Ashkenaz was in the late thirteenth century. (To Yuval's p. 378, n. 202 add Y. Lange, "Pisqei R. Yiẓḥaq mi-Corbeil," *Ha-Ma'ayan* 16 [1976]: 95.
47. Fines paid by those who embarrassed scholars (the *litra zahav*) were given to the scholars in Sepharad throughout the Middle Ages. In Ashkenaz there is no real evidence for the exercise of this privilege until the late fourteenth century; see Yuval, *Rabbanim ve-Rabbanut,* 392–93. See also Breuer, "Ha-Yeshivah ha-Ashkenazit," 16, and Dinari, *Ḥakhmei Ashkenaz,* 22–25.
48. For the routine of daily study in local *battei midrash* in Ashkenaz, see I. A. Agus, *The Heroic Age of Franco-German Jewry* (New York, 1965), 331–36. A provision of the *Taqqanot Shum* was promulgated to ensure that laymen would continue to study each day. See the text in L. Finkelstein, *Jewish Self-Government in the Middle Ages* (repr. New York, 1964), 231. Cf. Baron, *A Social and Religious History of the Jews,* 11:55; *SḤB,* sec 17; *SḤP,* sec. 462; *Semag, 'aseh* 12; and *RMB,* ms. Amsterdam, no. 240. A passage in R. Moses Mintz, *Responsa* (Salonika, 1802), no. 117, attributed to Raban, describes the procedure for holding a *siyyum* in a *yeshivah* or study hall. Local laymen would be invited to participate when the study of a new tractate was begun as well. See also J. Katz, *Massoret u-Mashber* (Jerusalem, 1958), 223–25. On the distinctions between *battei midrash* and *yeshivot* in the eighteenth and nineteenth centuries, see S. Stampfer, *Shalosh Yeshivot be-Lita* (Ph.D. diss., Hebrew University, 1981), 5–8.
49. On wandering students in medieval Ashkenaz, see E. E. Urbach, *Ba'alei ha-Tosafot,* 1:144, 154–56, 165–66, 208–10, 261, 321, 347–48, 438, 466; and vol. 2, esp. 526–28; *SḤP,* secs. 776, 798, 995, 1479, 1495, *Sefer Miẓvot Qatan* no. 136; *Tosafot Ketubot* 61b–62a (and *Tosafot R. Samson of Sens,* and *Tosafot ha-Rosh*), s.v. *ha-talmidim yoẓ'in;* N. Golb, *Toledot ha-Yehudim be-'Ir Rouen Bimei ha-Beinayim* (Jerusalem, 1976), 25, 37–40; M. Gordon, *Collegial Relationships among Ashkenazic Jewish Scholars* (Ed.D. diss., Yeshiva University, 1977), 56–62; and M. Breuer, "Niddudei Talmidim va-Ḥakhamim," *Tarbut ve-*

Hẹvrah be-Toledot Yisrael Bimei ha-Beinayim (*Qovez̩ Ma'amarim le-Zikro shel Ḥayyim Hillel Ben-Sasson*), ed. R. Bonfil, et al. (Jerusalem, 1989), 445–68. See also R. Ḥayyim Or Zarua' (*Responsa* [Leipzig, 1860], no. 183 [fol. 62a]), who suggests, based on a ruling of his father, that young men who travel afar to study Torah are exempt from fulfilling certain religious precepts as long as they are on the way to, or are already in, their teacher's abode. (R. Ḥayyim himself disagrees. See responsum no. 163, end and J. Katz in *Qiryat Sefer* 31 [1956]: 16.) See also *Sefer Tashbez̩* (Warsaw, 1876), no. 433. For an earlier reference to traveling students, see Rashi's *Commentary to Shir ha-Shirim* 5:16 (ed. J. Rosenthal), in *S. K. Mirsky Jubilee Volume* (New York, 1947), p. 169. Cf. Rashi to *Berakhot* 64a, s.v. *ein lahem menuḥah* and the Pietistic commentaries to Deuteronomy 33:9–10 in *SḤP,* sec. 1484; R. Eleazar Roqeaḥ, *Commentary to Shemot,* ed. S. Kanevsky (Jerusalem, 1981), 286; and Abraham b. Azriel, *Arugat ha-Bosem,* ed. E. E. Urbach, 3:117. See also *Bava Batra,* 8a. On wandering students in general society, see M. Chenu, *Nature, Man, and Society in the Twelfth Century,* 270–73; L. K. Little, *Religious Poverty and the Profit Economy in Medieval Europe,* 27; C. Haskins, *Studies in Medieval Culture* (repr. New York, 1965), 7–23, 99–102; and H. Waddell, *Wandering Scholars* (New York, 1954), 184–91.

50. See chap. 5, n. 7.
51. See the elegy of R. Eleazar Roqeaḥ for his wife Dolce in A. M. Habermann, *Gezerot Ashkenaz ve-Z̩arefat,* 164–65; Breuer, *Rabbanut Ashkenaz,* 19; and idem, *Ha-Yeshivah ha-Ashekanzit,* 11–12.
52. *SḤP,* sec. 1495; cf. I. Ta-Shema in *Bar Ilan* 14–15 (1977): 110. See also *SḤP* secs. 919, 1283, 1327.
53. See chap. 5, nn. 10–11.
54. See, e.g., *SḤP,* secs. 765, 778–79, 1493. See also *Sefer Or Zarua',* vol. 1, no. 762 (responsa). On a wife's providing support for her husband's studies (e.g., through the use of her dowry), see *RMC,* nos. 93–94, *SḤB,* sec. 874, and above, n. 51. (On the roles of the family and the wife in supporting the education of the son and the husband in nineteenth-century Lithuania, see E. Etkes, "Mishpaḥah ve-Limmud Torah be-Ḥugei ha-Lomdim be-Lita ba-Me'ah ha-19," *Zion* 51 [1986]: 87–106.)
55. See *Sefer Or Zarua', Pisqei Bava Mez̩i'a,* no. 244. See *Teshuvot R. Gershom,* ed. S. Eidelberg, no. 71, and above, n. 15. See also Breuer, *Ha-Yeshivah ha-Ashkenazit,* 46–47. Sources refer to both students (*baḥurim*) and *melammedim* who came to a particular town and rented rooms there. See *Sefer Or Zarua',* vol. 2, no. 172 and the

parallel sources cited above, chap. 1, n. 40; and E. Kupfer, *Teshuvot u-Pesaqim,* 325.

56. The responsum of R. Asher b. Yeḥiel (signed jointly by R. Asher, David b. Moses ha-Kohen, and Yissakhar b. Yequtiel) is published in R. Meir of Rothenburg, *Responsa,* ed. M. Bloch (Berlin, 1891), ms. Prague, no. 883, 321–22. It is also found (with a lacuna filled in) in a collection of R. Asher's responsa in ms. Paris Heb.421/1. See E. E. Urbach, "She'elot u-Teshuvot ha-Rosh be-Kitvei Yad uvi-Defusim," 141.

57. R. Asher answered in similar fashion another question concerning the lending at interest of funds earmarked for Torah study; see his *Responsa* 13:10. This is probably the case involving the rabbinically prohibited *bayit de-nakkaita* referred to by Rosh in the responsum cited in the above note. He also responded similarly to a question from Valladolid concerning the investment of funds donated for the general upkeep of the synagogue or to pay the salaries of synagogue functionaries, funds to purchase a *lulav* and the other species, funds to provide shrouds for poor people, as well as funds for Torah study. See his *Responsa* 13:17, supplemented by the Jerusalem ms. of R. Asher's responsa published by Urbach, "She'elot u-Teshuvot," 12–13, 17. The questioners indicate that with respect to lending at a fixed rate (*ribbit qeẓuẓah*) to Jews, which is normally prohibited by Biblical law, different opinions have been rendered; see the next note.

58. See *RMC,* no. 58 = *RMP,* no. 147. Cf. Agus's translation in his *R. Meir of Rothenburg,* 1:258 (no. 198). The unidentified responsum, 13:10, described in the previous note was probably sent by a Spanish community. R. Meir did compose several responsa permitting the investment of charity funds in partnership with Jews (*karov lisekhar*), a practice normally prohibited by rabbinic decree. See *RML,* no. 425 = *RMB* (Parma), no. 476, *RML,* no. 234, *RMC,* no. 109. In *RMC,* no. 101 and *RMP,* no. 73, R. Meir emphatically prohibits the lending of charity funds at a definite rate of interest, which is biblically proscribed. He indicates that he is not publicizing the prohibition since this practice is a widespread custom; he hopes that it will be curtailed in the future. (R. Asher cites this ruling of R. Meir and concurs; see his *Responsa* 13:8). It stands to reason that these rulings would apply equally to charity funds earmarked for Torah study. The question of whether money donated to charity can be lent out at a definite rate of interest directly to Jews, ignoring the biblical prohibiton, was addressed by earlier Ashkenazic authorities. R. Yoel and Rabiah prohibited such a practice while R. Isaac Or Zarua' permitted it (*Sefer Or*

Zarua', Hilkhot Ẓedaqah, no. 30 [1:18], cited by R. Meir in *RML,* 425, *RMB* [Parma], 476). In these sources, R. Meir questions R. Isaac Or Zarua's position and rejects it. Cf. *Teshuvot Maimuniyyot* to *Sefer Mishpatim* no. 14. A certain R. Ḥayyim b. Makhir attacks R. Meir's position that rabbinically prohibited interest is permitted for the sake of charity funds (cited in *RML,* no. 425 = Parma, no. 476; see Agus, *R. Meir of Rothenberg* 1:260, no. 202). He maintains that the one instance where the Talmud permits such a practice (funds of orphans) cannot be viewed as paradigmatic. Note that even these issues are not discussed in any northern French sources.

59. See Breuer, *Ha-Yeshivah ha-Ashkenazit,* 14–16. Cf. W. J. Courtenay "The Effect of the Black Death on English Higher Education," *Speculum* 55 (1980): 696–714 and B. Rosensweig, *Ashkenazic Jewry in Transition* (Ontario, 1975), 77–78. Where assistance was offered only to the poor students, it was from communal funds and covered all the needs of these students. The funds were disbursed through the head of the academy. On the term *haspaqah* in medieval Jewish sources, see G. Cohen, ed., *Sefer ha-Qabbalah,* 135 (nn. to lines 55–56).
60. See, e.g., R. Moses Mintz, *Responsa,* no. 33 and the statement of R. Menaḥem of Merseburg in S. Assaf, *Meqorot le-Toledot ha-Ḥinnukh be-Yisrael,* vol. 4, no. 20 (p. 16).
61. See Katz, *Massoret u-Mashber,* 224–25, 229, 266–67.
62. Of course, any scholar who was truly indigent was eligible to receive outright charity. On the question of preference for indigent scholars in the allocation of charity, see *SḤP,* sec. 860, 862, 919, 921; H. Soloveitchik, "Three Themes," 344, n. 107 and 337, n. 86; see also below, chap. 6.
63. R. Solomon Ibn Adret, *Responsa* 1:669. See the position of R. Isaac Or Zarua', above, n. 58. Cf. Rashba 3:291, 4:64, and 5:249. See also the responsum of Ramban in S. Assaf, *Sifran shel Rishonim* (Jerusalem, 1935), 101 (no. 68).
64. A *heqdesh* fund specifically designated for educational needs is found only in Spanish sources. See R. Asher b. Yeḥiel, *Responsa* 59:5; R. Nissim Gerondi (Ran), *Responsa,* no. 75; above, chap.1, n. 38.
65. See R. Asher b. Yeḥiel, *Responsa* 3:13 and Rashba, *Responsa,* vol. 5, no. 249. See also I. Ta-Shema, "Shipput 'Ivri u-Mishpat 'Ivri ba-Me'ot ha-Yod Bet/Yod Gimmel bi-Sefarad," *Shenaton ha-Mishpat ha-'Ivri* 1 (1975): 365–66. A responsum of Maimonides described a store that was constituted so that all the profits from its sales could be used to support scholars. See *Teshuvot ha-Rambam,* ed. J. Blau, 2:371 (no. 210). The Jewish communities of the Geniza lands generally main-

tained a very extensive system of economic and communal support for scholars. See S. D. Goitein, *Sidrei Ḥinnukh,* chaps. 4, 7.

66. R. Meir ha-Levi, *Responsa Or Ẓaddiqim,* no. 241 (and see the text published by Ta-Shema in *Qiryat Sefer* 44 [1969]: 431); R. Asher b. Yeḥiel, *Responsa* 7:4. See also S. Assaf, *Meqorot le-Toledot ha-Ḥinnukh be-Yisrael,* 2:56, n. 2.
67. See M. N. Adler, *The Itinerary of Benjamin of Tudela* (London, 1907), 3–4.
68. See I. Twersky, *Rabad of Posquières,* 25. Cf. the Provençal practices described by Radaq in *Qoveẓ Teshuvot ha-Rambam,* vol. 3, *Iggerot Qena'ot* (Leipzig, 1859), fol. 3b. Note that if *Sefer Ḥuqqei ha-Torah* is of Provençal origin, the reference in it to an academy supported by taxes paid by all members of the community and providing completely for all the needs of its mature students would be in character with contemporary Provençal practice; if the document is of Ashkenazic origin, such an academy would seem to be a great innovation. There are, however, conflicting passages within *SḤH* as to whether students contribute anything toward their educational costs. See App. A, lines 32–35, 93–97.
69. See above, nn. 27, 31. See also Rashba, *Responsa* 1:386.
70. See above, n. 26.
71. Scholars were also hired in Spain by patrons who wanted to be taught relatively simple material. See R. Isaac Alfasi, *Responsa,* no. 223, and Rashba, *Responsa* 2:260.
72. There is one Ashkenazic source from Nuremberg in the late fourteenth century recording the contribution of a wealthy man who gave seventy marks for the synagogue, seventy for the *ner tamid,* twenty for the cemetery, twenty for *ma'ot ḥittim,* and twenty for the *baḥurim* who study with the *rav;* see S. Salfeld, *Das Martyrologium des Nürnberger Memorbuches,* 87. That same document records a few incidental contributions to *talmidim* and *'ameilei Torah* and many small contributions *lilmod/le-limmud ne'arim* (pp. 87–93). These contributions, according to the text, went toward supplying either texts of the Pentateuch or teachers for what were obviously younger students. Cf. *SḤP,* sec. 664. On these charity lists, see A. Neubauer, "Le Memorbuch de Mayence," *REJ* 4 (1882): 7–8 and Y. Yuval, "Terumot mi-Nuremberg li-Yerushalayim," *Zion* 46 (1981): 182, 186–87. See also S. Spitzer, "Pesaqim u-Teshuvot Rabboteinu be-Ashkenaz be-Dor shele-aḥar Gezerot Quf-Tet (1349)," *Moriah* 8:8–9 (1979):9–10. We have already seen that greater organization and more systematic means of economic assistance were to be found in elementary and advanced Ashkenazic education after 1348; see above, nn. 21, 59–61 and chap. 1, nn. 43, 46, 52; also see be-

low, chap. 4, nn. 12, 50, 68. See also *Terumat ha-Deshen,* no. 342. In addition, outlying areas of Ashkenaz, even in the pre-1348 period, exhibit a greater concern for the support of education; see above, chap. 1, n. 33.

73. See *SḤP,* sec. 806 and I. Ta-Shema in *Bar Ilan* 14–15 (1977): 99.

Notes to Chapter 4

1. N. Golb, "Les Écoles Rabbiniques en France au Moyen Age," *Revue de l'histoire des religions* 102 (1985): 243–65. In large measure Golb's article reviews and sharpens the main points of his earlier article, "Nature et destination du monument hebraique découvert a Rouen," *PAAJR* 48 (1981): 101–61, itself a summary article of Golb's research extending over the previous decade. See above, chap. 1, n. 43, and Golb, *Toledot ha-Yehudim be-ʿIr Rouen Bimei ha-Beinayim* (Tel Aviv, 1976), 36–40. [In 1985, the University of Rouen published a revised version of Golb's Hebrew volume in French entitled, *Les Juifs de Rouen au Moyen Age.* See F. Talmage's review in *AHR* 92 (1987):648.]
2. See App. A.
3. Golb, "Les Écoles Rabbiniques," 246.
4. Golb claims that the great number of biblical and Talmudic scholars in northern France proves the existence of large, well-structured academies. His reasoning is dubious at best. See chap. 1. See also J. Shatzmiller, "Les écoles dans la litterature rabbinique," in *Art et archéologie des Juifs en France mediévale,* ed. B. Blumenkranz (Toulouse, 1980), 137–42. (Thirteenth-century linguist R. Abraham of Béziers' reference to an emissary from the communities of "Ẓarefat" who showed up at R. Abraham's own Perpignan collecting funds for the instruction of poor children [cited by Golb in "Nature et destination," 124, n. 31] sheds no light on practices in northern France. To a resident of Perpignan, which was considered to be part of the Spanish Jewish orbit, Ẓarefat often refers solely to southern France. See, e.g., R. Nissim b. Reuben Gerondi, *Responsa,* no. 75, and H. Gross, *Gallia judaica,* 369, 537–38. Supporting this usage in the case at hand are the fact that R. Abraham indicates that the messenger came "to the people of this land" [treating Perpignan as a separate entity], coupled with the fact that he notes that the messenger presented a letter of introduction signed by a former colleague still residing in Béziers named R. Joseph b. Meshullam. Cf. *Shirei Avraham ha-*

Bedersi, ed. A. M. Habermann [Jerusalem, 1969], 24 and B. Z. Dinur, *Yisrael ba-Golah* vol. 2, pt. 3, p. 335, n. 93. See above, chap. 3, n. 68.)

5. See S. Albeck, "Yaḥaso shel Rabbenu Tam li-Veʿayot Zemanno," *Zion* 19 (1954): 132–33, 140; M. Breuer, *Rabbanut Ashkenaz Bimei Ha-Beinayim,* 10–15; S. W. Baron, "Rashi and the Community of Troyes," *Ancient and Medieval Jewish History* (New Brunswick, 1972), 276; idem, *A Social and Religious History of the Jews,* 5:62–68; and I. A. Agus, *The Heroic Age of Franco-Germany Jewry* (New York, 1969), 331–33. Cf. A. Grossman, "Yerushat Avot be-Hanhagah ha-Ruḥanit shel Qehillot Yisrael Bimei ha-Beinayim," *Zion* 50 (1985): 208. A great scholar who headed a *beit midrash* might also serve his home community as an *adam ḥashuv* (preeminent scholar) for the promulgation of ordinances; or he might be consulted by an entire region in matters of *halakhah.* See, e.g., *Teshuvot Ḥakhmei Ẓarefat ve-Lothaire,* ed. J. Mueller, p. 11. On the function and nature of the *adam ḥashuv,* the *ḥaver ʿir,* and figures with related titles, see Y. Handelsman, "The Views of Rabiah on Communal Leadership" (in Hebrew), *Zion* 408 (1983): 27–40. While academy heads might also sit on the communal "boards," power to make decisions concerning self-government resided with the community, not with the scholar. See Y. Baer, "Ha-Yesodot veha-Hatḥalot shel Irgun ha-Qehillah ha-Yehudit Bimei ha-Beinayim," *Zion* 15 (1950): 30–31 and A. Grossman, "Yaḥas Ḥakhmei Ashkenaz ha-Rishonim la-Qahal," *Shenaton ha-Mishpat ha-ʿIvri* 2 (1975): 176–94. Cf. R. Ḥayyim Or Zaruaʿ, *Responsa,* nos. 65, 110, 222. On an attempt by a community to interfere with a scholar's jurisdiction in matters of Jewish law and the sharp reaction of R. Meir of Rothenburg, see I. A. Agus, *Teshuvot Baʿalei ha-Tosafot* (New York, 1954), no. 62.
6. The brothers of Evreux made their position known in a letter reproduced by R. Aharon ha-Kohen of Lunel in his *Orḥot Ḥayyim* (repr. Jerusalem, 1957), p. 64b:

> והר׳ שמואל (צ״ל משה) מאיורא רבו של ר׳ יונה ז״ל ואחיו ר׳ שמואל מאיורא כתבו באגרותיהם מיום שגלו אבותינו וחרב בית מקדשנו . . . אין לנו עוד לומר מורא רבך כמורא שמים וכל הדינים הראויין לעשות תלמיד לרב נתבטלו. כי הגמרות והפירושים והחידושים והחבורים הם המורים אנשים. והכל לפי פקחות הלבבות. ולכך היו רגילים שבעירם יחזיק תלמיד מדרש ולא אמרי׳ בהא כל המורה הלכה בפני רבו חייב מיתה. וכן יסתור התלמיד להם אם יוכל לפי פלפול. ע״כ מלשונם. [מן הנוסח שהובא בשו״ת מהרשד״ם חו״מ סי׳ א: . . . כי הספרים והחיבורים והפידושים הם המורים לנו. והכל לפי פקחות השכל והסברא ועל כן נהגו בעירם לקבוע התלמיד מדרש לעצמו. וכן אין לומר תלמיד אל יורה.]

Cf. E. E. Urbach, *Ba'alei ha-Tosafot,* 1:251, 480–81 and M. Breuer, *Rabbanut Ashkenaz,* 15–16. The related formulations of Ri are recorded in *Sefer ha-Semaq mi-Ẓurich,* ed. Y. Har-Shoshanim (Jerusalem, 1973), 275–76. The only concern of the brothers of Evreux was the status of the prohibition against a student deciding matters of law in the presence of his teacher. On this issue, the view of Ri that the full force of this prohibition could be sustained only during the Talmudic period adumbrated the brothers' position. (Indeed, Tosafists generally attempted to minimize the effects of this prohibition in their own day; see below, n. 11). But even if the brothers' position in this matter was not universal, the assumption is that a scholar can open an academy on his own. Cf. *Tosafot Gittin,* 54a, s.v. *R. Yoḥanan omer; Tosafot ha-Rosh,* s.v. R. *Yoḥanan omer;* and the parallel *Tosafot* in *Menaḥot,* 23b and *Bava Qamma,* 117b. For other examples of the expressions *litpos yeshivah* or *liqboa'/lehaḥaziq midrash,* which refer to the opening of a school by a scholar in this period, see the sources cited by G. D. Cohen, *Sefer Ha-Qabbalah* (New York, 1967), 135, n. 39. To these add ms. Bodl. 1103, fol. 78; R. Ḥayyim Or Zarua', *Responsa,* no. 164 (p.55); *Sefer ha-Yashar,* ed. S. Rosenthal (Berlin, 1898), 93; *Megillat Aḥima'aẓ,* ed. B. Klar, p. 17; the passage from ms. Bodl. 1208 published by S. Eidelberg in *Talpiyyot* 6 (1955): 707; and *Nimmuqei Yosef* to *Bava Batra,* 116a, s.v. *darash R. Pinḥas.* See also below, n. 35.

7. *RMP,* 137.
8. Aptowitzer, *Mavo la-Rabiah,* 16.
9. R. Isaac bar Sheshet Perfet, *Responsa,* no. 271.
10. See M. Breuer "Ha-Semikhah ha-Ashkenazit," *Zion* 33 (1968): 17, n. 13 and J. Katz, *Halakhah ve-Qabbalah* (Jerusalem, 1986), 208–10.
11. On the liberal attitude of Tosafists to the Talmudic prohibition of *talmid al yoreh bifnei rabbo,* see *Tosafot Sanhedrin,* 5b, s.v. *ella; Tosafot Eruvin,* 62b–63a, s.v. *afilu; Tosafot R. Pereẓ 'al Massekhet Eruvin,* ed. J. Wilman (New York, 1983), 62b, s.v. *R. Ḥisda orei be-Kafri; Semaq mi-Ẓurich,* 275–76; R. Meir me-Rothenburg, *Teshuvot, Pesaqim u-Mihagim,* ed. I. Z. Kahana, vol. 2 (Jerusalem, 1960), no. 189 (pp. 252–53); I. A. Agus, *Teshuvot Ba'alei ha-Tosafot* (New york, 1954), no. 62; *Sefer ha-Yashar le-Rabbenu Tam* (*Teshuvot*), 93, 105; and Urbach, 1:77. Cf. Ramban, *Hilkhot Talmud Torah* 5:1–4 (Ramban would be totally opposed to the position of the brothers of Evreux) and G. Blidstein, "Heter Hora'ah be-Mishnat ha-Rambam," *Tarbiz* 51 (1982): 581–87. See also *Beit Yosef* to *Yoreh De'ah,* sec. 242, s.v. *ve-lo,* citing a responsum of Mahariq (no. 167); *Teshuvot R. Abraham b. Isaac Av Bet Din,* ed. J. Kafaḥ (Jerusalem, 1962), no. 66. Cf.

Urbach, 1:446. The general aversion of Ashkenazic scholarship to centralized forms of *pisqei halakhah* would also tend to give students more freedom in deciding matters of law. See I. Ta-Shema in *Qiryat Sefer* 55 (1980): 194–97.

12. This formal, institutionalized privilege is thus a late development. See below, n. 48. Indeed, the term *liqboaʿ yeshivah* takes on new significance in post-1348 Ashkenaz, when the communities gradually began to regulate the opening of study halls and academies. See Breuer, "Ha-Semikhah ha-Ashkenazit," 41; idem, *Ha-Yeshivah ha-Ashkenazit,* 9–11, 17–18.
13. The Geonim received support from their *reshuyot,* as the exilarchs did. See S. Abramson, *Ba-Merkazim uva-Tefuẓot bi-Tequfat ha-Geonim,* 9–20 and A. Grossman, *Rashut ha-Golah bi-Tequfat ha-Geonim* (Jerusalem, 1984), 100–101. There is a letter of appointment for a Gaon dated 1209 (published by A. Ben-Jacob in *Zion* 15 [1950]: 67) that also extended to him the right to collect taxes, *li-ẓerakhav ule-ẓorkhei yeshivato.* The right to collect taxes was normally given to the exilarch alone. Scholars differ as to whether this privilege belonged to the Gaon in the earlier period when the exilarchate was more powerful or was usurped now by the stronger Gaonate. See Grossman, *Rashut ha-Golah,* 48–50 and sources on 105 and nn. 71–72, 105, 121. It is not clear in all of these references whether the Geonim were collecting taxes for the government or for their own use. See also S. Baron, *A Social and Religious History of the Jews,* 5:50–52.
14. Breuer, "Ha-Yeshivah shel Yemei ha-Beinayim," *Ḥinnukh ha-Adam ve-Yiʿudo* (Jerusalem, 1967), 147, based on the formulations of S. D. Goitein, *Sidrei ha-Ḥinnukh* (Jerusalem, 1962), chap. 7. Cf. ms. Bodl. 1103, fols. 90v, 91r, 98v. See also S. Assaf, *Tequfat ha-Geonim ve-Sifrutah* (Jerusalem, 1955), 42–45, 57–61, 66–70.
15. On the status of Ramerupt and Troyes after R. Tam, Dampierre after Ri and R. Elḥanan, and Sens after R. Samson (despite the fact that all left capable students who could continue their work), see H. Gross, *Gallia judaica,* 168–70, 238–41, 636–38, 662. For a reference to *yeshivat R. Tam,* see R. Zeraḥyah ha-Levi, *Sefer ha-Ma'or* to *Ḥullin,* 61a and below, n. 35. Razah (*Ma'or ha-Gadol* to *Ḥullin,* 12b) also refers to commentaries that he found *mi-yeshivato shel Rabbeinu Shelomo* (= Rashi). See also *Sefer Rabiah,* ed. V. Aptowitzer, 1:360 and *RML,* no. 425 (end). Cf. S. Assaf, "Sefer Pesaqim le-Ri ha-Zaqen, R. Tam u-She'ar Baʿalei ha-Tosafot," in *M. Kaplan Jubilee Volume* (New york, 1952), 21. Troyes, in the years prior to Rashi, was a town without an academy and was not considered a seat of scholarship. See S.

Eidelberg, "Qehillat Troyes Lifnei Zemanno shel Rashi," *Sura* 1 (1954): 48–51. N. Golb's claim in *REJ* 136 (1977): 545–47 that Ri and other important Tosafists did not teach and compose their important works in small villages like Dampierre (as Urbach says they did) but rather in larger centers like Paris is without basis. See below, n. 21.

16. See, e.g., the entries in S. Albeck's introduction to *Sefer Raban* (repr. Jerusalem, 1975): *Ḥakhmei Vermaiza, Magenẓa, (Narbonne), Regensburg, Reinus; Zeqeinei Ashpira, Magenẓa (Narbonne, Provinẓa); Geonei Magenẓa.* See also I. Ta-Shema, " ʿAl Perushei R. Gershom Me'or ha-Golah la-Talmud," *Qiryat Sefer* 53 (1978): 356–59 and B. Z. Dinur, *Yisrael ba-Golah,* v. 2, 6:90.
17. Two of them were Rashbam's relatives, and the other two are not especially important scholars. See Urbach, 1:46 and V. Aptowitzer, *Mavo la-Rabiah,* 292.
18. On the coterie of scholars in Paris c. 1200, see Urbach, 1:274, 318–22, 348 and E. Kupfer, *Teshuvot u-Pesaqim* (Jerusalem, 1973), 296–97, 325–26. See also R. W. Southern, "The Schools of Paris and the School of Chartres," in *Renaissance and Renewal in the Twelfth Century,* ed. R. L. Benson and G. Constable (Cambridge, 1982) and A. L. Gabriel, *Garlandia: Studies in the History of Medieval Universities* (Notre Dame, 1969), 1–6.
19. The text is reproduced in L. Finkelstein, *Jewish Self-Government in the Middle Ages,* 153.
20. See above, n. 15. Cf. Urbach, 1:313, regarding sources cited by the author of the commentary on the *Sifra* attributed to R. Samson of Sens. The author often cites *Sifrei Lunel, Ḥakhmei Lunel,* and *Ḥakhmei Provence.*
21. The so-called *Tosafot Sens* to various tractates of the Talmud do not weaken my argument. This title always refers to the *tosafot* that emanated from the study hall of R. Samson of Sens, the scholar who made Sens a recognized place. See Urbach, 1:272 and pp. 22–24. See also Urbach, 2:584–85 (regarding *Tosafot Touqes*) and p. 643. In any event, R. Samson's *tosafot* are sometimes called *Tosafot R. Samson of Sens* or *Tosafot Rashba* (= R. Samson b. Abraham). Needless to say, titles of *tosafot* texts assigned by copyists, printers, and editors do not conform to any pattern.
22. See H. Soloveitchik, "Three Themes in the Sefer Ḥasidim," *AJS* Review 1 (1976): 347 and below, chap. 6.
23. J. N. Epstein, "Perush ha-Riban u-Perushei Worms," *Tarbiz* 4 (1933): 11–34, 153–92.
24. A. Grossman, *Ḥakhmei Ashkenaz ha-Rishonim,* 412–15.

25. Ibid., 437–38. The financial arrangements between students and teachers in the pre-Crusade period were similar to those in the Tosafist period. See above, chap. 3, nn. 50–55. The students were not communally subsidized. See M. Breuer, "Le-Ḥeqer ha-Tippologiyah shel Yeshivot ha-Ma'arav Bimei ha-Beinayim," in *Studies in Jewish Society in the Medieval and Early Modern Periods,* ed. E. Etkes and Y. Salmon (Jerusalem, 1980), 49–50; idem, *Rabbanut Ashkenaz,* 14.
26. See *Sefer Or Zarua',* vol. 2, no. 275. See also the annotated text and parallel sources found in *Teshuvot Rabbenu Gershom,* ed. S. Eidelberg (New York, 1955), 98–100. Cf. *Arukh ha-Shalem,* ed. S. Kohut, p. 11; Grossman, *Ḥakhmei Ashkenaz ha-Rishonim,* 120; and I. A. Agus, "Rabbinic Scholarship in Northern Europe," in *World History of the Jewish People: The Dark Ages,* ed. C. Roth (Ramat Gan, 1966), 193–94; E. Kupfer, *Teshuvot u-Pesaqim* (Jerusalem, 1974), 314–15; and I. Ta-Shema, "Halakhah, Minhag, u-Massoret be-Yahadut Ashkenaz ba-Me'ot ha-Yod Alef/Yod Bet," *Sidra* 3 (1987): 137–38.
27. *Sefer Ma'aseh ha-Geonim,* ed. A. Epstein and J. Freimann (Berlin, 1910), no. 27; see also nos. 57 (pp. 48 = *Sefer ha-Pardes,* no. 20), 61 (p. 52 = *Sefer Or Zarua'* 2:464). Cf. *Teshuvot Rashi,* ed. I. Elfenbein (New York, 1943), no. 73 (p. 94).
28. *Commentary of R. Asher b. Yeḥiel to Rosh ha-Shanah* 4:11.
29. See M. Breuer, "Le-Ḥeqer," 45–48, and cf. I. Ta-Shema, "Halakhah, Minhag," above, n. 26. The seemingly more restrained reactions and responses of students to their teachers reflected in the rabbinic literature of the pre-Crusade period was likely a function of the relatively unencumbered method of study in that period. Tosafist dialectic obviously encouraged students to raise questions and suggest alternate interpretations. In addition (or perhaps as a result) the already laconic pre-Crusade rabbinic literature generally preserved less "audience participation" than Tosafist literature did. See below, chap. 5. Ta-Shema's overall point that determinations in matters of *minhag* became more closely tied to Talmudic-academic study in the Tosafist period is well taken.
30. See Urbach, 1:264. Cf. Twersky's review of Urbach's first edition in *Tarbiz* 26 (1957): 226. On the translation of the terms *ḥaverim* and *talmidim* in this text as "older students" and "younger students," see Aptowitzer, *Mavo la-Rabiah,* 307 and Urbach, 1:405, n. 52.
31. I. Agus, *Teshuvot Ba'alei ha-Tosafot,* 69.
32. *Sefer Or Zarua', Pisqei Avodah Zarah,* no. 262. While a number of the questions and responses discussed above were related to synagogue services (e.g., the saying of kaddish and the sounding of the shofar),

they were matters of *halakhah,* not purely issues of custom or liturgy. To be sure, even leading Tosafists could not control the services in the synagogue. Thus, R. Ephraim of Regensburg left the synagogue when the cantor did something improper in the course of the service. See *Sefer Rabiah,* 2:260 (*Megillah,* no. 851) and Urbach, 1:201. At the same time, those selected to be cantors were often important scholars. See M. Breuer, *Rabbanut Ashkenaz,* 15 and M. Frank, *Qehillot Ashkenaz u-Vattei Dineihem,* 25–26. Add *SḤP,* sec. 1759 and *Sefer Amarkal,* ed. N. Coronel, 22. The cases discussed here would support the claim that a separate synagogue for teachers and their students (*beit kenesset shel baḥurim*)—for which there is documentation after 1348—did not exist in the earlier period. These student synagogues were perhaps a function of the greater degree of scholarly organization in that period, although they were still closely linked to the synagogue of the community. See M. Breuer, *Ha-Yeshivot be-Ashkenaz,* 19–21 and M. Gordon, *Collegial Relationships* (see chap. 3, n. 49), 63. At the same time, however, communal services were sometimes held in *battei midrash.* The "*beit midrash* of R. Yehudah b. Kalonymus" was used as a place to hold services by those who lived in the part of Mainz that was cut off from the area of the main synagogue as a result of the First Crusade. See A. M. Habermann, *Gezerot Ashkenaz ve-Ẓarefat,* 104. See also Agus, *R. Meir of Rothenburg,* 1:25, n. 51; *RMB,* ms. Amsterdam, no. 55 (= Parma 289) and *Mordekhai* to *Shavu'ot,* no. 750; *Commentary of R. Asher b. Yeḥiel* to *Berakhot* 1:7; and R. Ya'akov Ḥazzan of London, *Eẓ Ḥayyim,* 1:57.

33. R. Eliezer b. Nathan, *Sefer Raban* (Prague, 1610), fol. 139d. Cf. R. Chazan, *European Jewry and the First Crusade* (Berkeley, 1988), 133–36 and A. Grossman, "The Historical Background to the Ordinances on Family Affairs Attributed to Rabbenu Gershom Me'or ha-Golah," *Jewish History,* ed. A. Albert and S. J. Zipperstein (London, 1988), 5 and 23, n. 45.
34. See also *Sefer Raban,* ed. S. Z. Ehrenreich (repr. Jerusalem, 1975), no. 19 (fol. 16d). Cf. Ta-Shema "Halakahah, Minhag," 102–3.
35. When R. Zeraḥyah ha-Levi refers to "R. Moshe b. Yosef *vi-yeshivato*" and to "R. Tam *vi-yeshivato,*" (*Sefer ha-Ma'or* to *Ḥullin,* 61a), he is probably referring not to R. Tam and his students but to R. Tam and those who side with him intellectually in his interpretation of the law. In R. Zeraḥyah's text the descriptions in question are preceded by the expression *al da'at kat R.———vi-yeshivato* and are followed by interpretations of various Talmudic passages leading to the formulation of halakhic position. Note that both groups in the Razah text are referred

to as R.———and *yeshivato.* Eliezer b. Nathan, *Sefer Raban* refers to "R. Isaac ha-Levi *u-benei yeshivato.*" The fact that Razah is a Provençal scholar may also be relevant; see below, n. 36. Breuer ("Le-Ḥeqer," 48–49, n. 22) accepts the solution of M. Frank that both the Raban and Razah texts are using the term *yeshivah* in the sense of a *beit din.* These scholars and their rabbinic courts rendered legal decisions in the cases before them. This solution would also accord with my overall argument. The terms *yeshivah* or *yeshivato* in *Sefer Rabiah,* 1:360; *Sefer Or Zarua',* vol. 1, no. 747; and *Responsa of R. Ḥayyim Or Zarua',* no. 90 are used by a student or a younger colleague as a sign of respect. See also Rashi to *Sanhedrin,* 110a, s.v. *ḥoleq al rabbo; Teshuvot Rashi,* ed. I. Elfenbein, no. 103 (p. 132); and *Sefer Or Zarua',* vol. 2, no. 140.

36. See *The Itinerary of Benjamin of Tudela,* ed. M. A. Adler (London, 1907), 3–5. See also A. Grabois, "Ha-Qeroniqah shel Almoni mi-Narbonne," *Proceedings of the Sixth World Jewish Congress* (Jerusalem, 1973), 2:83–84; B. Z. Benedikt, "R. Moshe b. Yosef mi-Narbonne," *Tarbiz* 19 (1948): 20–21; idem, "Le-Toldotav shel Merkaz ha-Torah bi-Provence," *Tarbiz* 22 (1951): 86–89, 93. Grabois is working with the anonymous twelfth-century Provençal supplement to *Sefer ha-Qabbalah.* On the date and provenance of this text, see chap. 1, n. 7. See also the text in Ha-Meiri's *Qiryat Sefer,* below, n. 43. Cf. M. Breuer, "Le-Ḥeqer," 49, n. 23 and Twersky, *Rabad of Posquières,* 22–23. Benedikt compares the system of *yeshivot* in Provence to the Babylonian academies. Just as we refer to Geonei Sura or Pumbeditha, it is possible to refer to the *roshei yeshivah* of the academy of Narbonne or to Ḥakhmei Lunel as a group.
37. On the support of elementary education in Provence, see Grabois, "Écoles et structures sociales des communautés juives dans l'Occident aux IX–XII siècles," in *Gli Ebrei Nell'alto Medioevo* (Spoleto, 1980), 937–62. See also the passage from a letter of Radaq cited in Assaf, *Meqorot,* 2:33. Cf. F. Talmage, *David Kimhi: The Man and His Commentaries* (Cambridge, 1975), 14–16, and above, chap. 1, n. 42.
38. See Benedikt in *Tarbiz* 22 (1951): 86–87, 103–4, and in *Tarbiz* 19 (1948): 21, n. 19. See also "Al Qavvim Ha-Meqoriyyim shel Torat Ḥakhmei Languedoc," in idem, *Merkaz ha-Torah bi-Provence* (Jerusalem, 1985), 185, nn. 9, 12. Cf. M. Frank, *Qehillot Ashkenaz u-Vattei Dineihen,* 126–27 and J. Katz, *Massoret u-Mashber* (Jerusalem, 1958), 228–29. In Provençal rabbinic literature the court was called *yeshivat zeqenim* and the academy was called *yeshivat talmidim.*
39. Ibn Daud, in the seventh section of his *Sefer Ha-Qabbalah* (trans. G. Cohen, pp. 63–93), takes note of generations of great scholars in

Moslem Spain and North Africa who were supported by patrons or paid by local communities; see above, chap. 3, n. 27. His evaluation of Torah study in Spain highlights the growing centers of study, not just the appearance of great scholars. See also I. Ta-Shema, "Shipput ʿIvri u-Mishpat ʿIvri ba-Me'ot ha-Yod Alef/Yod Bet bi-Sefarad," *Shenaton ha-Mishpat ha-ʿIvri* 1 (1974): 354.

40. For the history of the academy at Lucena, see E. Ashtor, *Qorot ha-Yehudim bi-Sefarad ha-Muslamit,* 1:202–3, 2:88–91 and *Sefer ha-Qabbalah,* trans. G. Cohen, pp. 84–86.

41. See Isaac Israeli (brother of R. Israel Israeli), *Yesod ʿOlam* (Berlin, 1777), *Ma'amar* 4, chap. 18, p. 86. Cf. R. W. Southern, *Medieval Humanism and Other Studies* (New York, 1970), 163.

42. See *Sefer ha-Qabbalah,* trans. G. Cohen, pp. 87–88; Menaḥem Ibn Zeraḥ, *Ẓedah la-Derekh,* 6; R. Menaḥem *Ha-Meiri, Commentary to Avot,* ed. B. Perag (New York, 1964), 55; and B. Septimus, *Hispano-Jewish Culture in Transition* (Cambridge, 1982), 20–23.

43. Cf. *Sefer ha-Manhig,* ed. Y. Raphael (Jerusalem, 1978), 2:723–36. See also Menaḥem ha-Meiri, *Qiryat Sefer,* ed. M. Hershler (Jerusalem, 1957), 45. Ha-Meiri reports that he is aware of a very accurate Torah scroll that was formerly in the possession of Ramah. Ramah testified that he had taken the trouble to send to "all the *yeshivot* [in Spain] and in the Maghreb and to *rabbanei Ashkenaz*" to verify his readings. (On this scroll, see I. Ta-Shema in *Qiryat Sefer* 45 (1970): 119–20.) While this text clearly conforms to our contention that *yeshivot* in Spain were more identified with their communities than the schools in Ashkenaz, where the teacher, not the institution, was most important, a note of caution must be sounded. The distinction in this case may simply be geographic. Ramah is a native of Spain and knows its schools well. His perception of Ashkenaz is of one large unit in which many scholars reside. This may also be true for Ibn Daud, who merely alludes to a few French scholars at the end of *Sefer ha-Qabbalah* after having described the academies in Spain in great detail. See *Sefer ha-Qabbalah,* 88–90. When the more balanced Provençal addendum to *Sefer ha-Qabbalah* (see above, n. 36) refers to *yeshivot* in various cities in Provence and then to *rabbanim* in northern France, the difference in terms is perhaps significant. See also the introduction of Menaḥem Ha-Meiri to his *Commentary to Avot,* 55–56.

44. R. Yehudah b. Barzilai of Barcelona, *Sefer ha-Shetarot,* ed. S. Z. H. Halberstam (Berlin, 1898), 131–32. On the actual use of these documents in Spain, see G. Cohen ed., *Sefer ha-Qabbalah,* 141, n. to line 408. See R. Isaac bar Sheshet, *Responsa,* nos. 192, 287, 377–79, 455.

R. Yehudah stresses that communal support for judges and scholars is both prevalent and obligatory; see above. chap. 3, n. 28.

45. See *Sefer Ha-Qabbalah,* trans. G. Cohen, pp. 85, 141, n. 408.
46. The documents of appointment described above, n. 44 are perhaps the best evidence for this. For the existence early on in Spain of communally salaried rabbis whose appointments were approved by the lay leadership, see A. A. Neuman, *The Jews in Spain* (Philadelphia, 1942), 2:86–91. See also S. Albeck, "Yesodot Mishtar ha-Qehillot bi-Sefarad ʿad Ha-Ramah (1180–1244)," *Zion* 25 (1960): 114–21. (For antecedents in the Geonic period, see S. Assaf, *Be-Ohalei Yaʿaqov* [repr. Jerusalem, 1966], 31–32).
47. Scholars have argued over whether a professionalized rabbinate was established when rabbinic appointments began or when a salary was paid. For Ashkenaz there are grounds to assume that the two developments were not simultaneous. There is also a controversy about what the title *rav* in Ashekanzic rabbinic literature represents. See the next note.
48. See Agus, *Teshuvot Baʿalei ha-Tosafot* (New York, 1954), 18–31; Urbach's review of Agus in *Qiryat Sefer* 30 (1955): 204–5; Agus's rejoinder in *JQR* 49 (1958–59): 219–20; M. Breuer, *Rabbanut Ashkenaz,* 9–22; S. Schwarzfuchs, *Études sur l'origin de la rabbinate au moyen âge* (Paris, 1957), 24–27; and Y. Y. Yuval, *Rabbanim ve-Rabbanut* (see chap. 1, n. 38), 9–16. Cf. above, n. 10.
49. See *Sefer Or Zaruaʿ* 1:113 (p. 40) and above, chap. 3, n. 45; Agus, *Teshuvot Baʿalei ha-Tosafot,* no. 90; *RMP,* no. 942.
50. By the sixteenth century, Ashkenazic communities supported and administered the academies, dictated the number of students who could study there, and in some instances even selected the students. Some communities appointed the academy heads. See Breuer, *Ha-Yeshivah ha-Ashkenazit,* 25–36, 55–56, and above, chap. 3, nn. 59–61.
51. See above, chap. 3.
52. See I. Ta-Shema, "Shipput ʿIvri," 364–65. See also L. Feldman, *Studies in the Life and Times of R. Nissim b. Reuben Gerondi of Barcelona* (Ph.D. diss., Columbia University, 1968), 45, 88, 131.
53. See Y. Baer, "Ha-Yesodot veha-Hatḥalot shel Irgun Ha-Qehillah ha-Yehudit Bimei ha-Beinayim," *Zion* 15 (1950): 36–37 and below, n. 62. Baer's assessment relates to the three major communal functions he had outlined: the preservation of relations with the ruling power, the securing of internal discipline and order, and the establishment of necessary economic controls (ibid., 32–35). According to R. Chazan (*Medieval Jewry in Northern France,* 20), the providing of educational and

welfare services was the fourth major function of the Jewish community. See S. Albeck, "Yaḥaso shel Rabbenu Tam li-Veʿayot Zemanno," *Zion* 19 (1954): 130–32, 136–37.

54. Ibid., 104–5; Chazan, *Medieval Jewry* 10–11, 31–32.
55. Ta-Shema, "Shipput ʿIvri," 354. Cf. idem, "Seder Hadpasatam shel Ḥiddushei ha-Rishonim la-Talmud," *Qiryat Sefer* 50 (1975): 334. Identification of Provençal scholars by their cities continues even after the relative number of important centers of study increases; see I. Twersky, *Rabad of Posquières,* 24.
56. See M. D. Chenu, *Nature, Man, and Society in the Twelfth Century* (Chicago, 1968), 270–73.
57. R. W. Southern, *Medieval Humanism and Other Studies,* 74–76. See also idem, "Schools of Paris," 114–18, 123, 128 and below, chap. 5, n. 30.
58. See I. Ta-Shema, "Shipput ʿIvri," 356–60, 369–72. See also B. Septimus, *Hispano-Jewish Culture in Transition* (Cambridge, 1982), 20.
59. For the comparative level and nature of scholarship in the Spanish academies and study halls, see Breuer, "Le-Ḥeqer," 45–48; I. Ta-Shema, "Seder Hadpasatam shel Ḥiddushei ha-Rishonim la-Talmud," 334–35; idem, "Shipput ʿIvri," 354–55, 360–65; and Urbach, 2:738–39. See also Ri Megash, *Responsa,* no. 114 and R. Isaac bar Sheshet, *Responsa,* nos. 375–76.
60. See I. Twersky, "The Mishneh Torah of Maimonides," *Proceedings of the Israel Academy of Sciences and Humanities* 5, no. 10 (Jerusalem, 1976): 268–70 and Septimus, *Hispano-Jewish Culture in Transition,* 47, 73 for statements of the Nasi Sheshet Beneviste to this effect. See also J. Faur, "Hora'at ha-Talmud ba-Massoret ha-Ḥinnukhit ha-Sefaradit," *Shevilei ha-Ḥinnukh* 35 (1975): 180–81, n. 19. Baer maintains throughout chap. 6 of his *A History of the Jews in Christian Spain* that the system of communal government in Spanish communities was based less on Jewish law and more on civil (Spanish) law as compared to the system of self-government in Ashkenazic communities. On illiteracy among Spanish Jewry, see Baer, *History,* 214–19. See also R. Judah b. Asher, *Zikhron Yehudah,* no. 49. See Y. Assis, "Pesha va-Allemut be-Ḥevrah ha-Yehudit bi-Sefarad," *Zion* 50 (1985): 221–40.
61. See Ta-Shema, "Shipput ʿIvri," 355, 370–72 and J. Katz, above, n. 10. Cf. idem, *Exclusiveness and Tolerance* (New York, 1961), 103–4 and B. Septimus, "Piety and Power in Thirteenth-Century Catalonia," in *Studies in Medieval Jewish History and Literature,* ed. I. Twersky (Cambridge, 1979), 1:215–18.
62. See S. Assaf, "Ḥalifat She'elot u-Teshuvot bein Sefarad u-Bein

Ẓarefat ve-Ashkenaz," *Tarbiz* 8 (1937): 162–66. It is not mere coincidence that several of the leading scholars in thirteenth-century Spain were trained by Tosafists or their students. See Urbach, 1:263–64, 479 and 2:660; B. Septimus, "Open Rebuke and Concealed Love: Naḥmanides and the Andalusian Tradition," in *R. Moses Naḥmanides; Explorations in His Religious and Literary Virtuosity,* ed. I. Twersky (Cambridge, 1983), p. 32; idem, *Hispano-Jewish Culture in Transition,* 31.

63. I have omitted Provence from this part of the discussion. The level of Talmudic studies in the academies of Provence seems to be quite high. At the same time, there is extensive communal support for education on all levels and the academies are identified with their communities. The problem with drawing any conclusions is that we simply do not know enough about the educational level of the average Provençal community and the proportion of scholars in any of the communities. Any attempt to portray the religiosity of Provençal Jewry must invariably rely solely on the evaluations and testimony of rabbinic scholars and academic leaders. See Twersky, *Rabad,* 22–29. The scholarly organization of the Geonim, which had no effect in Ashkenaz, may have affected Provence as well as Spain. See above, n. 36.
64. Ta-Shema, "Al Petur," (see chap. 3, n. 19), 317–20. Ta-Shema draws an interesting comparison to scholarly and clerical privileges in general medieval society. See also R. W. Southern, *Western Society and the Church in the Middle Ages,* 178, 194 and P. Kibre, *Scholarly Privileges in the Middle Ages* (Cambridge, 1962), 7–16, 325–28.
65. While the ability of the relatively small Ashkenazic communities to produce so many scholars is impressive, it should be noted that the density of scholarship in Ashkenaz was not quite as great as is sometimes thought. Compare the view of Agus (*The Heroic Age of Franco-German Jewry* [New York, 1969], esp. 310–16) with the more sober view of Grossman (*Ḥakhmei Ashkenaz ha-Rishonim,* 21–23). Regarding the neglect of certain *miẓvot,* see J. Katz in *Qiryat Sefer* 31 (1956): 15; Twersky, *Rabad,* 24; and Urbach, 1:82–83, 134–35. Moreover, the rosy picture Agus paints of Ashkenazic society as being completely free from most physical and social abuses has to be modified. See A. Grossman, "Avaryanim ve-Allamim ba-Ḥevrah ha-Yehudit be-Ashkenaz ha-Qedumah," *Shenaton ha-Mishpat ha-'Ivri* 8 (1981): 135–44 and Y. Baer, "Ha-Megammah ha-Ḥevratit ha-Datit shel Sefer Ḥasidim," *Zion* 1 (1937): 42, n. 56. See also the sources cited in H. J. Zimmels, *Ashkenazim and Sephardim,* 3d ed. (London, 1976), 253). See now Z. E. Rokeah, "Crime and Jews in Late Thirteenth-Century England:

Some Cases and Comments," *HUCA* 55 (1984): 95–158. On complaints in the thirteenth century that scholarship in Ashkenaz was losing ground, see below, chap. 5, n. 49.

66. See *Ẓedah la-Derekh* 1:4:21 and B. Septimus, "Tax Law," (see chap. 3, n. 24), 330–31.
67. Katz, *Halakah ve-Qabbalah.* cf. S. Albeck "Yaḥaso shel Rabbenu Tam," 134–35.
68. See M. Breuer, "Ha-Semikhah ha-Ashkenazit," *Zion* 33 (1968): 15–46.

Notes to Chapter 5

1. See I. Ta-Shema, "Al Seder Hadpasatam shel Ḥiddushei ha-Rishonim," *Qiryat Sefer* 50 (1975): 334–35 and the literature cited in n. 32; idem, in *Bar Ilan* 14–15 (1976): 107.
2. R. Menaḥem Ibn Zeraḥ, *Ẓedah la-Derekh* (Warsaw 1880), 6; Solomon Luria, *Yam shel Shelomoh,* intro. to *Ḥullin.* See also Urbach, 1:114 (n. 1), 251–52.
3. On communal size in Ashkenaz, see above, chap. 1, n. 47. Cf. A. Grossman, "Haggirat Yehudim el Germanyah ve-Hityashvutam ba-Me'ot 9–11," in *Haggirah ve-Hityashvut be-Yisrael uva-Ammim,* ed. A. Shinan (Jerusalem, 1982), 126–27.
4. See Ha-Meiri, *Beit ha-Baḥirah ʿal Massekhet Avot,* ed. B. Z. Perag (Jerusalem, 1964), 52–53 and Rashi to *Sanhedrin,* 7b, s.v. *shishim gibborim.* The *Ẓedah la-Derekh* text maintains that each of the sixty students (who studied with Ri) had mastered a different tractate of the Talmud. When Ri lectured, his students could immediately call attention to any other Talmudic passages that appeared to contradict the *sugya* at hand. This structure would account for the wide range of questions that raised in *tosafot* texts. See J. Katz in *Qiryat Sefer* 31 (1956): 15. Katz, who doubts the historicity of the *Ẓedah la-Derekh* description, argues that the wide scope and large number of Talmudic contradictions found in *tosafot* emanating from the study hall of Ri are due in part to the many questions preserved from the study halls of R. Tam and his contemporaries. M. Breuer ("Le-Ḥeqer" [see chap. 4, n. 25], 48, n. 20) notes that R. Solomon Luria names only nine Tosafists in his well-known responsum on the ancestry of Ashkenazic scholarship. The fact that R. Solomon based his responsum on an earlier

Spanish source (see J. N. Epstein, "Ha-He'eteq shebi-Teshuvat Rashal 29, Mi Ḥibbero?" *Ha-Qedem* 1 [1907]: 129–30) would not preclude his adding additional scholars who were known to him.

5. M. Breuer, "Le-Ḥeqer," 51–55.
6. See *RMC,* no. 108; R. Meir of Rothenburg, *Teshuvot, Peqasim, u-Minhagim,* ed. I. Z. Kahana, 3:134; *Responsa of Maharil,* no. 94; and I. A. Agus, *R. Meir of Rothenburg,* 1:25.
7. On students who resided in their teacher's home, see the sources cited in Breuer, "Le-Ḥeqer," 49–51. To these add *SḤP,* secs. 149, 798, 803, 1478; *SḤB,* secs. 973, 992. On the numerous opportunities for learning through observation and service (*shimmush*) that were available to students who lived in the home of their teacher, see M. Breuer, *Ha-Rabbanut be-Ashkenaz,* 15 and M. Gordon, *Collegial Relationships* (see chap. 3, n. 49), n. 49), 37, 46–54, 74–76. Cf. R. W. Southern, *The Making of the Middle Ages,* 177–94; J. W. Baldwin, *Masters, Princes, and Merchants* (Princeton, 1970), 117–49.
8. *Tosafot Qiddushin,* 33b, s.v. *ein talmid ḥakham.*
9. See *Tosafot 'Eruvin,* 72a, s.v. *u-modin,* as clarified by *Sefer Or Zarua',* vol. 2, no. 172 and *SḤP,* sec. 1416. Cf. *Tosafot R. Pereẓ,* ed. S. Wilman, s.v. *u-modin; Responsa of R. Jacob Weil,* no. 10; Urbach, 1:605; and *Teshuvot ha-Rashba ha-Meyuḥassot leha-Ramban,* no. 220. See also *Haggahot Maimuniyyot* [*Hag. Maim.*] *'Eruvin* 4:7(2); *RMP,* no. 558; *Hag. Maim. Shabbat* 12:5; *Sefer Or Zarua',* vol. 1, no. 478; E. Kupfer, *Teshuvot u-Pesaqim* (Jerusalem, 1973), 325.
10. See L. Finkelstein, *Jewish Self-Government in the Middle Ages,* 169. See also *RMP,* no. 971; R. Samson b. Ẓadoq, *Sefer Tashbeẓ* (Warsaw, 1876), no. 5; *SḤP,* sec. 968; *Responsa of R. Moses Mintz,* no. 42. On married students in the academies, see *SḤP,* secs. 954, 1526, 1985; *Siddur Ḥasidei Ashkenaz,* ed. M. Hershler, pp. 264 (= *Responsa of Rashi,* ed. I. Elfenbein, no. 100), 296; Rashi, *Berakhot* 17a, s.v. *ve-natrin le-gavraihu; SḤR,* p. 137 (= *SḤP,* sec. 375); *RMP,* no. 539; *Sefer ha-Orah,* ed. S. Buber, no. 143, (p. 224); and *Teshuvot Rashi,* ed. I. Elfenbein, no. 200. Some students returned home only for the periods of the major festivals. See N. Golb, *Toledot ha-Yehadim be-'Ir Rouen Bimei ha-Beinayim,* 36–38. The practice in many academies was to begin the study of a new tractate in the months of *Ḥeshvan* and *Iyyar.* See *Semaq,* no. 136 and *RMB,* no. 755 (p. 319). Cf. *Sefer Ḥuqqei ha-Torah,* below, App. A lines 83–84 and the sources cited in B. Dinur, *Yisrael ba-Golah,* vol. 2, pt. 6, pp. 37–38.
11. Even among the married students who lived in town with their families, some slept in a room at the academy and returned home only for

the Sabbath or at other intervals. See *Sefer Tashbeẓ,* no. 6: (= *Mord. Shabbat* no. 294): "Those young men [*baḥurim*] who go from place to place to study, and are not near their wives, must light the Sabbath candles with the blessing. . . . But one who is in the same city with his wife need not light candles in his room because his wife is lighting for him." See the variant readings in *Qoveẓ ʿal Yad* 11 (1985): 203 and R. Meir of Rothenburg, *Teshuvot, Pesaqim, u-Minhagim,* ed. I. Z. Kahana, 1:209. See also the description found in *Sefer Miẓvot Gadol, ʿaseh,* 64. On the historicity of this description, see J. Katz in *Qiryat Sefer* 31 (1956): 14. Cf. H. Soloveitchik, "Three Themes in the *Sefer Hasidim,*" *AJS Review* 1 (1976): 335, n. 73. This description implies that the students slept during the week in the place where they studied. Cf. the similar passage in *Sefer Or Zaruaʿ, Hilkhot Shabbat,* 2:67. See also the practice of Maharil cited by Assaf, *Meqorot,* 1:8, and *Sefer Ḥuqqei ha-Torah* (see App. A), lines 102–7.

12. Note the source describing the home–study hall of R. Tovia of Vienne cited in E. E. Urbach, *Baʿalei ha-Tosafot,* 1:487.
13. See Urbach, 1:22–24 and 2:676–80, 689–90, 738–40; Breuer, "Le-Ḥeqer," 45–48; Ha-Tosafai, "Ha-Pilpul," *Ha-Shiloaḥ* 19 (1908): 138–42.
14. See A. Grossman, "Yiḥus Mishpaḥah be-Ashkenaz ha-Qedumah," in *Studies in the History of Jewish Society in the Middle Ages and in the Modern Period,* ed. E. Etkes and Y. Salmon (Jerusalem, 1980), 9–23; idem, "On the Early Sages of Ashkenaz," *Immanuel* 15 (1982): 75–76; and H. Soloveitchik, "Three Themes," 339–54. Grossman argues that a good measure of academic freedom existed in the pre-Crusade academies despite the heavy emphasis on *yiḥus* as the determinant for leadership. Both Grossman and Soloveitchik maintain that the German Pietists also viewed good lineage as a prerequisite for spiritual leadership.
15. See M. Breuer, *Ha-Rabbanut be-Ashkenaz,* 11 and H. H. Ben-Sasson in *Beḥinot* 9 (1956): 44. See also I. Ta-Shema in *Meḥqerei Yerushalayim be-Maḥshevet Yisrael* 2 (1982–83): 418, n. 8. Grossman claims ("Yiḥus Mishpaḥah be-Ashkenaz ha-Qedumah," p. 14, n. 15) that Rashi might not have ascended to as prominent a position had the pre-Crusade period not been disrupted, because he was not descended from an important family. Cf. S. K. Mirsky, *Bein Zeriḥah li-Sheqiʿah* (New York, 1951), 71, who maintains that Rashi was descended from an important family of scholars in the pre-Crusade period and was related to several important scholars of the period. A view similar to that of Mirsky is held by S. Schwarzfuchs, "L'opposition Tsarfat-

Provence: La formation du Judaisme du Nord de la France," in *Hommage à Georges Vajda,* ed. G. Nahon and C. Touati (Louvain, 1980), 144. Cf. Grossman, "Haggirat Yehudim", 113–14 and n. 12.

16. On the importance of *yiḥus* for the appointment of communal leaders in the teachings of the German Pietists, see *SḤP,* sec. 17, 18, 37, 38, 50, 1493.
17. See I. Ta-Shema, "Sifriyyatam shel Ḥakhmei Ashkenaz Benei ha-Me'ah ha-11/ha 12," *Qiryat Sefer* 60 (1985): 298–309 and Urbach, 2:699–714.
18. See Urbach, 2:715–16. Cf. Ta-Shema in *Tarbiz* 55 (1985): 61–75 for one of the few examples of a commentary to Midrash in the twelfth century. On the much greater extent of commentaries to Midrash in the eleventh century, see Grossman, *Ḥakhmei Ashkenaz ha-Rishonim,* 418. Midrashim were also used to interpret *piyyut* in the twelfth century; but interpretation of *piyyut* was primarily the province of *pashtanim,* the German Pietists, or earlier German scholars who were conncected to the pre-Crusade period. See Urbach, *Arugat ha-Bosem,* vol. 4 (on the connection between *piyyut* and *torat ha-sod,* see esp. p. 73). Cf. Grossman, *Ḥakhmei Ashkenaz ha-Rishonim,* 422; H. Soloveitchik, "Three Themes," 352 and n. 131 regarding R. Tam; see also below, n. 136.
19. See B. Septimus, *Hispano-Jewish Society in Transition* (Cambridge, 1982), 50–51, 64–65; Ta-Shema in *Sefunot* 18 (1984): 99–100; idem., "Sefer Ha-Maskil- Ḥibbur Yehudi/Ẓarefati Bilti Yadua' mi-Sof ha-Me'ah ha-13," *Meḥqerei Yerushalayim* 2 (1982–83): 416–38 and the literature cited in nn. 3–4; M. Saperstein, *Decoding the Rabbis* (Cambridge, 1980), 7; Grossman, *Ḥakhmei Ashkenaz ha-Rishonim,* 424. There are no descriptions of any philosophical studies by the Tosafists in Urbach's *Ba'alei ha-Tosafot.* Cf. M. Idel, "Perush Mizmor 19 le–R. Yosef Bekhor Shor," *Alei Sefer* 9 (1981): 63–69. On the work of the enigmatic R. Moses Taku, see J. Dan's introduction to the Merkaz Dinur transcription of *Ketav Tamim* ms. Paris H 711 (Jerusalem, 1984), 9–14, 26–27.
20. Some messianic speculation and use of gematria for messianic predictions as well as for exegetical purposes was traditional, although these enterprises were almost always inspired by, or connected with, the German Pietists. See A. Marx in *Ha-Ẓofeh le-Ḥokhmat Yisrael* 5 (1921): 184–92; G. Cohen, "Messianic Postures of Ashkenazim and Sefardim," in *Studies of the Leo Baeck Institute* (New York, 1967), 128–32; and G. Scholem, *Major Trends in Jewish Mysticism,* 100. Urbach refers to *torat ha-sod* or *qabbalah* only in regard to the German Pietists or to scholars who were connected with them or with

their esoteric traditions. Cf. J. Katz in *Qiryat Sefer* 31 (1956): 16. See also G. Scholem, *Reshit ha-Qabbalah bi-Provence* (Tel Aviv, 1948), 162–63, 260 and below, n. 63.

21. See J. N. Epstein, "Tosafot Ashkenaziyyot ve-Italqiyyot Qedumot," *Tarbiz* 12 (1941): 190; Urbach, above, n. 13; Ta-Shema in *Alei Sefer* 2 (1976): 89–90.
22. See Ben-Sasson's review of Urbach in *Beḥinot* 9 (1956): 44; Ha-Tosafai, "Ha-Pilpul"; H. Soloveitchik, "Three Themes," 339; idem, "Can Halakhic Texts Talk History?" *AJS Review* 3 (1978): 178; and, most emphatically, idem, "Rabad of Posquières: A Programmatic Essay," in *Studies in the History of Jewish Society in the Middle Ages and in the Modern Period,* ed. E. Etkes and Y. Salmon (Jerusalem, 1980), 19: "Dialectic, dormant for three quarters of a millennium, was rediscovered by Rabbenu Tam and R. Isaac of Dampierre, and the two proceeded to do to the work of Abbaye and Rava what those *amoraim* had done to the Mishnah."
23. Grossman, *Ḥakhmei Ashkenaz ha-Rishonim,* 343, 419.
24. J. N. Epstein, "Perushei Worms u-Perushei Mayence," *Tarbiz* 4 (1937): 159. See also Urbach, 1:41–43.
25. See Urbach, 1:22, 48–56, 166–73 and J. Frankel, *Darko shel Rashi be-Perusho la-Talmud,* 203, n. 2. Riban's commentaries (which were sometimes called *tosafot*) seem more like addenda to Rashi's commentaries that were composed in Rashi's presence than critical *tosafot.* See Urbach, 1:38–41; I. Ta-Shema, "Ketav Yad Parma 933," *Alei Sefer* 5 (1978): 98. Riban's role is a transitional one and requires further investigation.
26. Interest in the rediscovered *Digesta* and the rest of the *Corpus iuris civilis* intensified in Europe after 1070. See S. Kuttner, *Harmony from Dissonance: An Interpretation of Medieval Canon Law* (Latrobe, 1960), 1–10; D. Knowles, *The Evolution of Medieval Thought* (New York, 1962), 156–67. Cf. B. Smalley, *The Study of the Bible in the Middle Ages,* 52–53.
27. Urbach, *Baʿalei ha-Tosafot* (Jerusalem, 1980); 2:744–52. In the first edition of his *Baʿalei ha-Tosafot* (1955) Urbach compares the Tosafists to the glossarists of Roman law (pp. 27–28). Noting some weaknesses in this comparison, he also compares them to Christian biblical scholars. Twersky, in his review of Urbach's book (*Tarbiz* 26 [1957]: 219–20), further questions both of these comparisons. Twersky briefly suggests that a better comparison might be made between the Tosafists and the canon lawyers. Urbach adopts this suggestion in his 1980 edition and also responds to several other criticisms made by Twersky in this area.

28. See Twersky, Review of *Ba'alei ha-Tosafot,* 218–19. Cf. Grossman, *Ḥakhmei Ashkenaz ha-Rishonim,* 423.
29. See D. Knowles, *The Evolution of Medieval Thought* (New York, 1962), 79–82; R. W. Southern, *The Making of the Middle Ages* (New Haven, 1953), 185–92; M. D. Chenu, *Nature, Man, and Society in the Twelfth Century* (Chicago, 1968), 300–309; J. Leclerq, *The Love for Learning and the Desire for God* (New York, 1961), 87–93. L. K. Little, *Religious Poverty and the Profit Economy in Medieval Europe* (Ithaca, 1978), 173–75. Cf. E. Touitou "Shittato ha-Parshanit shel Rashbam 'al Reqa ha-Meẓi'ut ha-Historit shel Zemanno," in *Iyyunim be-Sifrut Ḥazal ba-Miqra uve-Toledot Yisrael,* ed. Y. D. Gilat et al. (Ramat Gan, 1982), 60–61.
30. G. Paré, A. Brunet, and P. Tremblay, *La renaissance du XIIème siècle: Les écoles et L'enseignment,* 18–38; Chenu, *Nature, Man, and Society;* Southern, *The Making of the Middle Ages,* 193–203; idem, "The Schools of Paris and the School of Chartres," in *Renaissance and Renewal in the Twelfth Century,* ed. R. L. Benson and G. Constable (Cambridge, MA, 1982), 113–32. Even the importance of Paris as a center of learning was based initially on the presence of well-known independent masters, not on the reputation of a single school. See also R. W. Hunt, "English Learning in the Late Twelfth Century," in *Essays in Medieval History,* ed. R. W. Southern (London, 1968), 106–8 and A. L. Gabriel, *Garlandia* (see chap. 4, n. 18).
31. Chenu, *Nature, Man, and Society,* 291–300; Paré, Brunet, and Tremblay, *La renaissance,* 110–23; J. W. Baldwin, *Masters, Princes, and Merchants,* 88–101; Knowles, *Evolution of Medieval Thought,* 174–75; and above, chapter four, n. 57.
32. Knowles, *Evolution of Medieval Thought,* 93–106; S. G. Kuttner, *Harmony from Dissonance,* 12, 24.
33. G. Leff, *Medieval Thought* (Manchester, 1962), 93–115; Knowles, *Evolution of Medieval Thought,* 116–40, 178–84.
34. Chenu, *Nature, Man, and Society,* 270–72; Little, *Religious Poverty,* 26–27. Cf. U. T. Holmes, "Transition in European Education," *Twelfth Century Europe and the Foundations of Modern Society,* ed. M. Clagett et al. (Madison 1961), 15–38. Regarding the notion of intellectual progress, see Chenu, *Nature, Man, and Society,* 310–33.
35. See Soloveitchik, "Three Themes," 342–43, 348–49.
36. See above, chap. 4.
37. See Y. Baer, "Rashi veha-Meẓi'ut ha-Historit shel Zemanno," *Tarbiz* 20 (1950): 326; idem in *Zion* 3 (1937): 5; E. Shereshevsky, "Rashi and Christian Interpretation," *JQR* 61 (1970–71): 76–86; A. Grabois,

"The Hebraica Veritas and Jewish-Christian Intellectual Relations in the Twelfth Century," *Speculum* 50 (1975): 332. D. Berger's skepticism about the degree of proof offered in these studies ("Mission to the Jews and Jewish Christian Contacts in the Polemical Literature of the High Middle Ages," *American Historical Review* 91 [1986]: 589, n. 86) is appropriate. See also Grossman, *Ḥakhmei Ashkenaz,* 424. Cf. S. Kamin, "Dugma be-Perush Rashi le-Shir ha-Sharim," *Tarbiz* 52 (1983): 58; idem, "Perush Rashi u-Perush Origen le-Shir ha-Shirim," *Shenaton la-Miqra ule-Ḥeqer ha-Mizraḥ ha-Qadum* 7–8 (1984): 246, n. 121; *SḤP,* 259; S. Kogut, "The Language in *Sefer Ḥasidim,* Its Linguistic Backround, and Methods of Research," *Studies in Medieval Jewish History and Literature,* ed. I. Twersky, (Cambridge, 1984), 2:98, 101; *Sefer Rabiah,* 2:253–56; S. Z. Leiman in *JQR* 74(1983): 191–92, n. 52; Urbach, 1:210–11; I. Ta-Shema in *Shenaton ha-Mishpat ha-ʿIvri* 6–7 (1979–80): 417–21; N. Golb, *Toledot ha-Yehudim be-ʿIr Rouen,* 136, n. 382, and below, n. 46.

38. See D. Berger, "Mission to the Jews," 576–91.
39. See B. Smalley, *The Study of the Bible in the Middle Ages,* 2d ed. (Oxford, 1951), 148–72, 175–76, 197–99, 234–35; J. Cohen, "Scholarship and Intolerance in the Medieval Academy: The Study and Evaluation of Judaism in European Christendom," *AHR* 91 (1986): 596–600. See also C. Leviant, *King Artus* (New York, 1969), 76–79. On Abelard's knowledge of Hebrew, see Grabois, "The Hebraica Veritas," 617, n. 20, and 628. Cf. P. Payer, ed., *A Dialogue of a Philosopher with a Jew and a Christian* (Toronto, 1979), 9 and D. Berger, "Mission to the Jews," 584. Abelard tells Heloise that he *listened* to a Jew teaching the Book of Kings; see *Patrologia Latina* vol. 178, col. 718.
40. E. Touitou, "Shittato he-Parshanit shel Rashbam," 48–74; idem, "Peshat ve-Apologetiqah be-Ferush ha-Rashbam le-Sippur Moshe sheba-Torah," *Tarbiz* 51 (1982): 227–38; S. Kamin, "Dugma be-Ferush Rashi," 54–58; idem, "Perush Rashi u-Ferush Origen," 229–48. See also M. Signer, "King/Messiah in Rashi's Exegesis of Psalms 2," *Prooftexts* 3 (1983): 273–78; Kamin, "Affinities between Jewish and Christian Exegesis in Twelfth-Century Northern France," *Proceedings of the Ninth World Congress of Jewish Studies,* ed. M. Goshen-Gottstein (Jerusalem, 1988), 141–55, and "Rashbam's Concept of the Creation in Light of the Intellectual Currents of His Time," in *Scripta Hierosolymitana,* vol. 31 [Studies in Bible], ed. S. Japhet (Jerusalem, 1986), 91–132.
41. See Urbach, 1:17 and R. Chazan, *Medieval Jewry in Northern France,* 10–11, 31–32. Grabois describes in vivid detail the close intellectual,

economic, and social contact that Jews had with Christians in several towns and cities and notes the presence of leading Jewish and Christian scholars in the same locale at the same time. See Grabois, "Hebraica Veritas," 620, n. 32, 625, n. 55, and 631–33.

42. D. Knowles, *Evolution of Medieval Thought,* 177–78. See also S. Kuttner, *Harmony from Dissonance,* 12–26; R. W. Southern, *The Making of the Middle Ages,* 205–6; G. Leff, *Medieval Thought,* 130–31. Cf. J. T. Noonan in *Traditio* 35 (1979): 145–72.
43. Regarding the attitiude of the German Pietists toward dialectic, see chap. 6. Their objections were similar to those of Rupert of Deutz. See above, n. 34.
44. *SḤP,* sec. 752. Urbach (2:745–46) implausibly maintains that this passage refers to contacts that Jews had with Christians in the area of biblical studies. See Kogut, "Language in *Sefer Ḥasidim.*"
45. Ta-Shema, "Miẓvat Talmud Torah ki-Veʿayah Ḥevratit/Datit be-*Sefer Ḥasidm,*" *Bar Ilan* 14–15 (1977): 107.
46. The *SḤP* passage demonstrates Jewish awareness of the dialectical method in Germany. Awareness on the part of Jews in northern France would appear to be even more likely. S. Albeck (*Zion* 19 [1954]: 112–13) suggests that R. Tam's somewhat radical programmatic statements and overall position concerning the need to resolve divergent sources and practices was perhaps the product of intellectual contacts with scholastics who held that it was necessary to harmonize all new speculations with accepted sources. Albeck assumes that this basic principle was clear enough and valuable enough to be attractive to the Jewish scholar who heard it from Christian colleagues. Cf. Urbach, 1:87. Y. Baer ("Ha-Megammah ha-Ḥevratit/Datit be-Sefer Ḥasidim," *Zion* 1 [1937]: 5–7, 20–29) maintains that the German Pietists adapted certain principles of Christian spirituality which they either read about in Christian theological literature or heard from preachers. See also H. Soloveitchik, "Three Themes," 316–17.
47. See Soloveitchik, "Three Themes," 347–48; idem, "Rabad of Posquières," 16. The period of creativity in Christian circles peaked in the last quarter of the thirteenth century. See D. Knowles, *Evolution of Medical Thought,* 291–317 and E. Gilson, *The History of Christian Philosophy in the Middle Ages* (New York, 1955).
48. Urbach, vol. 2, chaps. 11 and 12, esp. pp. 521, 571–73, 596. See also I. Ta-Shema in *Alei Sefer* 4 (1977): 26–41.
49. See R. Ḥayyim Or Zaruaʿ, *Responsa,* no. 163. (Cf. Urbach; in *Qiryat Sefer* 31 [1956]: 16; Katz and J. N. Epstein in *REJ* 61 [1911]: 226). Cf. also R. Asher b. Yeḥiel, *Responsa* 20:27; R. Isaac of Corbeil,

Ammudei Golah, intro.; *Sefer Or Zarua*ʿ 1:416; and Urbach, 2:585–86. R. Pereẓ writes that *ein anu benei Torah kemo ha-rishonim;* but this may be part of a general Tosafist perception (expressed by some already in the twelfth century) that their best scholarship did not qualify them as true scholars as compared to those of the Talmudic period and thus did not entitle them to the prerogatives of Torah scholars. See *Tosafot R. Pereẓ* to *Beiẓah* 6a, s.v. *ha'idna; Tosafot Ḥagigah* 22b, s.v. *ke-man;* Urbach, 1:233; *Sefer Yere'im ha-Shalem,* no. 116; the sources cited in Urbach, 1:481, n. 14; and above, chap. 3. As a result of this self-perception, Tosafists advised that they were no longer capable of discerning some halakhic distinctions or performing certain legal functions. See, e.g., *Haggahot Asheri Sanhedrin* 3:28; *Tosafot Bekhorot,* 36b, s.v. *pesaq; Darkhei Moshe, Yoreh De'ah* 57:11. See, generally, H. J. Zimmels, "The Significance of the Statement 'We are not acquainted any more' As Echoed in Rabbinic Literature," *Leo Jung Jubilee Volume,* ed. M. M. Kasher et al. (New York, 1962), 223–35 and Y. Dinari, *Ḥakhmei Ashkenaz be-Shilhei Yemei ha-Beinayim* (Jerusalem, 1984), 17–40. See also Urbach, 1:391, 2:529; and I. A. Agus, *Teshuvot Ba'alei ha-Tosafot,* 37, 175–76, 189, and below, chap. 6. On rowdiness among students, see Urbach, 1:487, 2:572. Cf. L. Rabinowitz, *The Social Life of the Jews in Northern France* (repr. New York, 1972), 225–29 and C. H. Haskins, *Studies in Medieval Culture* (repr. New York, 1965), 49–71.

50. I. Ta-Shema, "Yediʿot Ḥadashot ʿal Tosafot Gornish ve-Inyanan," *Alei Sefer* 2 (1976): 84–90 and Urbach, 2:783ff.
51. See now A. Arieli's note in *Alei Sefer* 16(1989): 149–50, and *Olat Shelomoh* (Petach Tikva, 1989), 1:14–17.
52. On the shortage of books caused by the burning of the Talmud and the effect of this shortage on Talmudic studies, see Urbach, 1:455–56, 482–84 and 2:633, 636, 656–57, 670–71. See also I. Ta-Shema, "Ketav Yad Parma 933 (Tosafot Ḥakhmei Angliyyah) ve-Erko," *Alei Sefer* 5 (1978): 100; *Tosafot Ḥakhmei Evreux 'al Massekhet Sotah* (Jerusalem, 1969), ed. J. Lifshitz, p. 13, n. 57. Cf. Urbach, 1:483, n. *21.
53. See the references in Urbach cited above, n. 52, and see also Urbach, 2:632, 655. Ta-Shema ("Ketav Yad Parma 933," 100, n. 21) maintains that Lifshitz' identification of *Tosafot Sens le-Sotah* as *tosafot* that were in fact produced at the academy of Evreux (see Lifshitz, *Tosafot Ḥakhmei Evreaux,* 13–16) is incorrect but cites no proof for this assertion. Urbach (2:291, 1:481, n. *17) accepts Lifshitz's identification. On the origin of *Tosafot Rashba le-Massekhet Menaḥot* in Evreux, see J. Lifshitz, ed., *Sanhedrei Gedolah* (Jerusalem, 1974), 6:34–37.

54. See, esp., Urbach, 2:579–99.
55. S. W. Baron, *A Social and Religious History of the Jews,* 9:65–71. Note that Urbach in the fourth, revised edition of his *Ba'alei ha-Tosafot* subtly modified the broad claim that he had advanced in the first edition that church statutes mandating the elimination of Jewish books led to the ultimate destruction of Jewish spiritual life in northern France. Compare p. 455 of the fourth edition to p. 377 of the first edition.
56. See H. Soloveitchik, "Three Themes," 339–47; Ta-Shema, "Miẓvat Talmud Torah," 98–109; and I. Marcus, *Piety and Society,* 102–6; and esp. *SḤP,* sec. 801:

    ובזמן הזה שאין חכמה, צריך לרב לפרש הכל. גם אם יכתוב פירושים יפרש הכל כדי שלא יהא יגיע לחשוב ויתבטל משאר דברי תורה.

57. See my *Educational Theory and Practice in Ashkenaz During the High Middle Ages* (Ph.D. diss., Yeshiva University, 1987), 176–80, 202–10 and I. Ta-Shema, "Ḥasidut Ashkenaz bi-Sefarad: Rabbenu Yonah Gerondi- Ha-Ish u-Foʿalo," in *Galut Aḥar Golah,* ed. A. Mirsky et al. (Jerusalem, 1988), 165–73. (Cf. Urbach, 1:483–84 and 2:569–70 and 671, n. 58*.)
58. On the systematic coverage of *Seder Qodashim* in the academy of Evreux, see Urbach, 1:481–82 and J. Lifshitz, *Tosafot Evreux 'al Massekhet Sotah,* 19.
59. See R. Shelomoh Luria, *Yam shel Shelomoh,* intro. to *Ḥullin.* See also his *Responsa,* no. 29 (description of R. Elyaqim ha-Levi).
60. See R. Menaḥem Ha-Meiri, *Bet ha-Beḥirah 'al Massekhet Avot,* ed. B. Perag, p. 54; *Bet ha-Beḥirah 'al Massekhet Miqva'ot,* ed. A. Sofer (Jerusalem, 1939), 1; R. Asher b. Yeḥiel, *Responsa,* 31:9; R. Isaac bar Sheshet, *Responsa,* no. 375. Cf. H. Soloveitchik, "Rabad of Posquières," 13–14, 25; I. Twersky, *Rabad of Posquières,* 15; *Introduction to the Code of Maimonides,* 205–10. A perusal of *Sarei ha-Elef,* ed. M. M. Kasher and D. B. Mandelbaum, 1:165–331, will show that the number of published Ashkenazic commentaries and different *tosafot* collections on the tractates in *Seder Qodashim* (especially tractates and sections that had little halakhic relevance) is markedly smaller than for other more mainstream tractates and orders. Cf. the final section of *Sefer Ḥuqqei ha-Torah,* App. A, and R. Isaac of Corbeil, *Sefer Miẓvot Qatan,* intro.
61. On R. Moshe's criticisms of R. Yehudah he-Ḥasid, see Urbach, 1:420–25 and J. Dan's introduction to the *Merkaz Dinur* edition of R. Moses, *Ketav Tamim* (ms. Paris H 711) (Jerusalem, 1984). Regarding

pilpul, see Urbach, 1:26 and Ta-Shema, "Miẓvat Talmud Torah," 104, n. 5.

62. See *SḤP,* secs. 1 (p. 2), 1509; cf. secs. 765, 1495.
63. See Y. Sussman, "Massoret Limmud u-Massoret Nusaḥ shel Talmud Yerushalmi," in *Meḥqarim le-Sifrut Talmudit le-Regel Melot Shemonim Shanah le-Shaul Liberman* (Jerusalem, 1983), 14, n. 11. Sussman maintains that a circle of thirteenth-century Spires scholars who were closely linked (and in most cases related) to the *Ḥasidei Ashkenaz* attempted to stretch the scope of study of the "three orders" to include *Qodashim* and many other relatively neglected areas such as *aggadah, piyyut, tefillah.* This circle produced commentaries to *Seder Qodashim, midreshei halakhah ve-aggadah,* and *Talmud Yerushalmi.* Sussman also notes (pp. 34–35) that the German Pietists, their relatives, and their students were practically the only *rishonim* to produce commentaries on *Yerushalmi Sheqalim.* See Urbach, 1:405, n. 20. There is one commentary to *Sheqalim,* ostensibly not from this group, which S. Lieberman (*Sefer ha-Yovel Likhvod A. Marx,* 295) attributed to a student of R. Samuel b. Shneur of Evreux. Both Urbach (1:405) and Sussman (p. 35) reject this identification and suggest that this commentary was authored by R. Eleazar Roqeaḥ or one of his circle. See also Urbach in *Qiryat Sefer* 31 (1957): 326–27; idem, *Ba'alei ha-Tosafot,* 1:482. If our argument concerning the brothers of Evreux is correct, Lieberman's attribution of the commentary to R. Samuel of Evreux can perhaps be retained.
64. See A. Grossman, *Ḥakhmei Ashkenaz ha-Rishonim,* 165–70. On the desire of the German Pietists to return to the intellectual values of the pre-Crusade period, see H. Soloveitchik, "Three Themes," 345–54 and below, chap. 6.
65. *Haggahot R. Pereẓ to Semaq,* sec. 11, n. 3.
66. Urbach, 1:480. See below, n. 71.
67. *Orḥot Ḥayyim* (repr. Jerusalem, 1957), 1:229 (end of the chapter entitled "Inyanim Aḥerim bi-Teshuvah"); *Kol Bo,* no. 66 (end), fol. 32a.
68. On the deeper meaning and centrality of the phrase *yir'at ha-ḥet* in the thought of the German Pietists, see H. Soloveitchik, "Three Themes," 326, and 334, n. 72.
69. T. Preschel ("Iggeret she-Yuḥasah be-Ta'ut la-Ramban," *Talpiyyot* 8 (1961): 49–53) argues convincingly that the core of the well-known epistle attributed to Nahmanides, *Shema beni mussar avikha,* was in fact written by R. Moses of Evreux. He notes the close parallel between the second half of the so-called *Iggeret ha-Ramban* and a section of the *Kol Bo* passage attributed to R. Moses of Evreux. The first

part of this letter may thus have been a later addendum, as Preschel argues with regard to some concluding phrases that do not appear in the *Kol Bo* text. The text that we can be certain was written by R. Moses of Evreux has four components. The fourth section is the one on *kavvanah.* The third says that the goal of Torah study should be to perform that which was studied. The second says that one should always assume that others are better than him and that he therefore must honor and speak respectfully to all others. One phrase in this section, *hitbayesh mi-kol adam va-adam,* might reflect the strong emphasis placed by Pietists on the need to tolerate humiliation (H. Soloveitchik, "Three Themes," 329). Another, "Do not look at a person's face when speaking to him," is found in a passage in sec. 53 of the Bologna edition of *Sefer Ḥasidim* (ed. R. Margaliyyot). The first section advises that anger should be avoided. This will lead to a constant state of modesty, which is to be pursued. Cf. Y. Baer, "Ha-Megammah ha-Datit/ha-Ḥevratit," 9–10.

70. *SḤB,* no. 754 and H. Soloveitchik, "Three Themes," 344–45.
71. R. Pereẓ to *Semaq,* no. 96; cf. Rabad to *Hilkhot Qeri'at Shema* 4:8 and esp. *Tosafot Berakhot* 17b, s.v. *Rav Shisha.* See Urbach, 1:481.
72. See *Siddur Ḥasidei Ashkenaz* (Jerusalem, 1972), ed. M. Hershler, 184 and also 88, n. 78.
73. See *Shittah ʿal Moʿed Qatan le-Talmido shel R. Yeḥiel mi-Paris,* ed. M. Zaks (Jerusalem, 1937), 2:113. R. Yedidyah may have been the teacher of R. Yehudah he-Ḥasid's son, R. Zal(t)man. See Urbach, 1:569, n. 25. R. Samuel of Evreux was the teacher of R. Isaac of Corbeil, who bore the title Ḥasid (Urbach, 1:572–73), and R. Meir of Rothenburg, who was under the influence of the German Pietists. See below, n. 85.
74. On the title Ḥasid and the connection of those who held it to the German Pietists or to their ancestors, see Urbach, 1:151, 228, 237. See also J. Dan, *Torat ha-Sod shel Ḥasidut Ashkenaz* (Jerusalem, 1968), 41. Regarding the mystical traditions of the scholars of Corbeil and the connection to German Pietism, see G. Scholem, *Reshit ha-Qabbalah bi-Provence,* 162–63, 260 and Dan, "*Iggeret Germaiza* u-Veʿayat ha-Pseudo Epigraphah ba-Qabbalah ha-Qedumah," in *Studies in Jewish Mysticism, Philosophy, and Ethical Literature,* ed. J. Dan et al. (Jerusalem, 1986), 111–38.
75. See Urbach, 1:485, n. 28* regarding *Sefer ʿal Ha-Kol,* an unusual handbook of legal decisions and customs devoted in large measure to the laws and the correct text (*nusaḥ*) of the prayers. See also *Sefer Zikkaron le–R. Shmuel Kalman Mirsky,* 187, 193–94. R. Moses himself

apparently composed a *siddur;* a fourth non-Tosafist brother, Judah, wrote *piyyutim.* See *Gallia judaica,* 40–41.

76. See J. Dan, "The Emergence of Mystical Prayer," in *Studies in Jewish Mysticism,* ed. J. Dan and F. Talmage (Cambridge, 1982), 87–107 and H. Soloveitchik,, "Three Themes," 330–35, 352–53. See also I. Ta-Shema in *Alei Sefer* 4 (1978): 31–34, 41 and Y. Kamelhar, *Rabbenu Eleazar Roqeaḥ* (Raisha, 1930), 67–73.

77. See the literature cited by B. Richler, "Al Kitvei ha-Yad shel Sefer Ha-Yir'ah ha-Meyuḥas le–R. Yonah Gerondi," *Alei Sefer* 8 (1981): 51, nn. 1–2. R. Aaron ha-Kohen of Lunel, in his *Orḥot Ḥayyim,* cites three passages from *Sefer Ḥayyei Olam* and attributes them to "Ri he-Ḥasid." Richler (pp. 52–54) notes that this work is attributed in some mss. to R. Isaac he-Ḥasid, in some to R. Yonah he-Ḥasid, and in some to R. Yehudah he-Ḥasid. In several mss. this work was copied right after *ʿAmmudei Golah/Semaq,* whose author, R. Isaac of Corbeil, was referred to as he-Ḥasid; see above, n. 73. See also Ta-Shema, "Ḥasidut Ashkenaz bi-Sefarad," 169.

78. See Urbach, 1:479; A. T. Shrock, *R. Jonah b. Abraham of Gerona* (New York, 1948), pp. 28–31; J. Lifshitz' introduction to *Tosafot Evreux ʿal Massekhet Sotah,* 21–22. To these add *Orḥot Ḥayyim, Hilkhot Tefillin,* sec. 4 (1:15) and *Ḥiddushei ha-Rashba li-Nedarim,* 80a, s.v. *hekhi.* On the composition of the remainder of Rabbenu Yonah's ethical corpus and its relationship to German Pietism, see I. Ta-Shema, "Ḥasidut Ashkenaz bi-Sefarad," 171, 181–88; J. Dan in *Meḥqerei Yerushalayim be-Maḥshevet Yisrael* 6 (1987): 130–31; idem, *Jewish Mysticism and Jewish Ethics* (Seattle, 1986), 28–75; idem, "Ha-Reqa ha-Raʿayoni le-Hitgabshutah shel Sifrut ha-Mussar ba-Me'ah ha-13," *Meḥqerei Yerushalayim* 7 (1988): 250–60; S. Shokek, *Sefer ha-Yashar be-Misgeret Sifrut ha-Mussar ha-ʿIvrit* (Ph.D. diss., Hebrew University, 1986), 29, 37–46, 64–72, 114–16, 135–44, 335–41; and now idem, "Ziqato shel Sefer ha-Yashar le-Ḥug Mequbbalei Gerona," *Meḥqerei Yerushalayim* 6 (1987): 337–66; A. Shrock, *R. Jonah,* 78–87, 143. R. Yonah is referred to as Ḥasid, but it is unreasonable to attribute this solely to his possible association with the German Pietists. See C. Chavel, *Rabbenu Moshe b. Naḥman,* 57; B. Dinur, *Yisrael ba-Golah,* vol. 2, pt. 3, pp. 251–52. On the connections between the esoteric teachings of Gerona and the German Pietists, see J. Dan, *Torat ha-Sod shel Ḥasidut Ashkenaz,* 116–28.

79. Richler ("Al Kitvei," 55) notes that of the forty extant manuscripts only five non-Ashkenazic ones (two of which were copied from the first edition) mention the name of R. Samuel. Since this work does

not usually cite names at all, it is possible that the reference to R. Samuel was a later addendum. Still, Richler (in his summary, p. 57) suggests on the basis of this citation that R. Yonah did write *Sefer ha-Yir'ah.* The attribution to R. Samuel may be confirmed by noting that R. Yosef Ḥaviva (*Nimmuqei Yosef, Hilkhot Ẓiẓit*—found in standard editions of the Talmud following *Massekhet Menaḥot*, fol. 12a) records a statement of Ritba who cites this view as a "comment of R. Yonah in the name of R. Moshe b. Shneur of Evreux." (The names of the brothers are associated with R. Yonah interchangeably.) On R. Yonah's presence in Ashkenaz see Ta-Shema in *Sinai* 66 (1970): 345–46, and "Ḥasidut Ashkenaz bi-Sefarad," 173–75. Cf. *Ma'aser Kesafim,* ed. C. Domb (Jerusalem, 1980), 24, 33. On his role in the Maimonidean controversy as an emissary sent to enlist the support of *rabbanei ẓarefat* for the position of the anti-Maimunists, see A. Shohat, "Berurim be-Parashat ha-Pulmus ha-Rishon 'al Sifrei ha-Rambam," *Zion* 36 (1971): 27–37.

80. Bodl. 875 (all Bodleian ms. numbers are according to A. Neubauer's catalog), contains *'Ammudei Golah* (= *Semaq*) followed by *Ḥayyei Olam* and a version of *Sefer Ḥasidim* that has predominantly French glosses; see below, n. 86. Bodl. 1098 and Breslau 255 also juxtapose *Sefer Ḥayyei Olam* and *Sefer Ḥasidut/Ḥasidim.* Bodl. 2343 and 1114 group it with *Shir ha-Yiḥud* and *Sod ha-Teshuvah le–R. Yehudah he-Ḥasid.* (On the composition of *Shir ha-Yiḥud* by a German Pietist, see J. Dan's introduction to the Jewish National and University Library's edition of this work [Jerusalem, 1981], 7–11). Bodl. 884 groups it with *Semaq* and *Ẓava'at R. Yehudah he-Ḥasid.* Bodl. 2274 places it next to R. Eleazar Roqeaḥ's *Hilkhot Teshuvah.* Regarding the use of *Sefer Ḥayyei Olam* in Ashkenaz, see I. Elfenbein ed., *Sefer Minhagim de-Vei Maharam mi-Rothenburg* (New York, 1938), xx.

81. Richler, "Al Kitvei," 52–54. The Ashkenazic mss. are from the thirteenth and fourteenth centuries and the Spanish ones are from the fifteenth and sixteenth. Richler shows (p. 54) that despite A. Loewenthal's claim that all the laws found in *Sefer ha-Yir'ah* correspond to positions taken by the commentary of the students of R. Jonah to *Hilkhot ha-Rif le-Massekhet Berakhot,* there are at least two cases where this is not true. This objection is weak because it is not clear that positions of the "students of R. Yonah" (= R. Shelomoh bar Ali; see C. Chavel, *Rabbenu Moshe b. Naḥman,* 69–70 and A. Neubauer, *Meqorot Le-Toledot ha-Yehudim,* 1:103; cf. I. Ta-Shema, "Ḥasidut Ashkenaz bi-Sefarad," 177) always correspond to positions attributed directly to R. Yonah. Also, in regard to the second contradiction

concerning the number of words in *Qeri'at Shema,* note that the position of *Sefer Ḥayyei Olam* corresponds precisely to that of R. Yehudah he-Ḥasid. See *Shibbolei ha-Leqet,* ed. S. Buber, p. 14. Perhaps R. Yonah favored the Ashkenazic custom while a student in Ashkenaz and reverted to the Spanish custom when he returned there to teach. See I. Ta-Shema, "E-l Melekh Ne'eman- Gilgulo shel Minhag," *Tarbiz* 39 (1969): 184–94. Cf. S. Z. Havlin in *Tarbiz* 40 (1970): 108, n. 6.

82. N. Bronznick. "Baʿaluto shel R. Yonah Gerondi ʿal Sefer Shaʿarei ha-Avodah ha-Nidpas," *Ha-Darom* 28 (1969): 238–42.

83. See S. Lieberman, ed., *Midrash Devarim Rabbah* (Jerusalem, 1965), 14–15 and 134n.

84. See A. Grossman, *Ḥakhmei Ashkenaz ha-Rishonim* (Jerusalem, 1981), 293. It should be noted that the stylistic and methodological differences between *Shaʿarei Avodah* and acknowledged works of R. Yonah noted by Bronznick are in many cases not significant. Moreover, Bronznick has reached conclusions concerning the authorship of *Shaʿarei Avodah* based upon a misjudgement of R. Yonah's relationship to Spanish *Kabbalah.* See J. Dan, *Jewish Mysticism* (see n. 78) and I. Ta-Shema, "Ḥasidut Ashkenaz bi-Sefarad," 190–91.

85. See E. E. Urbach, *Baʿalei Ha-Tosafot,* 4th ed. (Jerusalem, 1980), 1:199, 207, 369–70, 375, 390, 437, 522, 564. See also Y. Sussman "Massoret Limmud," (above n. 63); Y. S. Lange, ed., *Taʿamei Massoret ha-Miqra le–R. Yehudah he-Ḥasid* (Jerusalem, 1981), 11; *Sefer Or Zaruaʿ* 2:281; N. Wieder, "*Barukh Hu (u-)Varukh Shemo*—Meqoro, Zemanno, ve-Nusaḥo," in *Iyyunim be-Sifrut Ḥazal, ba-Miqra uve-Toledot Yisrael,* ed. Y. Gilat et al. (Ramat Gan, 1982), 277–80; I. Ta-Shema, "*Sefer ha-Maskil*—Ḥibbur Yehudi Ẓarefati Bilti-Yaduaʿ mi-Sof ha-Me'ah ha-13," *Meḥqerei Yerushalayim be-Maḥshevet Yisrael* 2 (1983): 428–32; idem, "Rabbenu Dan mi-Galut Ashkenaz asher bi-Sefarad," in *Studies in Jewish Mysticism, Philosophy, and Ethical Literature,* ed. J. Dan and J. Hacker (Jerusalem, 1986), 385–94; E. Zimmer, "Moʿadei Nesi'at Kappayim," *Sinai* 100 (1987): 405–8. There was some contact between R. Yehudah and R. Eleazar and older contemporaries who studied in northern France. See Urbach, 1:161, 214, 237. Urbach (1:408–9) asserts that the teachings of Roqeaḥ spread quickly throughout Christian Europe, carrying with them the message of German Pietism—though he also admits that Roqeaḥ is not mentioned much by subsequent French halakhists. But the only source adduced by Urbach to support his claim is the statement of Ramban in his letter of 1232 to the *rabbanei Ẓarefat* that

he knows that a particular theological text of Roqeaḥ from which he has cited is "to be found amongst you." See R. Ẓadoq ha-Kohen, *Divrei Soferim* (Bnai Brak, 1967), 55. On the significance of this passage in regard to the spread of Roqeah's kabbalistic teachings, see J. Dan, "Le-Ḥeqer ha-Aggadot ʿal R. Eleazar mi-Worms," *Sinai* 74 (1974): 171–77. On the impact of Roqeaḥ's esoteric works upon the kabbalistic schools in both Provence and Gerona, see above, n. 78.

86. See I. Marcus in *PAAJR* 45 (1978): 152–53; idem, Introduction to *Sefer* Ḥasidim [ms. Parma H3280] (Jerusalem, 1985) 10 n. 11. For the existence of small pietistic circles in northern France and England that produced mystical treatises bearing similarities to esoteric works of German Pietism, see G. Vajda, "R. Elḥanan Isaac b. Yaqar mi-London veha-Ideologiyyah ha-Noẓrit shel Zemanno," in *Proceedings of the Third World Jewish Congress* (Jerusalem, 1969), 315; E. Kupfer, "Le-Toledot Mishpaḥat R. Moses bar Yom Tov mi-London," *Tarbiz* 40 (1970–71): 385–87; J. Dan in *Qoveẓ ʿal Yad* n.s. 6 no. 1 (1966): 201; idem, "The Ashkenazi Ḥasidic Gates of Wisdom," in *Hommage à G. Vajda* (above, n. 15), 183–89; M. Saks, *Pisqei R. Eliyyahu mi-London,* 39–41; and C. Roth, *The Intellectual Activities of Medieval English Jewry* (London, 1948), 62–64.

87. See Urbach, 1:466–70; J. Katz, *Exclusiveness and Tolerance,* 102–5; I. Ta-Shema, "Ḥasidut Ashkenaz bi-Sefarad," 170–71. It is interesting to note that while R. Moses of Coucy and Rabbenu Yonah, both inspired by the German Pietists, were among the very few prominent medieval Jewish scholars to call for, and actually attempt, public preaching on matters of religious observance, their views on how far to pursue the sinner differed. As opposed to Maimonides' position (and that of R. Eliezer of Metz), both R. Moses of Coucy and the author of *Sefer Ḥasidim* felt that the obligation to rebuke another was in effect only if the critic thought that his words might be heeded. See H. Soloveitchik, "Three Themes," 336, n. 82; I. Marcus, *Piety and Society,* 87–88; Yassif, "Ha-Sippur," (chap. 2, n. 29), 243–44, n. 53. R. Yonah's view on the requirement to offer rebuke even when it will not be heeded is closer to the Maimonidean position. See B. Septimus, "Piety and Power in Thirteenth-Century Catalonia," in *Studies in Medieval Jewish History and Literature,* ed. I. Twersky (Cambridge, MA, 1979), 215–21. Cf. N. Lamm, "Hokheaḥ Tokhiaḥ et Amitekha," *Gesher* 10 (1982): 170–76 and Y. Baer, "Ha-Megammah ha-Datit/ha-Ḥevratit," 1–10.

88. See I. Ta-Shema, "Qavvim le-Ofyah shel Sifrut ha-Halakkah be-Ashkenaz be-Me'ot ha-Yod Gimel/Yod Daled," *Alei Sefer* 4 (1977):

32–34; idem, "Miẓvat Talmud Torah ki-Veʿayah Ḥevratit-Datit be-Sefer Ḥasidim," *Bar Ilan* 14–15 (1977): 104–6; and H. Soloveitchik, "Three Themes," 349–51.

89. R. Isaac of Corbeil, who studied at Evreux, also had some affinity to the German Pietists. See above, nn. 73, 74, and 80 and I. Ta-Shema, "Hasidut Ashkenaz bi-Sefarad," 168, n. 8.
90. See above, n. 49.
91. H. Soloveitchik, "Three Themes," 350–54.
92. In addition to the degree of influence, the very presence of German Pietists in the communities of northern France remains an open question. The Pietist critiques of French liturgical practices and intellectual proclivities (see above, n. 76, and chap. 6) do not prove that there were any Pietists who actually lived in northern France. The French practices that were anathema to the Pietists could easily have been criticized from afar. Cf. I. Marcus, *Piety and Power* (Leiden, 1981), 168, n. 80.
93. *Tosafot Qiddushin,* 30a s.v. *la ẓerikha; Sanhedrin,* 24a s.v. *belulah;* and *Avodah Zarah,* 19a s.v. *yeshallesh.* See also R. Ḥayyim Yosef David Azulai (*Shem ha-Gedolim* [Warsaw, 1876], 116), who attributed the following statement to R. Tam: "I will engage in interpretation of the Talmud, as my revered grandfather did. But biblical interpretation I will not undertake for I have not the capacity to do it." The ordinance attributed to R. Tam by S. Assaf, *Meqorot le-Toledot ha-Ḥinnukh be-Yisrael,* 1:4, implying that only those who could not study Talmud should study Scripture, was an ordinance of the Rhineland communities issued in the 1220s. See L. Finkelstein, *Jewish Self-Government in the Middle Ages,* 231, and above, chap. 1, n. 37. Cf. F. Talmage, "Keep Your Sons from Scripture: The Bible in Medieval Jewish Scholarship and Spirituality," in *Understanding Scripture,* ed. C. Thoma and M. Wyschogrod (New York, 1987), 84–86.
94. *Sefer Ha-Galui,* ed. H. J. Mathews (Berlin, 1887), 2. R. Tam may have been the author of a *peshat* commentary to Job. He offered "*peshat*" interpretations to a number of biblical verses and authored a grammatical treatise responding to the works of Dunash and Menaḥem. See A. Poznanski, *Mavo ʿal Ḥakhmei Ẓarefat Mefarshei ha-Miqra* (Berlin, 1813), 53–54 and Urbach, 1:107–10. The relatively meager amount produced by R. Tam in grammatical and biblical studies does not significantly diminish R. Joseph's claim. See Urbach, 1:107–8. Urbach has perceptively noted the familial influence on Rabbenu Tam's involvement in these disciplines.
95. See *Teshuvot ha-Geonim,* ed. J. Mussafia (Lyck, 1864), no. 9; *Teshu-*

vot ha-Geonim- Sha'arei Teshuvah, ed. Z. Leiter, no. 55; *Maḥẓor Vitry,* ed. S. Hurwitz, 26; and *Shibbolei ha-Leqet,* ed. S. Buber, no. 44. On the position of R. Amram Gaon cited by *Tosafot Qiddushin and Avodah Zarah,* cf. *Ozar ha-Geonim,* ed. B. M. Lewin, 82.

96. *Bait Ha-Talmud* 4 (1885): 344. The will was published by S. Schechter.
97. See above, chap. 1, n. 89. See also U. Simon, "R. Avraham Ibn Ezra-Bein ha-Mefaresh le-Qor'av," in *Proceedings of the Ninth World Congress of Jewish Studies,* ed. M. Goshen-Gottstein (Jerusalem, 1988), 40–42. After his demand for grammatical study of the biblical text, R. Yehudah advises that the portion of the week be studied with Rashi's commentary and "other commentaries" and that Midrash should also be studied regularly.
98. A. Grossman, *Ḥakhmei Ashkenaz ha-Rishonim,* 419–20. See also I. Ta-Shema, "Halakhah, Minhag, u-Massoret be-Yahadut Ashkenaz ba-Me'ot ha-Yod Alef-Yod Bet," *Sidra* 3 (1987): 122.
99. Grossman, *Ḥakhmei Ashkenaz,* 64–66, 74, 226, 250, 353.
100. Ibid., 96. Familiarity with midrashic literature was also required. See above, n. 18.
101. Ibid., 154–57, 187, 430–32; cf. 342, 396. See also Grossman, "Haggirat Yehudim el Germaniyah ve-Hityashvutam Bah ba-Me'ot 9–11," in *Haggirah ve-Hityashvut be-Yisrael uva-Ammim,* 112, n. 9. This type of usage was curtailed in the mid–eleventh century.
102. Grossman, *Ḥakhmei Ashkenaz ha-Rishonim,* 62–63, 158–61, 419. See also R. Bonfil, "Tra due mondi: Prospettive di ricerca sulla storia culturale degli Ebrei nell 'Italia meridionale nell 'alto medioevo," *Italia judaica* (1983): 151–57.
103. Grossman, *Ḥakhmei Ashkenaz ha-Rishonim,* 226, 289, 412. Cf. D. Berger's review in *Tarbiz* 53 (1984): 484, n. 7.
104. Grossman, *Ḥakhmei Ashknaz ha-Rishonim* 240, 249–50.
105. See Grossman, "Ha-Pulmus ha-Yehudi/Noẓri veha-Parshanut ha-Yehudit la-Miqra be-Ẓarefat be-Me'ah ha-12," *Zion* 51 (1986): 60. According to Grossman (*Ḥakhmei Ashkenaz,* 420), the *peshat* methodology of Rashi is not really new but rather an approach that he learned from his teacher R. Ya'akov b. Yaqar.
106. For a description of the so-called Tosafist commentaries to the Torah, see S. Poznanski, *Mavo,* 92–119. A more complete list of published sources and especially of manuscripts is compiled in *Tosafot ha-Shalem,* ed. J. Gellis, 1 (1982), 1:11–38. The list contains all biblical commentaries written by Tosafists, including *peshat* commentaries, such as those of Rashbam and Yosef Qara, and works of German Pietists as well. Y. S. Lange ("Perush Ba'alei ha-Tosafot 'al

ha-Torah— ms. Paris 48," *Alei Sefer* 5 [1978]: 73–74) has noted that a comprehensive study of the content, style, and historical and cultural development of the Tosafist commentaries is still a desideratum.

107. The Tosafist commentary published by S. Abramson exemplifies this type. See S. Abramson, ed., *Ba'alei Tosafot 'al ha-Torah* (Jerusalem, 1974), esp. 7–11.

108. See S. Poznanski, *Mavo,* 93–114 and M. Greenberg, "Parshanei Ẓarefat," in *Encyclopedia Miqra'it,* 8:702. Cf. E. Touitou, "Al Gilgulei ha-Nusaḥ shel Perush Rashi la-Torah," *Tarbiz* 56 (1987): 238–41. When *pashtanim* are quoted in the Tosafist commentaries, they are simply incorporated into the flow of the text. See below, n. 129.

109. The verses in the early part of Genesis, many of which are not analyzed in Talmudic literature, are particularly fruitful for the exegete interested in *remez* and gematria. These methodologies are associated with the German Pietists. Many of their comments appear in Tosafist commentaries; indeed, some are occasionally attributed to Tosafists. See J. Dan, *Torat ha-Sod shel Ḥasidut Ashkenaz,* 65–70, 220–21 and A. Epstein in *REJ* 53 (1909): 196–97. See also E. E. Urbach, ed., *Arugat ha-Bosem,* 4:110, 152–54 and above, n. 20.

110. See *Tosafot Berakhot,* 8b, s.v. *R. Yose; Tosafot R. Yehudah Sir Leon,* s.v. *yashlim; Sefer Or Zarua'* 1:12 (p. 22); *Haggahot Maimuniyyot, Hilkhot Tefillah* 3:300.

111. *Sefer Ha-Yashar,* ed. S. Rosenthal, no. 47:1. (On the implications of this source for the larger conflict between R. Tam and R. Meshullam, see Urbach, 1:71–82.) R. Eleazar Roqeaḥ may also have referred to this type of weekly lecture; see A. M. Habermann, *Gezerot Ashkenaz ve-Ẓarefat,* 164. See also S. Schechter, "Notes on a Hebrew Commentary to the Pentateuch in a Parma Manuscript," in *Semitic Studies in Memory of Alexander Kohut,* ed. S.W. Baron and A. Marx (Berlin, 1897), 486.

112. See *Sefer Miẓvot Gadol,* end of *'aseh* 19 (Venice, 1547, fol. 103:3) and *Commentary of R. Asher b. Yeḥiel* to *Berakhot* 1:8. Cf. *Shibbolei ha-Leqet,* no. 71 and the introduction to *Sefer Miẓvot Qatan* (*'Ammudei Golah,* Constantinople, 1510).

113. See M. Ahrend, "Perush Rashbam le-Iyyov?" *Alei Sefer* 5 (1978): 46–47. See also N. Leibowitz, *Iyyunim be-Sefer Shemot* (Jerusalem, 1975), 497–524 and above, n. 106. There is a degree of correlation and consistency between Rashi's biblical and Talmudic commentaries. See E. Touitou's review of Y. Florsheim, *Rashi la-Miqra be-Perusho la-Talmud* in *Tarbiz* 52 (1983): 360–63.

114. The Book of Job, for example, merited a half dozen commentaries of this type. See M. Sokolow in *JQR* 72 (1981): 153–55. Cf. F. Talmage, "Mi-Kitvei R. Avigdor Qara ve-R. Menaḥem Shalem," in *Hagut u-Ma'aseh*, ed. A. Greenbaum and A. Ivry (Haifa, 1982), 50, n. 12. On the works of Menaḥem bar Ḥelbo, see Poznanski, "Pitronei R. Menaḥem bar Ḥelbo le-Kitvei ha-Qodesh," in *N. Sokolow Jubilee Volume* (Warsaw, 1904), 389–439. On Yosef Qara's works, see M. Ahrend, *Le commentaire sur Job de R. Yoseph Qara* (Hildesheim, 1978), 180–84. Rashbam authored commentaries on a number of biblical books outside the Pentateuch (although there are questions regarding the attribution to him of certain extant northern French commentaries). See S. Japhet and R. B. Salters, *Perush Rashbam le-Qohelet* (Jerusalem, 1985), 13–26.
115. See A. Grossman, "Ha-Pulmus ha-Yehudi/Noẓri," 57–60; E. Touitou, "Shittato ha-Parshanit shel Rashbam," 48–72; and Touitou's review of Ahrend's *Le Commentaire sur Job de R. Yoseph Qara,* in *Tarbiz* 51 (1982): 524–26. Cf. Y. Baer, "Rashi veha-Meẓi'ut ha-Historit shel Zemanno," in *Sefer Rashi,* ed. Y.L. Maimon (Jerusalem, 1956), 489–502; J. Rosenthal, "Ha-Pulmus ha-Anti Noẓri be-Rashi 'al ha-Tanakh," in his *Meḥqarim u-Meqorot* (Jerusalem, 1967), 101–16; E. I. J. Rosenthal, "Anti-Christian Polemics in Bible Commentaries," *JJS* 11 (1960): 115–35; my "Trinitarian and Multiplicity Polemics in the Biblical Commentaries of Rashi, Rashbam, and Bekhor Shor," *Gesher* 7 (1979): 11–37; S. Kamin, "Perush Rashi 'al Shir ha-Shirim veha-Vikkuaḥ ha-Anti Noẓri," *Shenaton la-Miqra ule-Ḥeqer ha-Mizraḥ ha-Qadum* 7–8 (1983–84): 244–48; M. Berger, *The Torah Commentary of R. Samuel b. Meir* (Ph.D. diss., Harvard University, 1982), 323–29. See also Urbach in *REJ* (1935): 73–74; idem, *Ba'alei ha-Tosafot,* 1:226, 2:745. Lipshutz and Segal held that *peshat* was primarily the outgrowth of Talmudic studies or other internal intellectual considerations. See the sources cited in Toitou, "Shittato ha-Parshanit shel Rashbam," nn. 1, 2, 12. See also H. H. Ben-Sasson's review of Urbach's *Ba'alei ha-Tosafot* in *Beḥinot be-Biqqoret ha-Sefarim* 9 (1955): 48–49; M. Greenberg, "Parshanei Ẓarefat," in *Encyclopedia Miqra'it,* 8:690; M. Berger, *The Torah Commentary of R. Samuel b. Meir,* 321–23; and M. Lockshin, *R. Samuel b. Meir's Commentary on Genesis* (Ph.D. diss., Brandeis University, 1984), 13–22.
116. See H. Soloveitchik in *PAAJR* 38–39 (1972): 242, n. 63; D. Berger in *AHR* 91 (1986): 589, n. 66; Urbach, *Ba'alei ha-Tosafot,* index, s.v. *vikkuaḥ 'im noẓrim;* idem in *REJ* 100 (1935): 50. The production of

polemical literature in this period was the province of *pashtanim* and specialists such as the members of the Official family. See J. Rosenthal, ed., *Sefer Yosef ha-Meqanne* (Jerusalem, 1970), 21–28.

117. See M. Bannitt, "L'étude des glossaires" (see chap. 1, n. 6); idem, "Les Poterim," (see chap. 1, n. 6).
118. M. Ahrend, *Le commentaire de R. Yosef Qara sur Job,* 2–3.
119. Touitou, "Shittato ha-Parshanit shel Rashbam," 60; idem, "Al Gilgulei ha-Nusaḥ shel Perush Rashi," 216. See now M. Ahrend, *Perush R. Yosef Qara le-Iyyov* (Jerusalem, 1988), 26–27, n. 25.
120. Rashi to *Shir ha-Shirim* 7:13, s.v. *nir'eh im parḥah ha-gefen* (= *Perush Rashi ʿal Shir ha-Shirim,* ed. J. Rosenthal, in *Sefer ha-Yovel Likhvod S. K. Mirsky,* ed. S. Bernstein and G. Churgin [New York, 1958], 182).
121. *Arugat ha-Bosem,* ed. Urbach, 3:289 and n. 17. Cf. Touitou in *Tarbiz* 52 (1983): 367 and *Tarbiz* 51 (1982): 525; and Banitt, "The Leʿazim of Rashi and of the French Biblical Glossaries," in *World History of the Jewish People,* vol. 11, *The Dark Ages,* ed. C. Roth (Ramat Gan, 1966), 291–96. See also I. A. Agus, "The Languages Spoken by Ashkenazic Jews in the High Middle Ages," *Joshua Finkel Festschrift,* ed. S. Hoenig and L. Stitskin (New York, 1974), 19–28. A form of the word *pittaron/liftor* is used in conjunction with *peshat* interpretations (especially by R. Yosef Qara) as well as polemical interpretations (see, e.g., *Sefer Yosef ha-Meqanne*). The origin of the meaning and precise use of these terms requires further study.
122. See Rashbam's commentary to Genesis 37:2 and S. Kamin, *Rashi: Peshuto shel Miqra u-Midrasho shel Miqra* (Jerusalem, 1986), 267–72.
123. The identification of Bekhor Shor as the Tosafist Joseph of Orleans is beyond question; see Urbach, 1:134.
124. See M. Ahrend, *Le Commentaire sur Job de R. Yosef Qara,* 13–23; A. Grossman, "Ha-Pulmus ha-Yehudi/Noẓri, 31–32; *Arugat ha-Bosem,* ed. Urbach, 4:13–15; and Urbach, *Baʿalei ha-Tosafot* 1:43. See also below, n. 128.
125. See Touitou, "Al Gilgulei ha-Nusaḥ," above, n. 108.
126. See A. Berliner, ed., *Rashi ʿal ha-Torah* (Frankfurt a.M., 1905), 10; S. Poznanski, *Mavo ʿal Ḥakhmei Ẓarefat Mefarshei ha-Miqra,* 54–57; M. Ahrend, *Le commentaire sur Job de R. Yosef Qara,* 2–3; E. Touitou, "Shittato ha-Parshanit shel Rashbam," 61, n. 76; M. Berger, *The Torah Commentary of R. Samuel b. Meir,* 195–205; M. Sokolow, "Ha-Peshatot ha-Mitḥaddeshim- Qetaʿim Ḥadashim mi-Perush ha-Torah la-Rashbam," *Alei Sefer* 10 (1984): 73–80; S. Japhet, *Perush Rashbam le-Qohelet,* 48–51. See also M. Ahrend,

Perush R. Yosef Qara le-Iyyov, 13–30. D. Rosin (*Perush ha-Torah asher Katav ha-Rashbam* [Breslau, 1882], 30) noted that Rashbam and Yosef Qara refer to each other in their commentaries only on rare occasions. See also Rosin, *R. Samuel b. Meir als Schrifterklerer* (Breslau, 1880), 72–74; G. Drori, "Shittato ha-Parshanit shel R. Yosef Qara li-Nevi'im Rishonim" (Master's thesis, Bar Ilan University, 1982), 180–81; and M. Ahrend, "R. Joseph Kara and his Notes on Rashi's Torah Commentary," *Le-Eyla,* Winter, 1988, pp. 30–33. Rashbam twice refers to questions that he received and was attempting to answer through his Torah commentary; but the questions appear to have been basic, non-scholarly queries concerning the interpretations of particular verse, to which he responded by offering *peshat* interpretations. See his commentary to Numbers 11:35, 30:2; and see Toitou, "Shittato ha-Parshanit shel Rashbam," 54, n. 30. Cf. *Teshuvot Rashi,* ed. I. Elfenbein, 1:1–6, esp. sec. 10 (= A. Geiger, *Melo Ḥofnayim,* 36). See also Poznanski, *Mavo,* 22–23. M. Ahrend (*Le commentaire sur Job de R. Yosef Qara,* 19) claimed that Qara's commentary to Job was the result of an oral presentation. M. Signer ("Exégèse et enseignment: Les commentaires de Joseph ben Simeon Kara," *Archives Juives* 18 [1982]: 60–63) argued that Qara's exegetical writings reflect his activity as a teacher of Scripture. The documentation of both Signer and Ahrend is somewhat sketchy and unconvincing. See also Ahrend, "Perush Rashbam le-Iyyov?" *Alei Sefer* 5 (1978): 46–47 and Touitou in *Tarbiz* 51 (1982): 525–27. Cf. J. Frankel, *Darko shel Rashi be-Perusho le-Talmud ha-Bavli* (Jerusalem, 1980), 284–96.

127. See Rashbam's commentary (ed. D. Rosin) to Genesis 1:1 and 37:2 and the preamble to Exodus 21. See E. Touitou, "Darko shel Rashbam be-Perusho le-Ḥeleq ha-Halakhi shel ha-Torah," *Millet* 2 (1986): 275–83.

128. See R. Yosef Qara's commentary to 1 Samuel 1:20. Qara notes that while those who follow rabbinic interpretation will reject his exegesis, the *maskilim,* who are faithful to the text, will accept it. On *maskilim* as those who study and interpret Scripture in its own light, see the critique of R. Abraham Ibn Ezra (which was adopted by R. Eleazar Roqeaḥ), below, chap. 6, n. 16. Rashbam, in the sources cited above, n. 127, also refers to those who prefer *peshat* interpretation as *maskilim.* Cf. Touitou, "Shittato ha-Parshanit shel Rashbam," 66, n. 122. The tension between Talmudists and *pashtanim* regarding scriptural interpretation was even sharper in Spain. See Moses Ibn Ezra, *Sefer ha-Iyyunim veha-Diyyunim,* ed. A. Halkin (Jerusalem, 1975), 227.

See also Yonah Ibn Janaḥ, *Sefer ha-Riqmah,* ed. M. Wilensky (Berlin, 1929), 10–19 and Judah b. Barzilai al-Barẓeloni, *Perush Sefer Yeẓirah,* ed. S. Z. H. Halberstam (Berlin, 1888), 5.

129. See Poznanski, *Mavo,* 55–75; Y. Nevo, "Yaḥasam shel Parshanei ha-Torah Baʿalei ha-Tosafot le–R. Yosef Bekhor Shor," *Sinai* 92 (1983): 97–108; and J. M. Orlian, *Sefer Ha-Gan* (Ph.D. diss., Yeshiva University, 1973), 54–61. (Note that the biblical commentaries of Rashbam and even those of Yosef Qara are not devoid of midrashic interpretations. See Touitou in *Tarbiz* 51 [1982]: 525.)
130. Compared to Rashbam, Bekhor Shor has fewer comments disagreeing with halakic interpretations of *Ḥazal;* see Y. Nevo, "R. Yosef Bekhor Shor Parshan ha-Peshat," *Sinai* 95 (1984): 271–77 and Urbach, 1:134–36.
131. See Lange's introduction to his edition of *Perushei ha-Torah le–R. Ḥayyim Paltiel* (Jerusalem, 1981), 10 and the collection of citations from R. Yosef Qara in Tosafist biblical commentaries in A. Berliner, *Pletat Soferim* (Breslau, 1872), Hebrew sec., 12–25.
132. Urbach, 1:146, 149, 263, 333–34, 460; 2:585. See also N. Golb, *Toledot ha-Yehudim be-ʿIr Rouen,* 116–18, 190–92. Cf. M. Breuer, "Minʿu Beneikhem min ha-Higgayon," in *Sefer Zikkaron le–R. David Ochs* (Ramat Gan, 1978), 251, n. 42. Breuer's blanket assertion that some Tosafists studied Scripture with their students is thus left unsubstantiated.
133. Urbach, 1:173.
134. Ibid., 195. See also p. 361 and Avraham b. Azriel, *Arugat ha-Bosem,* ed. Urbach, 1:167, n. 1. Cf. Breuer, "Minʿu Beneikem," 251, n. 43. The passage in the article of Ben-Sasson (to which Breuer refers as proof for the fact that many Ashkenazic scholars were masters of the biblical text and involved in its interpretation) concerns the German Pietists, who are not representative in this issue. See chap. 6.
135. Urbach, 1:40, 44, 59, 110.
136. See Urbach, 1:146, 151, 263, 270, 460 and A. Grossman, "Perush ha-Piyyut le–R. Aharon b. Ḥayyim ha-Kohen," *Be-Oraḥ Mada: Sefer Zikkaron le–Aharon Mirsky,* ed. Z. Malachi (Lod, 1986), 451–68. On R. Yosef Qara's *piyyut* commentaries, see Urbach, *Arugat ha-Bosem,* 4:3–23 and Grossman, "Pulmus anti-Noẓri be-Perushav shel R. Yosef Qara la-Miqra ule-Piyyut," *Proceedings of the Ninth World Congress of Jewish Studies* (Jerusalem, 1986), 75–77. Commentaries to *piyyut* were also authored by twelfth-century German scholars who were directly linked with the pre-Crusade period. The German Pietists attempted to rekindle interest in *piyyut.* See above, n. 18.

137. Urbach, 1:387. Urbach doubts whether in fact this is Rabiah's commentary. See Aptowitzer, *Mavo la-Rabiah,* 184–85.
138. See above, n. 87.
139. On *derashot* in Ashkenaz, see J. Elbaum in *Qiryat Sefer* 48 (1973): 340–47, and ms. Bodl. 340, fol. 143–61. Note that the *Derashot R. Ḥayyim Or Zarua'* quoted in *Responsa of Maharil, Minhagei Maharil,* and *Terumat ha-Deshen* are halakhic with homiletical introductions. See N. Goldstein, *R. Ḥayyim Eliezer b. Isaac Or Zarua'—His Life and Works* (D.H.L. diss., Yeshiva University, 1959), 36–37 and J. Gellis, *Tosafot ha-Shalem le-Parshat Va-Yeḥi* (Jerusalem, 1985), 105, 198, 227. The commentary on most of the books in *Nevi'im* and *Ketuvim* attributed to the Italian Tosafist R. Isaiah di Trani is possibly the work of his grandson, R. Isaiah the Younger. This commentary makes use of the commentaries of Rashi, Ibn Ezra, and Radaq and contains Italian glosses. In any event, R. Isaiah the Elder's provenance and backround make him an exception among the Tosafists, as is this commentary when compared to other Tosafist works. See I. Ta-Shema in *Encyclopedia Judaica,* vol. 9, cols. 73–74; E. Z. Melammed, "Le-Perush Nakh shel R. Isaiah mi-Trani," *Meḥqarim ba-Miqra uva-Mizraḥ ha-Qadum,* ed. Y. Avishor and J. Blau (Jerusalem, 1978), 279–301; S. Z. Leiman, "Aḥaronei ha-Parshanim bi-Sepharad uvi-Provence u-Farshanei Italyah," in *Encyclopedia Miqra'it,* 8:708; and Urbach, 1:413, 435.
140. Profiat Duran, *Ma'aseh Efod* (Vienna, 1865), 41. Cf. M. Lockshin, *R. Samuel b. Meir's Commentary on Genesis,* 395–96.
141. See also the critique of R. Abraham Ibn Ezra, below, chap. 6, n. 16. Cf. F. Talmage, "Keep Your Sons from Scripture," 86–87. Talmage views the works of the twelfth-century northern French exegetes as clear evidence for pervasive Ashkenazic biblicism and maintains that Duran's critique concerning the absence of biblical studies in Ashkenaz was directed only against the Ashkenazic scholars of the fourteenth century. Needless to say, I do not agree with these assessments.

Notes to Chapter 6

1. See, e.g., pp. 20, 40–41, 45–46, 50, and 75–76 above.
2. Y. Baer, "Ha-Megammah ha-Datit ha-Ḥevratit shel Sefer Ḥasidim," *Zion* 3 (1937): 10–14. Cf. above. chap. 2, n. 29.

3. Ibid., 20–22, 43. Cf. M. Breuer, *Ha-Rabbanut be-Ashkenaz Bimei ha-Beinayim* (Jerusalem, 1976), 16.
4. H. Soloveitchik, "Three Themes," 339–40.
5. Ibid., 345–52.
6. I. Ta-Shema, "Miẓvat Talmud Torah ki-Veʿayah Ḥevratit Datit be-Sefer Ḥasidim," *Bar Ilan* 14–15 (1977): 98–103, 109–112. In the areas of pedagogy and teacher-students relations, *Sefer Ḥasidim* addresses such issues as teacher haughtiness and incompetence, the need for teachers to be able to judge and respond to the different intellectual abilities of their students, and the level of devotion required of teachers. In addition to the sources cited by Ta-Shema, see *SḤP,* secs. 794–96, 764 (*SḤB,* 276), 782–86, 815 (see also *Sefer Raziel ha-Gadol* [Amsterdam, 1700], fol. 9a), 1496, 828, 830 1491, (*SḤB,* sec. 1007). (Cf. *Sefer Or Zaruaʿ, Pisqei Bava Meẓiʿa,* nos. 245–46 and *Mordekhai, Bava Meziʿa,* no. 343).
7. Ta-Shema, "Miẓvat Talmud Torah" 103–6. Cf. Ta-Shema, "Qavvim le-Ofyah shel ha-Sifrut ha-Rabbanit be-Ashkenaz be-Me'ot ha–13–14," *Alei Sefer* 4 (1977): 31–34, 41. Ta-Shema's position regarding pietistic educational theory reflects his stand on the much-debated question of the scope of *Sefer Ḥasidim*'s intended audience and the nature (or very existence) of its social focus. This question was first discussed by J. N. Simhoni, "Ha-Ḥasidut ha-Ashkenazit Bimei ha-Beinayim," in *Ha-Ẓefirah* (Warsaw 1917), sec. 13. In addition to the studies of Baer, Ta-Shema, and Soloveitchik (see above, nn. 1, 4, 6), see H. H. Ben-Sasson, "Ḥasidei Ashkenaz ʿal Ḥaluqat Qinyanim Ḥomriyyim u-Nekhasim Ruḥaniyyim Bein Benei ha-Adam," *Zion* 35 (1970): 61–79; G. Scholem, "Three Types of Jewish Piety," *Ariel* 32 (1973): 17–21; and I. Marcus, *Piety and Society* (Leiden, 1981). Cf. J. Dan's review of *Piety and Society,* "Toratam ha-Mussarit veha-Ḥevratit shel Ḥasidei Ashkenaz," *Tarbiz* 51 (1982): 323–24 and J. Katz, *Exclusiveness and Tolerance,* 103–5. See now Marcus's introduction to the Dinur Center publication of *Sefer Ḥasidim* (Jerusalem, 1985), 23–24 (based on ms. Parma H 3280) and to *Dat ve-Ḥevrah be-Mishnatam shel Ḥasidei Ashkenaz* (Jerusalem, 1987), 15–23.
8. Ta-Shema, "Miẓvat Talmud Torah," 104, 108, and esp. 109: "The dialectic method is beneficial and upright in theory. But its actual use by the unqualified causes lapses in conduct, e.g., boastfulness"; cf. Ta-Shema's English summary, p. 121 and also T. Alexander, *Sipporet ve-Hagut be-Sefer Ḥasidim* (Ph.D. diss., University of California, Los Angeles, diss., 1976), 73, 246. See also Soloveitchik, "Three Themes," 342, 348–50, and 343, n. 106; *SḤP,* sec. 811; and *Perush*

ha-Roqeaḥ la-Haggadah shel Pesaḥ, ed. M. Hershler (Jerusalem, 1984), 153.

9. *SḤP,* sec. 1478: "If one [teacher] has *tosafot* and the other teacher does not, the first teacher should not say, 'I will not lend him mine' so that the other students will come to study with him." Cf. *SḤP,* sec. 664, and Ta-Shema, 112–13; *SḤP,* secs. 15 (p. 21), 746, 1739.
10. Ta-Shema, "Miẓvat Talmud Torah," 104. See above, chap. 2, n. 54.
11. *SḤP,* sec. 752 censures those who imitate non-Jewish dialectical methods in their Talmudic studies. See above, chap. 5, n. 44.
12. I. Marcus (*Piety and Society,* 103–5) maintains that *Sefer Ḥasidim* does not criticize the dangers inherent in the study of dialectic per se but rather the study of dialectic developed by non-Pietists. See also his introduction to ms. Parma H 3280, pp. 22–23. Marcus's assertion is based on his theory that R. Yehudah he-Ḥasid directed the large portion of *Sefer Ḥasidim* that he composed to the spiritual leaders of the German Pietists. See Marcus, "Ḥibburei ha-Teshuvah shel Ḥasidei Ashkenaz," in *Studies in Jewish Mysticism, Philosophy, and Ethical Literature,* ed. J. Dan and J. Hacker (Jerusalem, 1986), 369–79; idem in *Tarbiz* 51 (1982): 319–25.
13. The critique is discussed briefly by M. Breuer, "Minʿu Beneikhem min ha-Higgayon," *Mikhtam Le-David* (Ramat-Gan, 1978), 251. Cf. H. H. Ben-Sasson, "Derekh Ḥadashah el ʿOlam ha-Genizah," *Zion* 41 (1976): 37 and F. Talmage, "Keep Your Sons from Scripture" (see chap. 5, n. 93).
14. Ms. Paris 772, fol. 21r, cited by E. E. Urbach in his introduction to R. Abraham b. Azriel, *Arugat ha-Bosem,* (Jerusalem, 1963), 4:111. Roqeaḥ uses the term *miqra* to refer to biblical books other than the Pentateuch. On the use of the term *miqra* in this manner, see *Sifrei,* ed. L. Finkelstein (repr. New York, 1969), *Ha'azinu,* sec. 317 (p. 359, line 14): "*zo Torah . . . zeh Miqra . . . zo Mishnah.*" See also the elegy *Mi Yittein Roshi Mayim* of R. Qalonymus b. Judah ha-Baḥur, a Qalonymide and ancestor of Roqeaḥ, in A. M. Habermann, *Gezerot Ashkenaz ve-Ẓarefat,* 67. R. Qalonymus mourns the loss of the great German scholars during the First Crusade who were thoroughly versed in *Torah, miqra, mishnah, aggadah.* Roqeaḥ also uses *miqra* in this way in his introduction to *Sefer Roqeaḥ* (repr. Jerusalem, 1967), 14: "If one cannot study Talmud, he should study midrashim, or *miqra* or *ḥumash.*"
15. See above, chap. 5. Cf. J. N. Epstein, "L'auteur du commentaire des chroniques," *REJ* 53 (1909): 189–99.
16. Abraham Ibn Ezra, *Yesod Mora, Shaʿar Rishon* (repr. Jerusalem,

1958), 1–3. Ibn Ezra also discusses the significance of the Aramaic Targum and linguistics and the priority to be given to their study.

17. On the relationship of the German Pietists to Ibn Ezra, and their use specifically of *Yesod Mora,* see Y. Dan, *Torat ha-Sod shel Ḥasidut Ashkenaz* (Jerusalem, 1968), 29–30, 51. Ibn Ezra composed *Yesod Mora* while in London in 1158.
18. See above, chap. 5, nn. 99–101, 105.
19. See above, chap. 5, nn. 98, 102–4.
20. See J. N. Epstein "L'auteur du commentaire," 198–99, n. 2 and J. Dan, "Sefer ha-Ḥokhmah le–R. Eleazar mi-Worms," *Zion* 29 (1964): 170–71.
21. *SḤP,* secs. 752, 820. Cf. H. Soloveitchik, "Three Themes," 313–20; Ta-Shema, "Miẓvat Talmud Torah," 109–10. Of course, *Sefer Ḥasidim* makes extensive use of the entire biblical corpus. One section of the Parma ms. (para. 1792–1874) entitled *Sefer ha-Ḥasidim be-Mishlei Shelomo* is devoted to pietistic interpretation of verses in the book of Proverbs. The study of *Nakh* is also included by R. Eleazar in his ideal educational curriculum; see *Sefer Roqeaḥ,* 11–14. Cf. *SḤP,* sec. 666. Roqeaḥ also commented extensively on all of the *Megillot* and on the *haftarot.* See his *Qiryat Sefer* (Lemberg, 1905) and n. 22.
22. On the biblical commentaries associated with the German Pietists, and the Tosafist biblical commentaries in which German Pietists are cited, see the following entries in the introduction of J. Gellis to his collection of Tosafist commentaries, *Tosafot ha-Shalem,* vol. 1 (Jerusalem, 1982): *Da'at Zeqenim* (p. 12); *Perush ha-Torah le–R. Yehudah he-Hasid,* (p. 16, to which add R. Yehudah's *Ta'amei Massoret ha-Miqra,* ed. I. S. Lange [Jerusalem, 1985]) cf. R. Meir of Rothenburg's *Ta'amei Massoret ha-Miqra* [p. 13], *Perush Ba'al ha-Turim 'al ha-Torah* [p. 16], and Oxford/Bodl. 271/5, 6 [p. 22]); *Perush ha-Roqeaḥ 'al ha-Torah* (p. 18); and *R. Eliezer* [sic] *mi-Germaizah* (p. 20), to which add the so-called commentary of R. Eleazar Roqeaḥ to the Pentateuch and the *Megillot* published in three volumes by S. Kanevsky [Bnei Brak, 1979–81]; the author utilizes the methodology of the Pietists but may not be R. Eleazar: see J. Dan in *Qiryat Sefer* 59 [1984]: 644); *Peshatim u-Perushim* (p. 19); Oxford/Bodl. 271/22 (p. 22); Oxford/Bodl. 945 (p. 23); Oxford/Bodl. 970/4–6 (p. 24); Oxford/Bodl. 1812/6 (p. 24); Vatican 45/1 (p. 26); Jerusalem 5138 (p. 27); London (Gaster) 10855/1 (p. 29); Leiden 4765 (p. 29); Moscow-Ginzburg 82/1 (p. 29); Moscow-Ginzburg 322/22 (p. 30); Jewish Theological Seminary 793, 899/1, 1062, 1065/3 (pp. 32–33); Strassberg (p. 38). See also the texts published by J. Dan in *Da'at,* 2:99–120; M. Hershler in *Sinai* 74 (1974): 193–200; M.

Lehmann in *Sinai* 71 (1972): 1–20 and his edition of the commentary of Roqeaḥ to Esther. On the methodology of the biblical interpretations of the German Pietists, see Epstein in *REJ* 53 (1909): 193–94; G. Brin, "Qavvim le-Perush ha-Torah shel R. Yehudah he-Hasid," *Te'udah* 3 (1983): 215–20; J. Dan in *Zion* 29 (1968): 175–80; and see now I. Marcus, "Exegesis for the Few and for the Many: Judah he-Ḥasid's Biblical Commentaries," *Meḥqerei Yerushalayim be-Maḥshevet Yisrael* 8 (1989): 1–24. See also the anonymous work *Te'amim shel Ḥumash,* originally attributed by I. Levi to R. Leontin, the teacher of R. Gershom, and published in *REJ* 49 (1904): 234–38. (Levi, in *REJ* 53 [1909]: 153–54, accepted the claim of A. Epstein, "Leontin und andere Namen in den Ta'amim shel Ḥumash," *MGWJ* 49 [1905]: 557–70, that this is a twelfth-century text. On its affinity to the work of the German Pietists, see J. N. Epstein in *REJ* 53 [1909]: 196–97.) Study of Midrash was also extremely important to the German Pietists. See J. Dan, *Torat ha-Sod shel Ḥasidut Ashkenaz,* 10–12, 20–22; E. E. Urbach, ed., *Arugat ha-Bosem* 4:155–76; and Soloveitchik, "Three Themes," 322–23.

23. *SḤP,* sec. 820. The importance of studying texts in a manner that will inculcate fear of heaven extends to older students as well; see *SḤP,* 752.
24. *SḤP,* secs. 745, 748, 765, 796, 824–25. Cf. I. Ta-Shema in *Bar Ilan* 14–15 (1976): 99–101. The claim of R. Ḥayyim b. Beẓalel (cited in Assaf, *Meqorot,* 1:43–44) that his ancestors, especially *Ḥasidei Ashkenaz,* encouraged their children to study Talmud exclusively was made in the course of a diatribe against those who do not study Hebrew grammar. He makes no specific charge regarding biblical studies. Cf. Talmage, "Keep Your Sons from Scripture." It should also be noted that contemporaries of R. Ḥayyim use the term *Ḥasidei Ashkenaz* to refer generally to their pious Ashkenazic predecessors in the high Middle Ages, not specifically to the German Pietists. R. Ḥayyim himself later repeats that grammatical studies had been neglected, especially in *medinat Ashkenaz.* See H. H. Ben-Sasson, *Hagut ve-Hanhagah* (Jerusalem, 1959), 12, 15, 59.
25. See *SḤP,* secs. 748, 796 and the introduction to *Sefer Roqeaḥ,* 11–13. See also the sources cited in Y. Sussman, "Kitvei-Yad u-Mesorot Nusaḥ shel ha-Mishnah," in *Proceedings of the Seventh World Congress of Jewish Studies* (Jerusalem, 1977), 3:224, n. 45 and 235–36, nn. 86, 88. Cf. above, chapter five, nn. 62–63.
26. See Roqeaḥ, *Commentary to Leviticus,* ed. S. Kanevsky, p. 266; idem, *Commentary to Numbers,* ed. Kanevsky, p. 33; idem, *Commentary to Deuteronomy,* ed. Kanevsky, p. 191; idem, *Commentary to Megillot,*

ed. Kanevsky, pp. 59 (Lamentations), 216 (Ecclesiastes); and *Commentary to Ruth* in *Genuzot* 2 (1985): 196.

27. See *Arugat ha-Bosem,* ed. E. E. Urbach, 3:289, and above, chap. 5, n. 128. See also Roqeaḥ's *Commentary to Ruth* in *Genuzot* 2 (1985): 211. Cf. Y. Sussman, "Kitvei-Yad u-Mesorot Nusaḥ," 223, n. 44; 225, n. 49; and 239, n. 93.
28. On the study of Mishnah in pre-Crusade Ashkenaz, see Sussman, "Kitvei-Yad," 235–36. While the sources cited above (notes 25–27) demonstrate that in the pietistic view Mishnah ought be studied as a separate discipline, the evidence is not unequivocal. *SḤP* does not list Mishnah as a discipline to be studied by one who cannot master Talmud (see *SḤP,* 825); see also above, n. 14 (end). Cf. Sussman, "Kitvei-Yad," 224–25. Moreover, although the recommendation by *Sefer Ḥasidim* that one should study the areas of Talmudic literature that are usually neglected (*SḤP,* secs. 1, 588) appears to urge the study of Mishnah *Zera'im* and *Tohorot,* only the study of *Seder Qodashim* is explicity mentioned by the author in this context and the reference is no doubt to the Gemara portion of *Seder Qodashim* as well. Cf. *SḤP,* sec. 1495, and above, chap. 5, n. 58.
29. See Y. Sussman, "Kitvei-Yad," 222–41; A. Kleinberger, *The Educational Theories of the Maharal of Prague* (in Hebrew) (Jerusalem, 1962), 135–36; Ta-Shema, "Miẓvat Talmud Torah," 110. Cf. Ta-Shema, "Shipput 'Ivri u-Mishpat 'Ivri," (see chap. 3, n. 65), 254 and B. Septimus, *Hispano-Jewish Culture in Transition* (Cambridge, MA, 1982), 16, n. 106.
30. Soloveitchik, "Three Themes," 347, n. 118.
31. R. Joseph Ibn Ezra, *Sefer Massa Melekh* (ms. Salonica 1601), pt. 4, fol. 38a. See A. David in *Qiryat Sefer* 45 (1970): 627–28; cf. H. H. Ben-Sasson in *Zion* 35 (1970): 66.
32. I. Ta-Shema, "'Al Petur Talmidei Ḥakhamim me-Missim Bimei ha-Beinayim," in *'Iyyunim be-Sifrut Ḥazal, ba-Miqra, uve-Toledot Yisrael,* ed. Y. D. Gilat et al. (Ramat Gan, 1982), 319. It should be noted that for Soloveitchik, the German Pietists are deviating from the pre-Crusade policy of not granting tax exemptions to scholars. To be sure, not all of the reasons given for this policy would still apply by the year 1200. See A. Grossman, *Ḥakhmei Ashkenaz ha-Rishonim* (Jerusalem, 1981), 411 and the review of D. Berger in *Tarbiz* 53 (1984): 482. For Ta-Shema, on the other hand, the pietistic policy regarding tax exemptions is a continuation of the pre-Crusade Ashkenazic position that remained in effect in nonpietistic circles as well through the fourteenth century. See above, chap. 3.

33. *RMP,* nos. 730, 932. Cf. Ta-Shema, "ʿAl Petur," 318.
34. See, e.g., *SḤP,* secs. 751, 762, 912, 1349. Cf. Soloveitchik, "Three Themes," 330–35, 344.
35. Ta-Shema does not address the Joseph Ibn Ezra text. There is no explicit indication in that text that scholars who are entitled to exemption are only those who study day and night and engage in no other pursuit whatever.
36. Ta-Shema, following this interperetation, characterizes the father's claim as a subterfuge. The son cannot be the claimant in this case, since he could not very well be both the completely dedicated student and the *nosei ve-notein* with the funds as well.
37. Cf. H. H. Ben-Sasson, "Ḥasidei Ashkenaz ʿal Ḥaluqat Qinyanim," 66.
38. Nonetheless, an alternate reading of *ein yadam* is possible. Sec. 807 may actually be suggesting that scholars who are totally devoted to their studies should be provided with all their needs. If so, perhaps the phrase in 1493 means that scholars need to spend time earning a livelihood because they cannot get the community to support them. Once they must spend time earning their livelihoods, they cannot indeed be exempted from taxes. See below, n. 46.
39. Ta-Shema, "ʿAl Petur," 313–14. Regarding Spanish influences on the German Pietists, see J. Dan, *Torat ha-Sod shel Ḥasidut Ashkenaz,* 28–32. See below, n. 55.
40. *SḤP,* secs. 1496, 810. Cf. I. Ta-Shema, "Miẓvat Talmud Torah," 110.
41. See *Sefer Or Zaruaʿ,* vol. 1, *Responsa,* no. 113 (p. 40). See now I. Ta-Shema, "Le-Toledot ha-Yehudim be-Polin ba-Meʾot ha-12/ha-13," *Zion* 53 (1988): 347–69.
42. We have noted that while Tosafists engaged in a theoretical discussion of the possible payment of temple functionaries from communal funds in response to a problem of Talmudic interpretation, R. Judah of Barcelona endorsed this method for paying judges and teachers. See above, chap. 3, n. 28. Cf. Rashba, *Responsa* 1:450.
43. *SḤP,* sec. 1838. Cf. *SḤP,*, sec. 826, 1474.
44. *SḤP,* sec. 765. See also *Sefer Toledot Adam ve-Ḥavvah* (Venice, 1553), 2:4 (end, fol. 23a); *Yosef Omeẓ* (Frankfurt, 1928), 273–75; M. Ber, "Issachar and Zevulun," *Bar Ilan* 6 (1971): 167–80; and R. M. Feinstein, "Teshuvah be-ʿInyan Shutfut Yissakhar u-Zevulun," *Moriah* 12 (1983): 89–100. Cf. *SḤP,* secs. 745, 774—a scholar should have someone to "manage his money." Cf. the formulation of R. Isaac Or Zaruaʿ above, chap. 3, n. 17.
45. *SḤP,* sec. 778; see also sec. 779. While these arrangements are private and not communal, they are part of the pietistic plan to encourage

individuals to take responsibility for the learning of others. All Jews are to be considered as one's children in terms of the responsibility to teach them (*SḤP*, sec. 801, end).

46. *SḤP*, sec. 1045. Cf. Ta-Shema, "Miẓvat Talmud Torah," 99. While *Sefer Ḥasidim* encourages all persons to work rather than to rely on charity, the scholar whose Torah knowledge is needed by many may allow himself to be supported by charity. See *SḤP*, sec. 1084. See also *SḤP* secs. 903–4. The claim that a scholar who imparts knowledge to the community is in effect a partner of the community and is thus the most worthy candidate for charity funds is implicit in *SḤP*, secs. 764, 860. *Sefer Ḥasidim* values greatly the charity that is given by people to worthy scholars. See *SḤP*, secs. 806, 862, 892, 919, 921, 1707. Cf. Soloveitchik, "Three Themes," 344, n. 107 and 337, n. 86. Note that a fifteenth-century Austrian rabbi, Isaac b. Eliezer, who advocates outright support for scholars (*Sefer ha-Gan* [Vienna, 1596], p. 5), claims (in his introduction) to have been influenced by *Sefer Ḥasidim*.
47. See above, chap. 4. Cf. *SḤP*, secs. 814, 1478–80.
48. *SḤP*, sec. 1484; see also sec. 1283.
49. *SḤP*, sec. 777.
50. *SḤP*, secs. 776, 798, 1495. See also the pietistic biblical commentaries cited above, chap. 3, n. 49.
51. *Commentary of R. Yonah* to *Proverbs* 17:24.
52. See I. A. Agus, "Morei ha-Talmud ve-Talmideihem ba-Ḥevrah ha-Yehudit be-Germanyah Bimei ha-Beinayim Kefi she-Meto'ar be–*Sefer Ḥasidim*, "in *Samuel Belkin Memorial Volume*, ed. M. Carmilly and H. Leaf (New York, 1982), 138–39. References to *roshei yeshivah* in *SḤP*, secs. 53 and 826 refer to earlier periods, as Agus notes. R. Isaac Or Zarua', in a gloss to *SḤP* (p. 126), cites his teacher R. Judah the Pious who told of the punishment meted out to a *rav gadol u-muvhaq la-rabbim* for berating worshippers whose lengthy recitation of the liturgy delayed his study. A passage in *SḤP* (sec. 1343) that is parallel to this part of the gloss seems to refer to an entirely different instigator. Cf. H. Soloveitchik, "Three Themes," 333–34, n. 70. It is possible that R. Isaac bestowed these titles on the scholar in his transcription of the incident. Note that later in the gloss, R. Isaac quotes R. Judah concerning a pious Jew in Worms whose name is mentioned, another convention never practiced by R. Judah in *Sefer Ḥasidim*. Even if R. Judah himself described the scholar in this way, the description is being used to underscore the impropriety of the scholar's actions, not to praise him. Cf. Agus, "The Use of the Term *Ḥakham* by the Author of *Sefer Ḥasidim* and its Historical Implications," *JQR* 61 (1966): 54–55.

53. H. Soloveitchik, "Three Themes," 343, n. 106.
54. See *SḤR,* 136, sec. 24.
55. The Pietists also wished to develop a more centralized process for halakhic decision making in Ashkenaz (see above, n. 7). Note that Spanish Jewry, whose educational organization was more centralized than in Ashkenaz, also produced and promoted all-encompassing halakic codes whose authority was meant to be universal. See I. Ta-Shema, "Qelitatam shel Sifrei ha-Rif, ha-Raḥ va-Halakhot Gedolot be-Ẓarefat uve-Ashkenaz ba-Me'ot ha-11/12," *Qiryat Sefer* 55 (1980): 197; idem, "Shipput ʿIvri," 354.

Notes to Appendix A

1. The text is found in ms. Bodl. 873, fol. 196r–199. See A. Neubauer, *Catalogue of Hebrew Manuscripts in the Bodleian Library* (London, 1886), 1:181. The manuscript was copied in 1309 in a German hand.
2. M. Güdemann, *Geschichte des Erziehungswesens und der Cultur der abendländischen Juden während des Mittelalters,* 1:92–106, 264–72. Cf. *MGWJ* 29 (1880): 427–30. Güdemann's transcription was copied by M. Friedman in *Beit ha-Talmud* 2 (1881): 61–63, 91–95 and S. Assaf, *Meqorot le-Toledot ha-Ḥinnukh be-Yisrael* (Tel Aviv, 1954), 1:9–16. More recently, a photo-offset and a punctuated transcription were published by N. Morris in his *Le-Toledot ha-Ḥinnukh shel Am Yisrael,* (repr. Jerusalem, 1977), 2:417–23. A more accurate transcription can be found in N. Golb, *Toledot ha-Yehudim be-ʿIr Rouen Bimei ha-Beinayim* (Jerusalem, 1976), 181–84.
3. See J. Dan in *Encyclopedia Judaica,* 14:1099–1100. More than twenty scholars have undertaken the identification of this text.
4. Cf. Güdemann, *Ha-Torah veha-Ḥayyim,* 218.
5. See D. Kaufmann, *Gesammelte Schriften,* 2:210–15; Assaf, *Meqorot,* 7. To support his view, Kaufmann cites a list of liturgical poems describing schools that were established and maintained under Babylonian influence in a manner similar to the system presented in *SḤH.* See the response of S. Z. H. Halberstam cited in Güdemann, *Ha-Torah veha-Ḥayyim* 219 and in Assaf, *Meqorot,* 9.
6. On the use of this term in medieval Jewish literature, see above, chap. 4, n. 6.
7. See B. Dinur in *Qiryat Sefer* 1 (1924): 107; idem, *Toledot Yisrael*

ba-Golah 1:3, p. 326, n. 38; S. Assaf, *Mi-Sifrut ha-Geonim* (Jerusalem, 1933), 4, n. 10; B. Z. Benedikt, "Le-Toledot Merkaz ha-Torah bi-Provence," *Tarbiz* 22 (1951): 98; and Twersky, *Rabad of Posquières* (Philadelphia, 1980).

8. Golb, *Toledot ha-Yehudim be-ʿIr Rouen,* 36–40.
9. G. Scholem, *Reshit ha-Qabbalah bi-Provence,* 84–91; *Ursprung und Anfänge der Kabbalah* (Berlin, 1962), 202–10; *Ha-Qabbalah bi-Provence* (*Ḥug ha-Rabad*), ed. R. Schatz (Hebrew University, 1964), 42–44; I. Twersky, *Rabad of Posquières,* 25–28.
10. I. Loeb in *REJ* 2 (1881): 159–60. Cf. Assaf, *Meqorot,* 1:7–8 and Twersky, *Rabad of Posquières,* 25.
11. Baron, *A Social and Religious History of the Jews,* 6:140–41, and 375, n. 163. While the document is never cited in subsequent medieval or modern rabbinic literature, there are some later works displaying similarities to *SḤH.* See S. Assaf, *Meqorot,* 1:8 and R. Samuel Kaidonover, *Emunat Shmuel* (Frankfurt, 1683), 37a. It is doubtful, however, that either of these sources was based on an actual remnant of the text of *SḤH.*
12. See above, n. 7; A. Grabois, "Écoles et strctures sociales des communautés juives," in *Gli Ebrei nell'alto medioevo* (Spoleto, 1980), 937–62; idem, "Les écoles de Narbonne au XIIIe siècle," in *Juifs et Judaisme de Languedoc* (Toulouse, 1977), 141–57.
13. See chap. 3.
14. See Twersky, *Rabad of Posquières.*
15. See *SḤP,* secs. 821–25 and *SḤH,* lines 38–46.
16. See *SḤP,* secs. 800, 828, 830, 1492, 1496. The formulations of both *SḤP* and *SḤH* are much sharper and more extensive than the relevant Yerushalmi passage, which neither text cites. Cf. *Sefer Or Zaruaʿ*, *Bava Meẓiʿa,* no. 245 and *Mordekhai* to *Bava Meẓiʿa,* no. 343.
17. *SḤP,* sec. 800. See also M. Breuer, "Le-Ḥeqer" (see chap. 4, n. 25), 50.
18. See *SḤP,* sec. 1474. Psalms 19:8, which opens the *SḤP* passage, is a leitmotif of *Sefer Ḥasidim.* An interpretation of this verse begins the other section in *SḤP* devoted to Torah study (747) as well. See also *SḤP,* secs. 805 and 1838. On the consecration of *kohanim* and *leviyim* to Torah study, cf. *SḤP,* sec. 806 and S. Kramer, *God and Man in the Sefer Ḥasidim* (New York, 1966), 237. The only other medieval text that interprets Deuteronomy 33:10 in this manner, to my knowledge, is the commentary attributed to R. Eleazar Roqeaḥ. *Sefer Ḥasidim* views the consecration of the sons of the Levites as a paradigm for all Jews to follow. Later in *SḤH* (lines 116–21), all parents are urged to consecrate their firstborn sons.

19. Cf. I. Twersky, *Introduction to the Code of Maimonides* (New Haven, 1980), 170–75.
20. Cf. D. Berger, *The Jewish-Christian Debate in the High Middle Ages* (Philadelphia, 1979), 27, n. 71.

Notes to Appendix B

1. *Maḥzor Vitry,* ed. S. Hurwitz, pp. 628–30 (cf. the variants in ms. Bodl. 1100, fol. 229r–230v); *Sefer Roqeaḥ,* no. 296; *Sefer Assufot,* ms. Mont. 134 (sec. 382), fol. 67r; ms. Hamburg 152, fol. 81r–82r (cf. A. N. Z. Roth, "Ḥinnukh Yeladim la-Torah be-Shavuʿot," *Yeda ʿAm* 11 [1966]: 9–12 and S. E. Stern, "Seder Ḥinnukh Yeladim le-Torah ule-Yir'ah mi-Beit Midrasham shel Ḥakhmei Ashkenaz," *Ẓefunot* 1:1 [1988]: 15–21); *Orḥot Ḥayyim* (pt. 2), ed. M. Schlesinger (Berlin, 1899), 24–25.
2. See I. Marcus, *Piety and Society* (Leiden, 1981), 113–14.
3. See also M. Güdemann, *Ha-Torah veha-Ḥayyim,* 1:91, n. 3.
4. *Sefer Mordekhai, Shabbat,* no. 369, and the variants in R. Meir b. Barukh, *Teshuvot, Pesaqim, u-Minhagim,* ed. I. Z. Kahana, 1:99–100.
5. See the text published by I. Levi in *REJ* 49 (1904): 237–38. For the dating of this text, see above, chap. 6, n. 22.
6. See M. Breuer, "Ha-Yeshivah shel Yemei ha-Beinayim," in *Ḥinnukh ha-Adam ve-Yiʿudo,* World Conference for Jewish Thought, vols. 9–10 (Jerusalem, 1967), 142–43; *Maḥzor Vitry,* 628, end of sec. 507 (cf. *SḤB,* 946); G. Scholem, *On the Kabbalah and its Symbolism* (New York, 1965), 135–37; A. Katz, "Talmud Torah ʿal ha-Nahar ve-ʿal ha-Mayim," *Yeda ʿAm* 11 (1966): 4–8; and I. Marcus, "Mothers, Martyrs, and Moneymakers: Some Jewish Women in Medieval Europe," *Conservative Judaism* 37 (1986): 43, n. 7.

Index